TEEN DREAMS

EMMANUEL D. FOUQUET

EDITION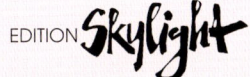

1st Edition 2025 in Paperback,
Copyright © 2025 by Edition Skylight

EDITION SKYLIGHT
Rosengartenstr. 13B
CH-8608 Bubikon/Zürich
Switzerland
Mail: info@edition-skylight.com
Web: www.edition-skylight.com

ISBN 978-3-03766-711-8

Bibliographic information published by Die Deutsche Bibliothek
Die Deutsche Bibliothek lists this publication in the
Deutsche Nationalbibliografie; detailed bibliographic data
are available in the Internet at http://dnb.ddb.de.

Printed in Bosnia and Herzegovina

PREFACE · AVANT PROPOS · VORWORT

Who wouldn't want to watch 18-year-old beauties discovering
their sexuality? Emmanuel Fouquet, for us the ever-curious spy on a
particularly hot assignment, the photographer for magazines
such as Penthouse and Hustler, encourages his young models in front of
the camera to do exactly what they do to themselves at home in
their erotically charged fantasies for this illustrated book. The shootings
are a real feast for the viewer. And we ask ourselves: how can the
photographer stay behind the camera …

Qui n'a pas envie de voir ces beautés de 18 ans découvrir leur sexualité ?
Emmanuel Fouquet, pour nous l'espion toujours curieux en
mission particulièrement torride, le photographe de Magazine comme
Penthouse et Hustler, incite pour ce livre de photos ses jeunes modèles à
faire devant l'appareil photo exactement ce qu'elles se font à la
maison dans leurs fantasmes chargés d'érotisme. Les shootings sont une
véritable fête pour le spectateur. Et nous nous demandons : comment
le photographe peut-il rester derrière l'appareil photo …

Wer möchte sie nicht dabei beobachten, die 18jährigen Schönheiten,
die ihre Sexualität entdecken? Emmanuel Fouquet, für uns der stets
neugierige Spion in besonders heissem Auftrag, der Fotograf für Magazine
wie Penthouse und Hustler, animiert für diesen Bildband seine
jungen Models vor der Kamera genau das zu tun, was sie zu Hause in ihren
erotisch aufgeladenen Fantasien mit sich anstellen. Die Shootings sind
ein wahres Fest für den Betrachter. Und wir fragen uns: wie kann
der Fotograf da hinter der Kamera bleiben …

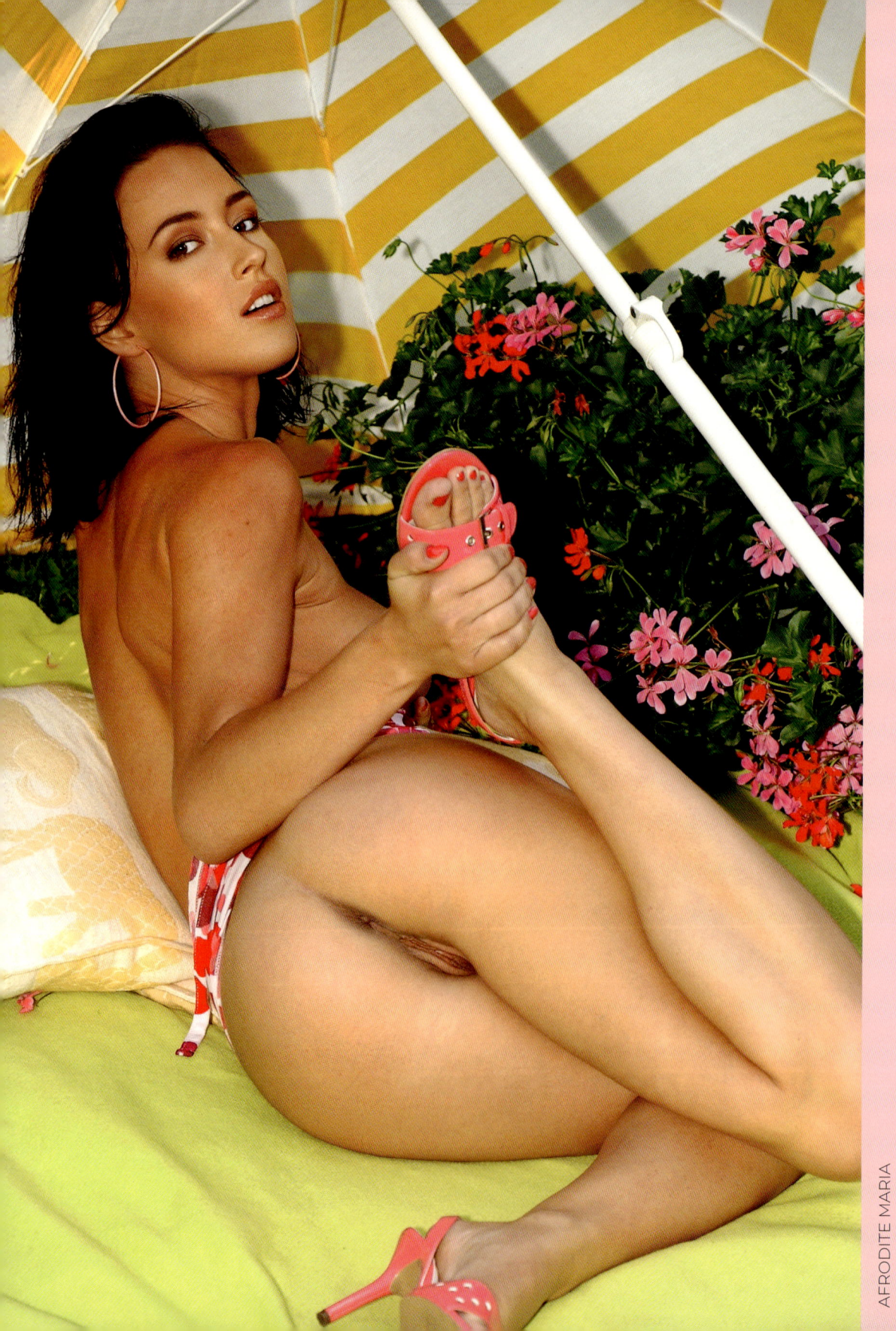

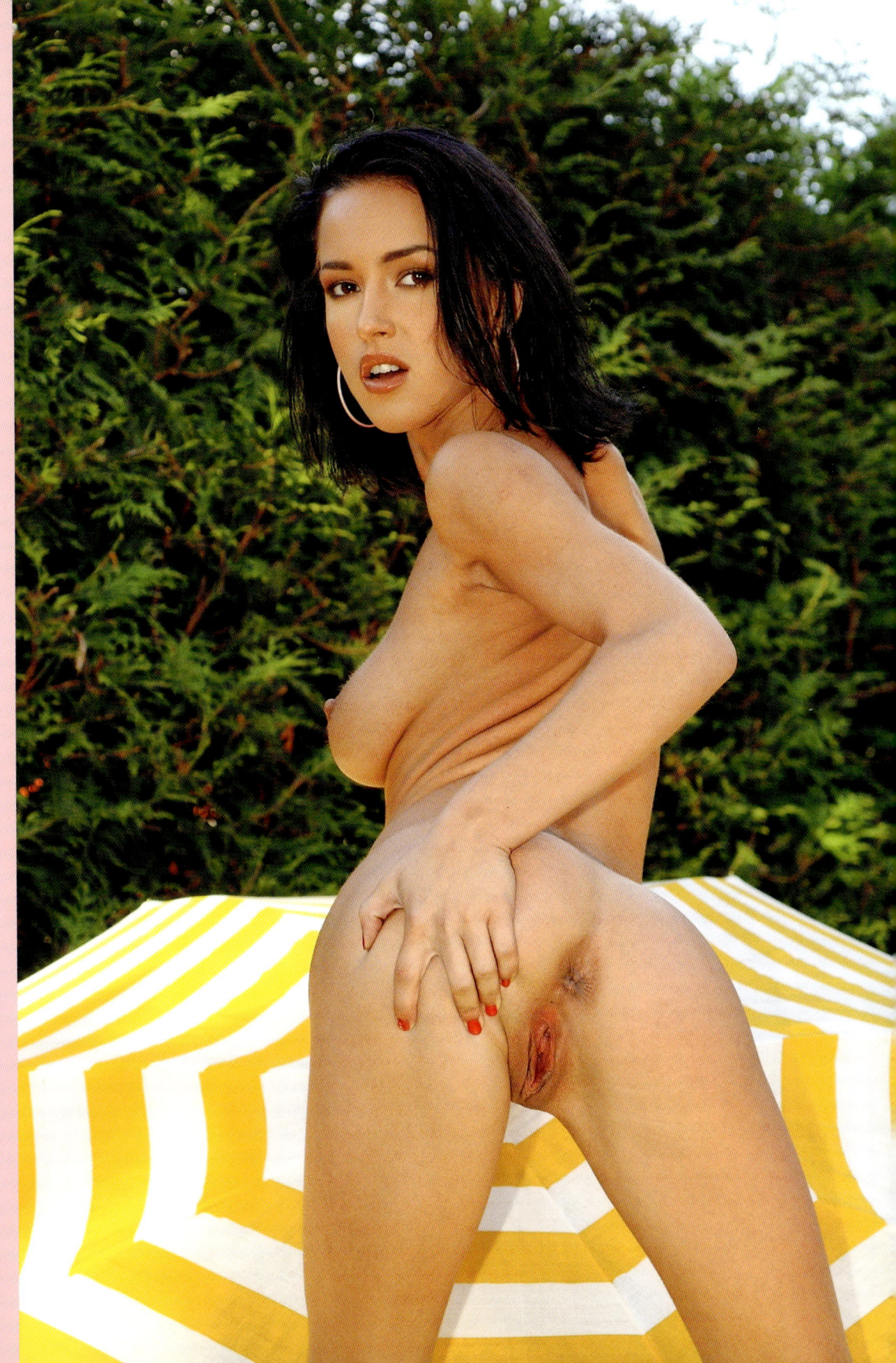

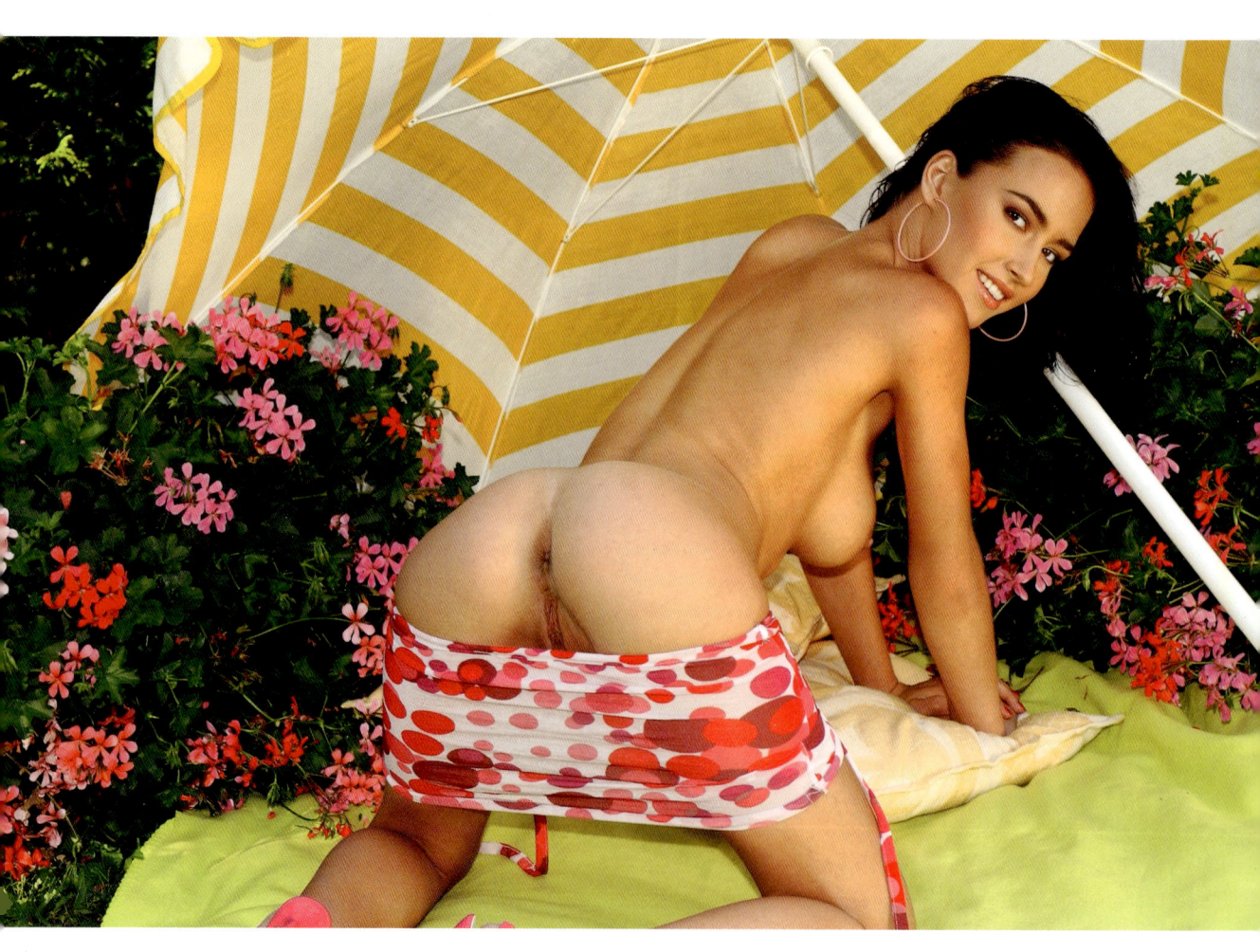

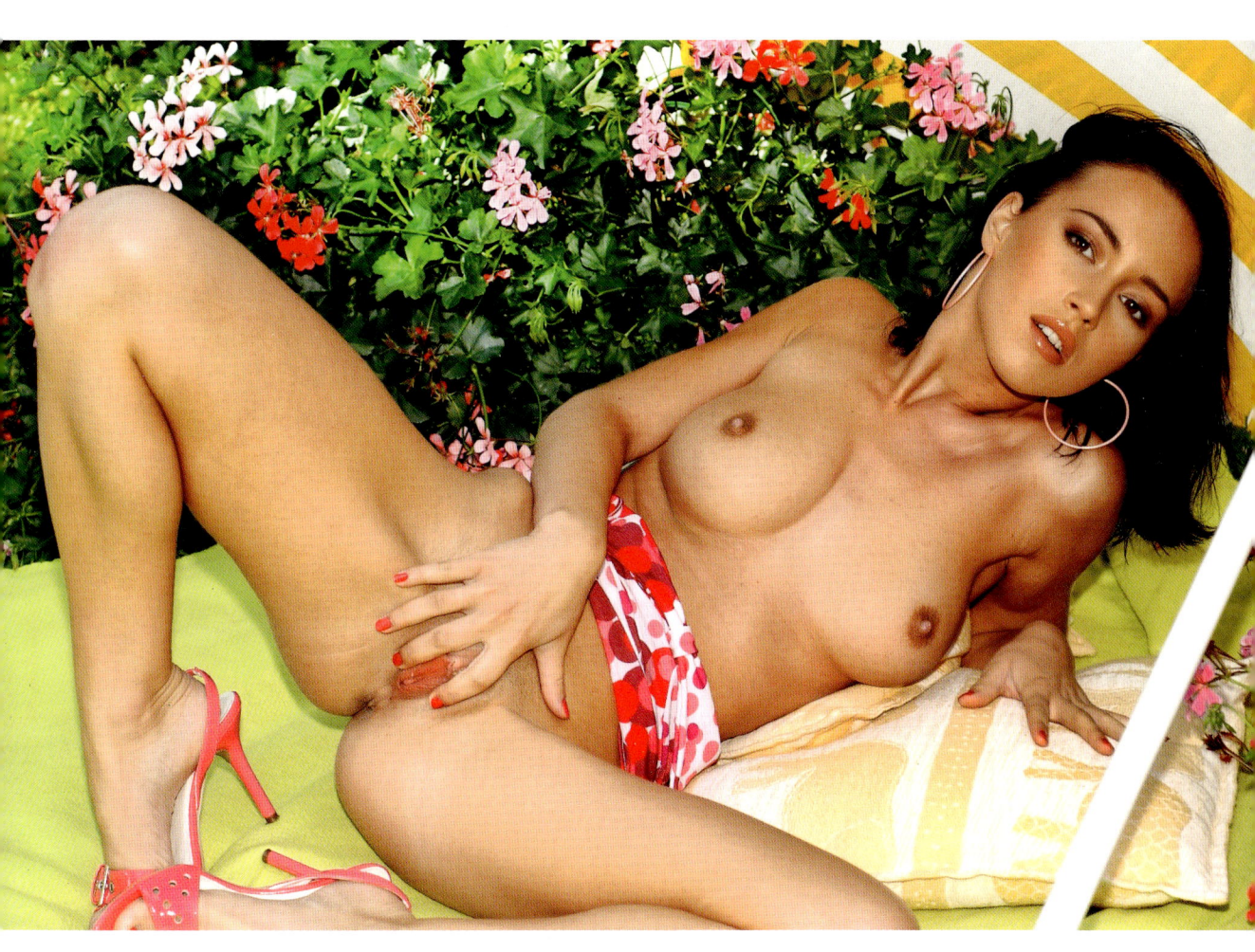

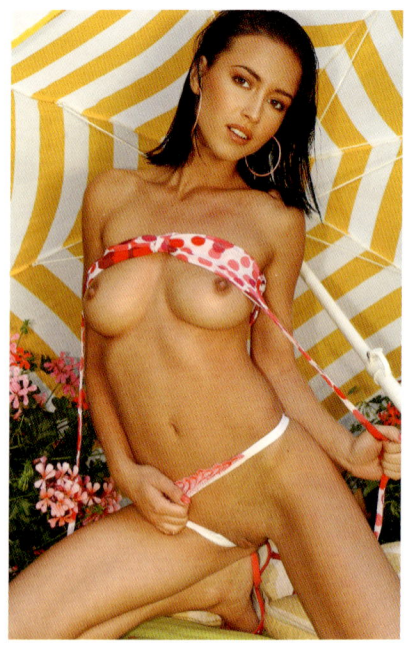 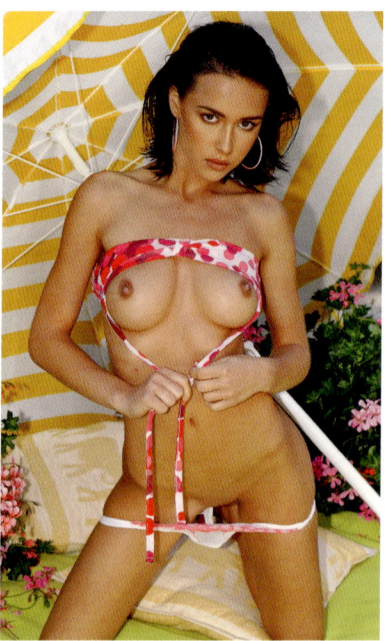 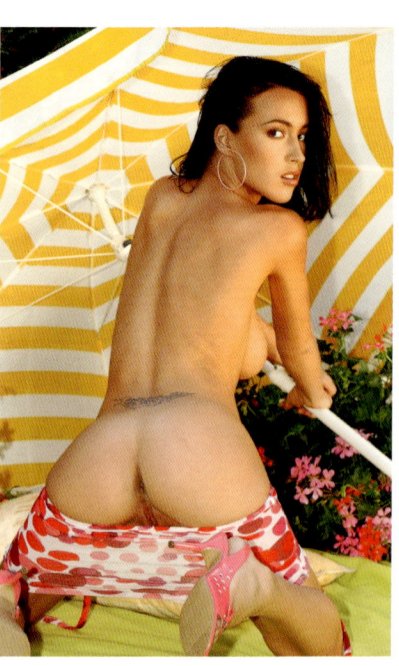

AFRODITE MARIA

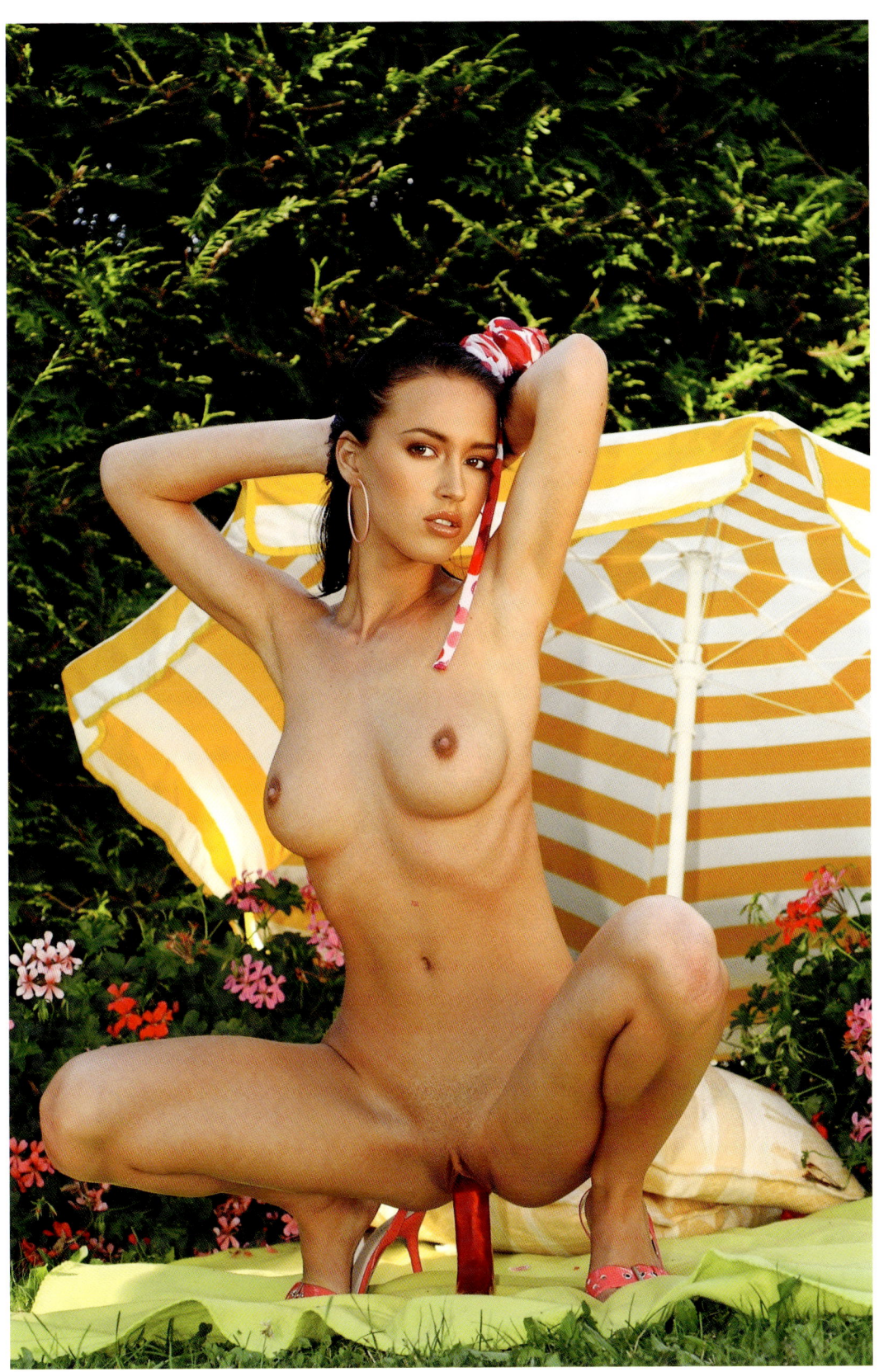

AFRODITE MARIA

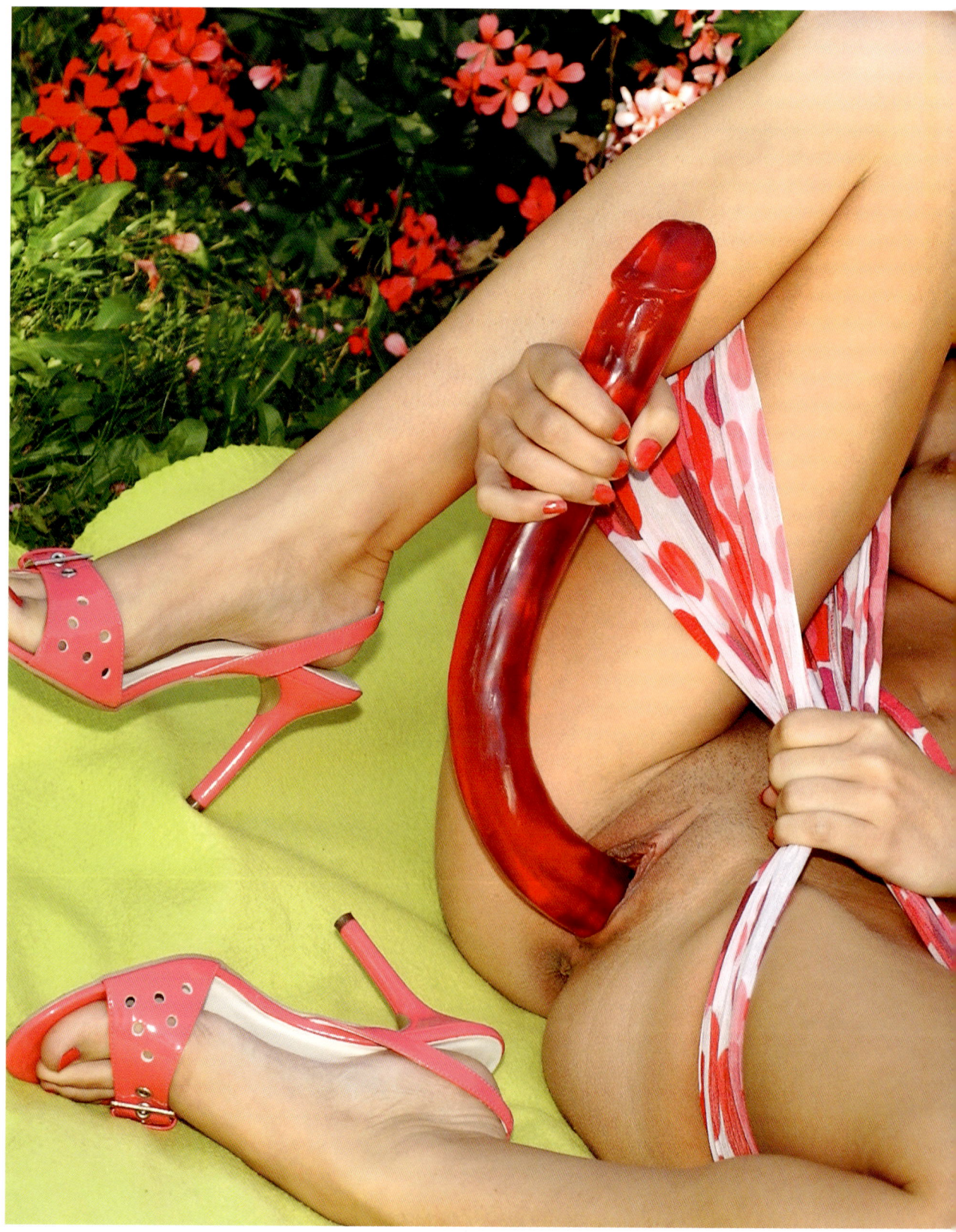

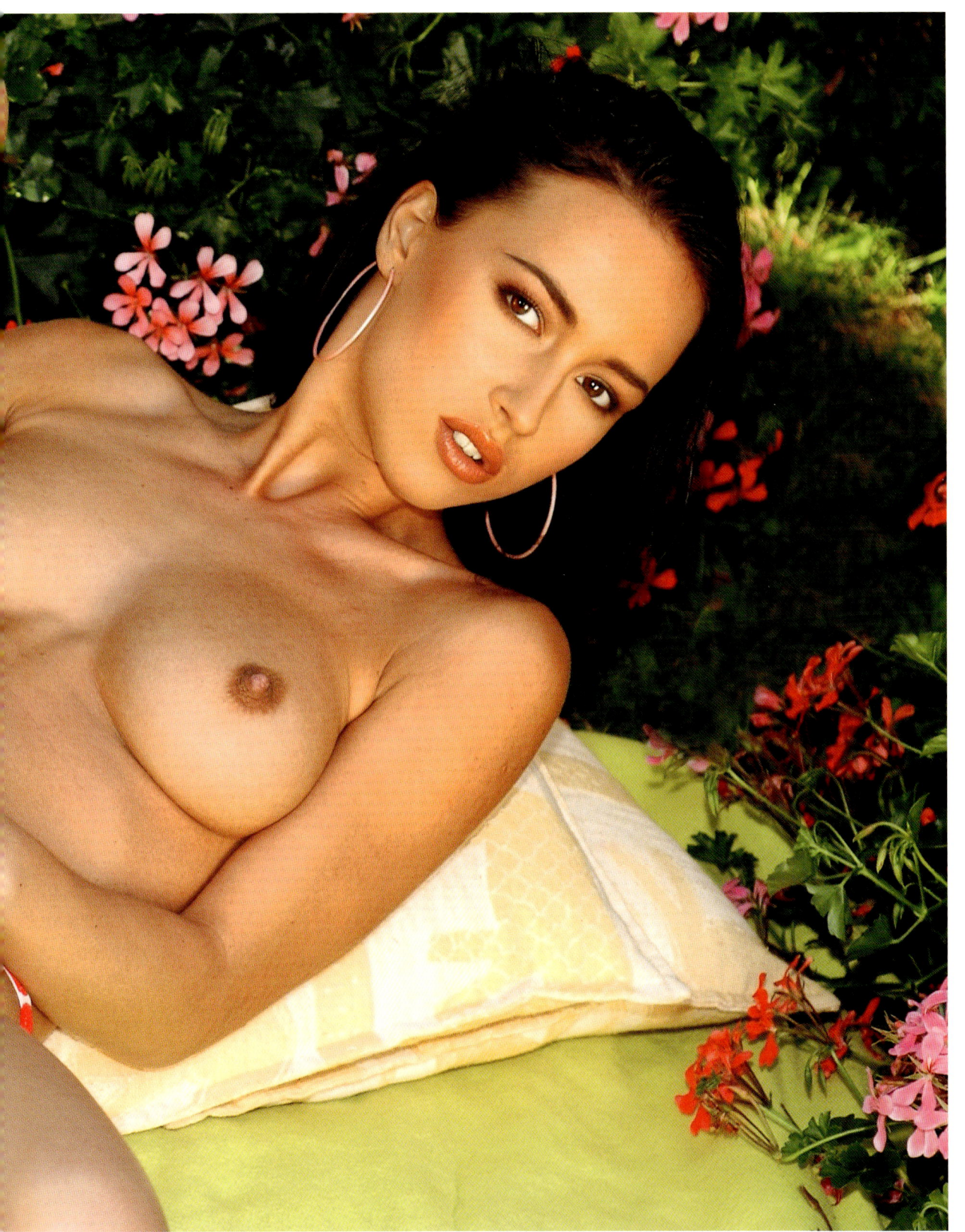

AFRODITE MARIA

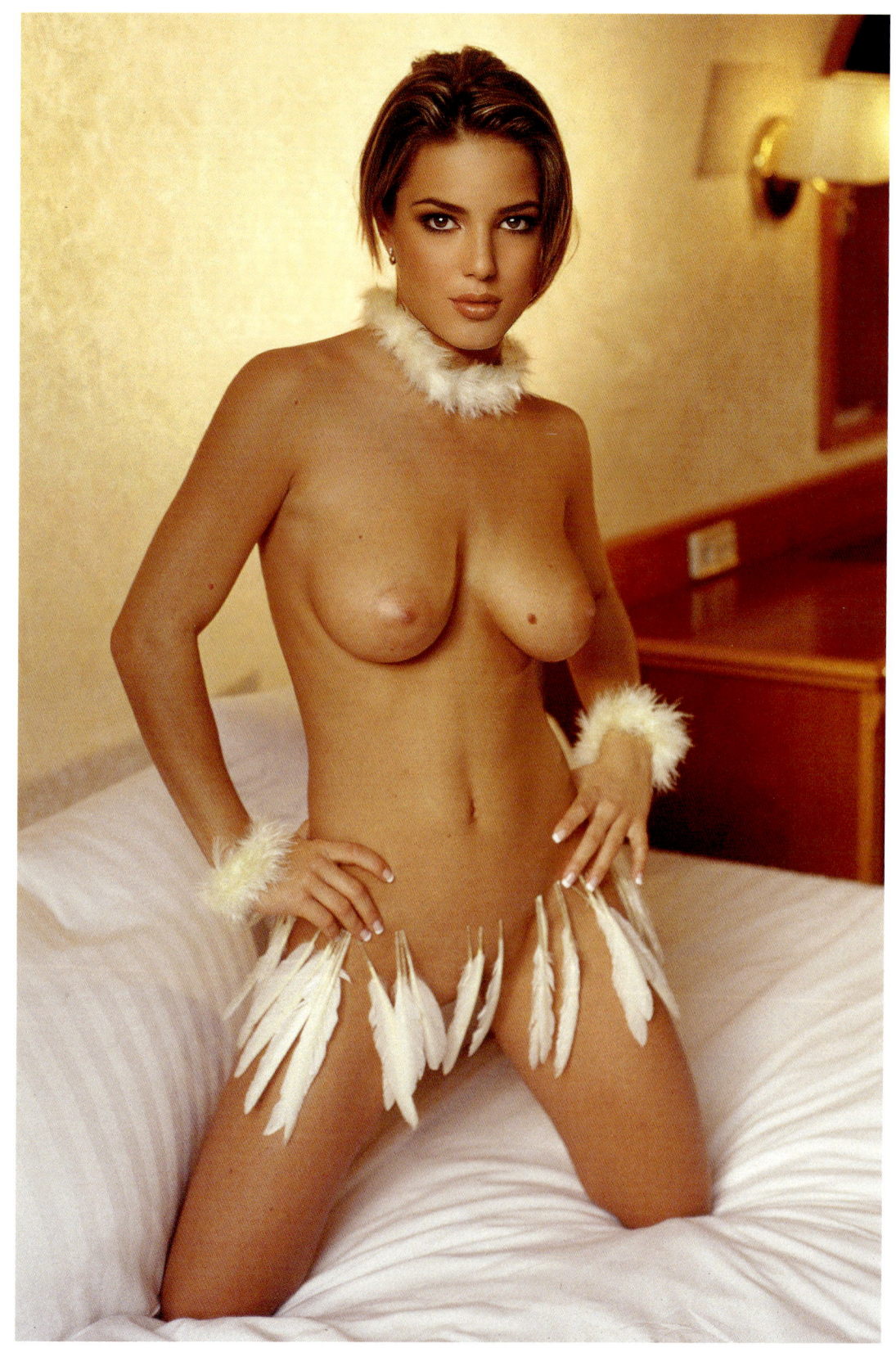

ALEXANDRA

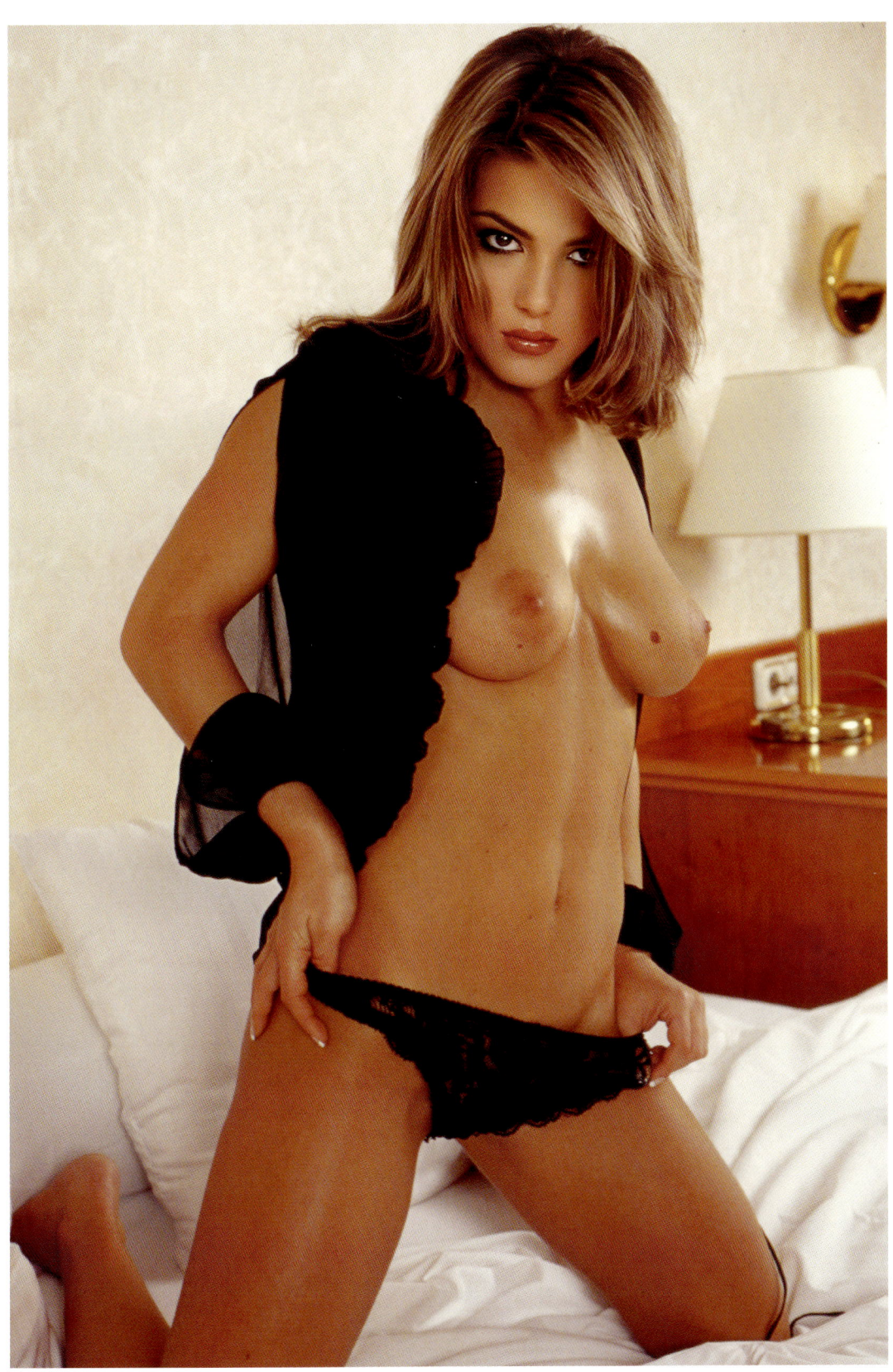

ALEXANDRA

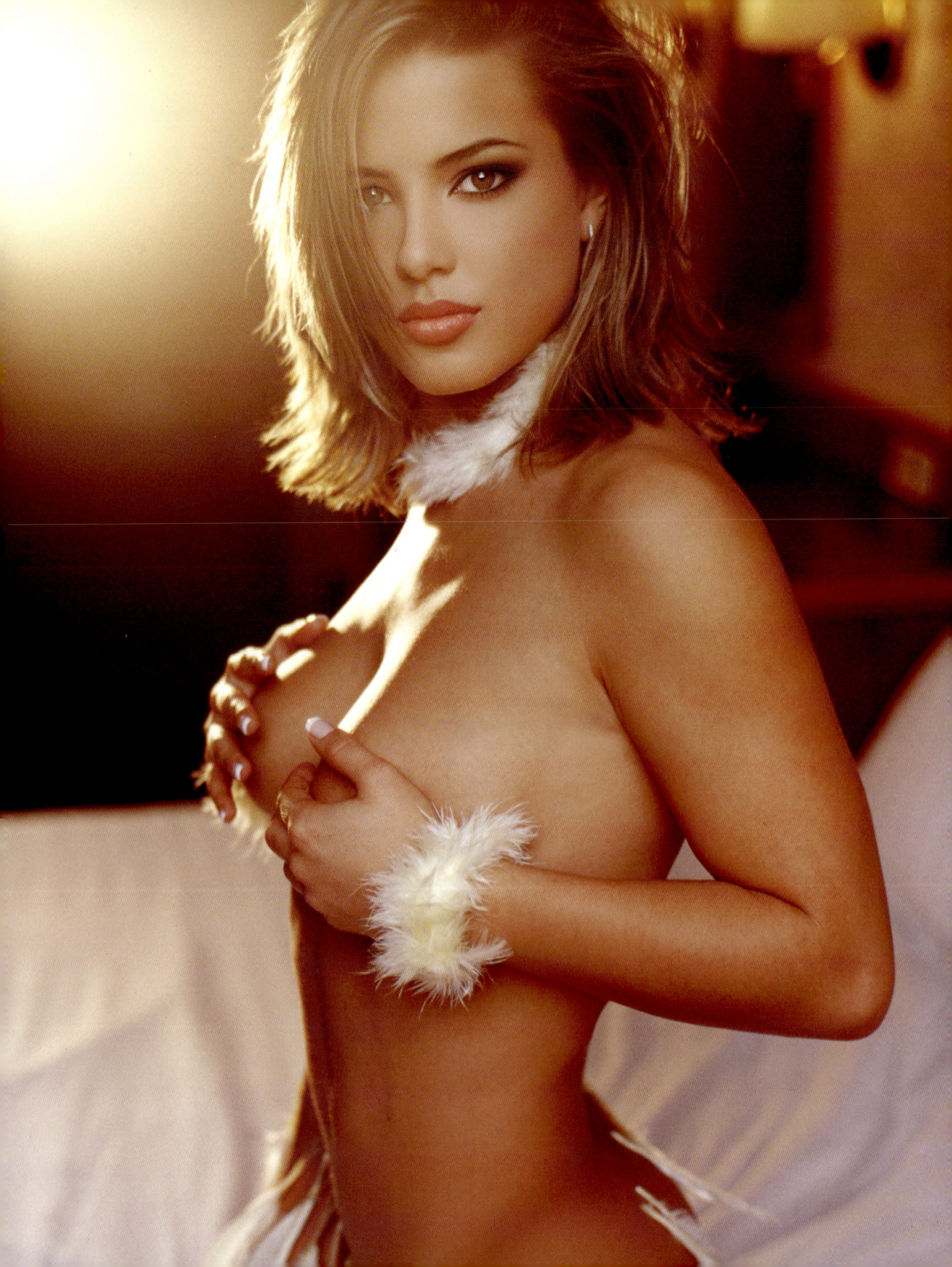

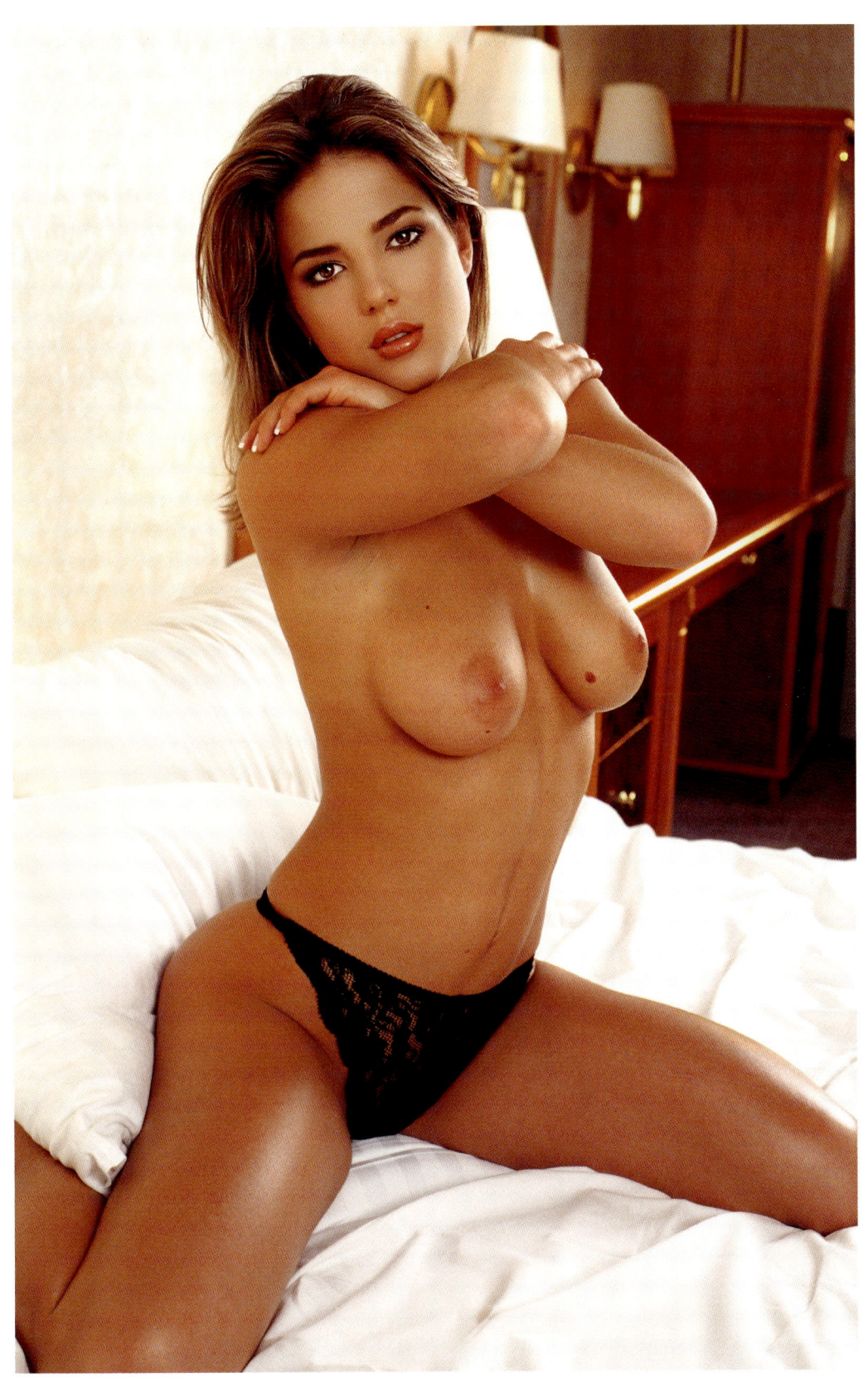

ALEXANDRA

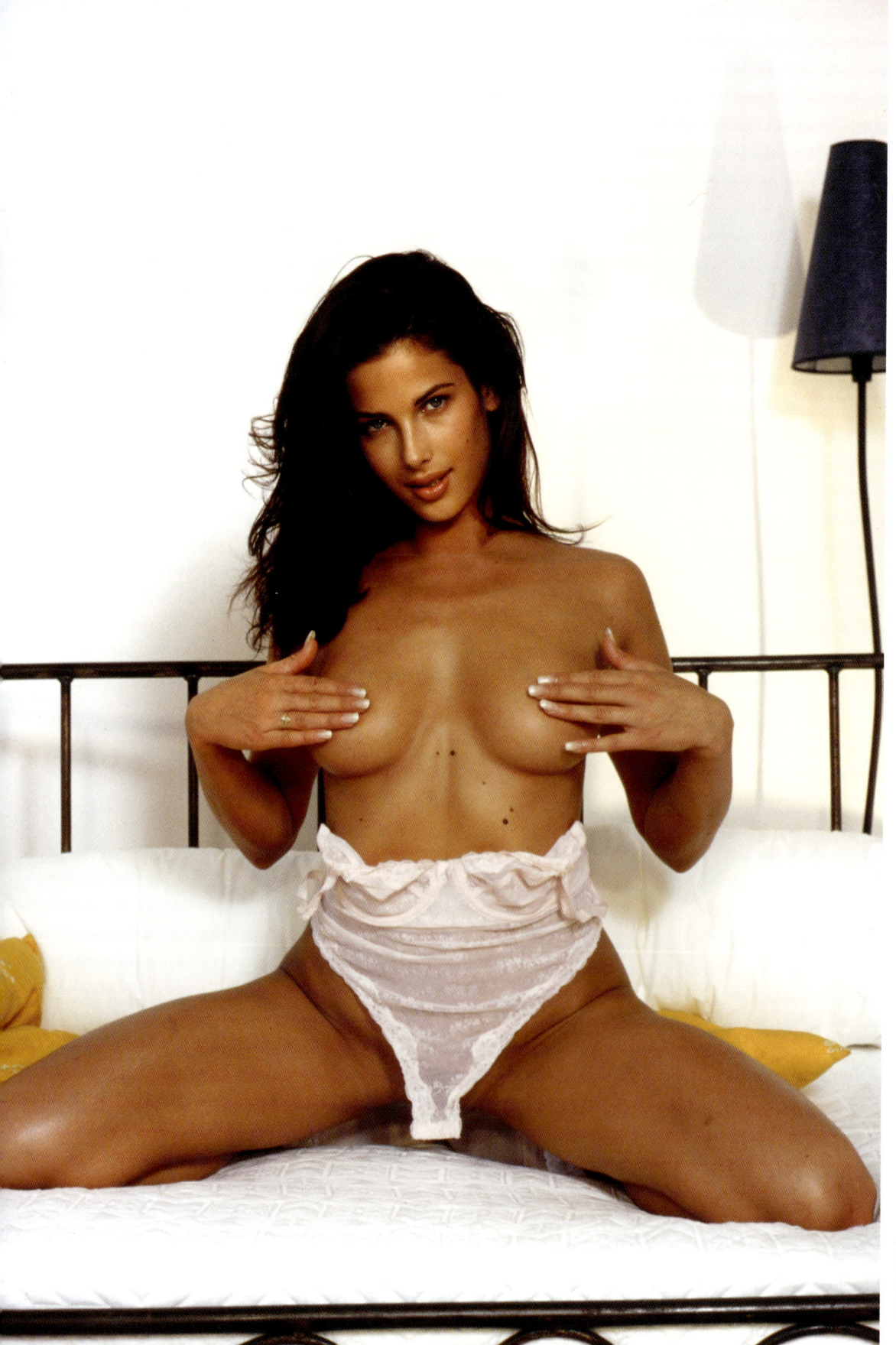

BARBARA

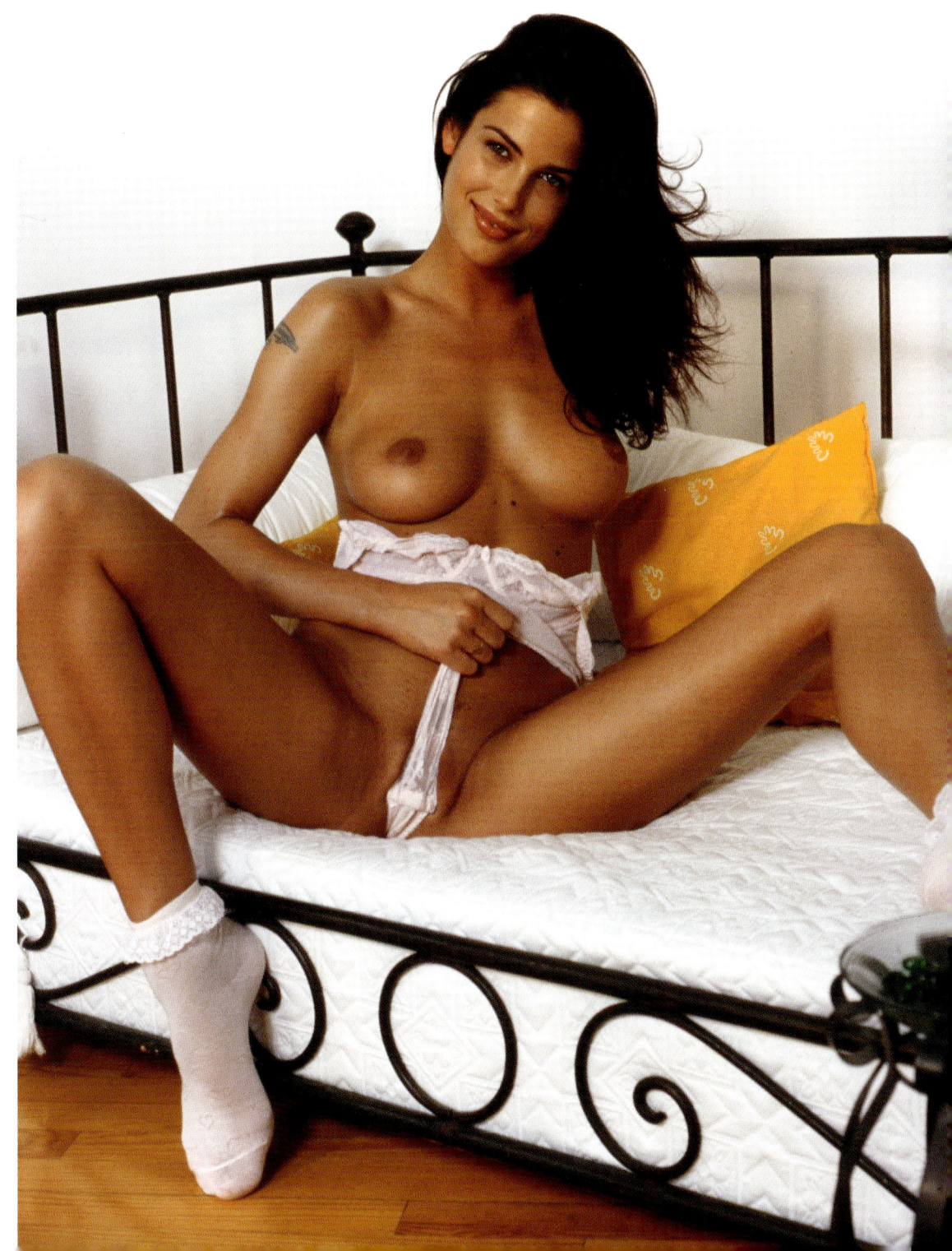

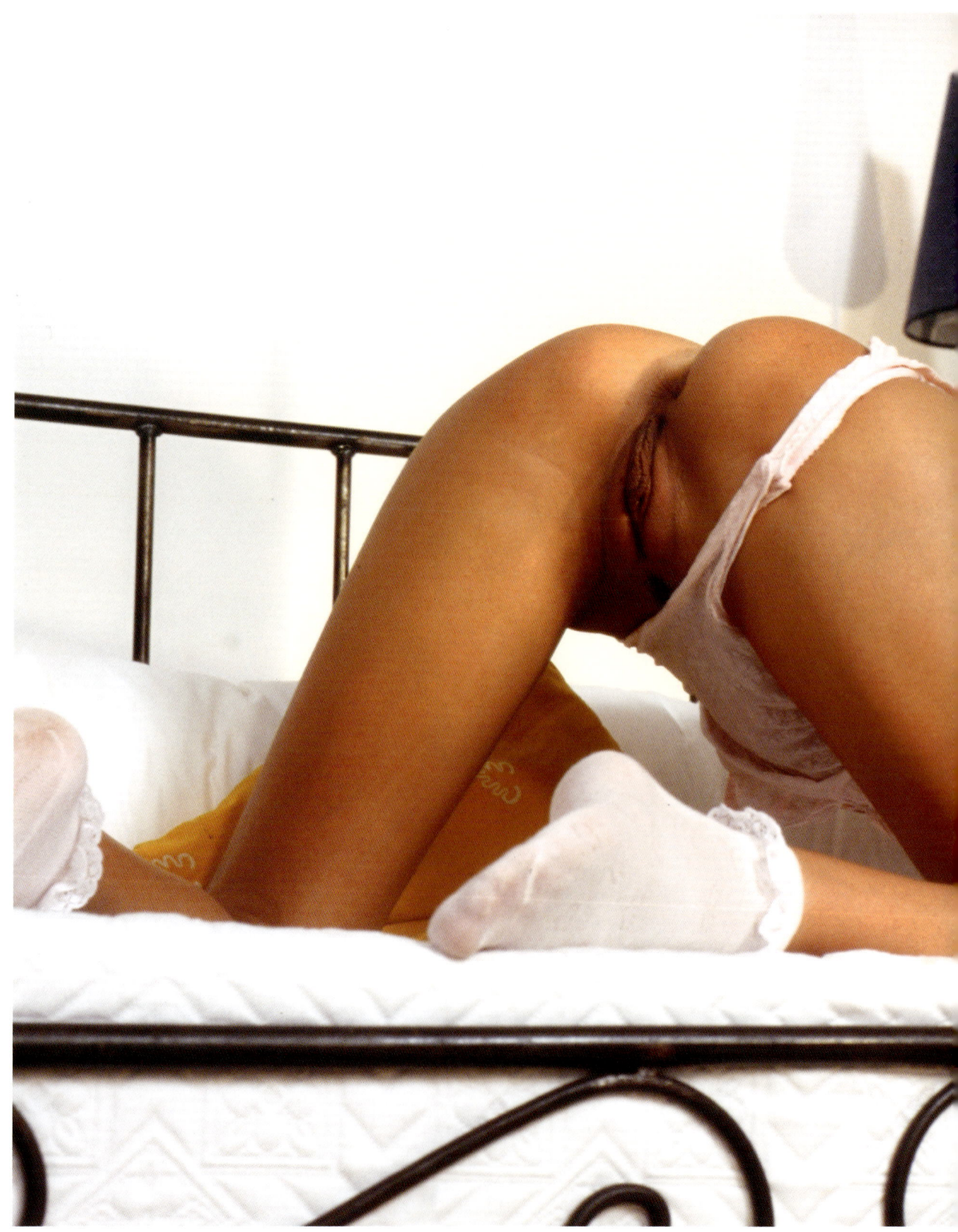

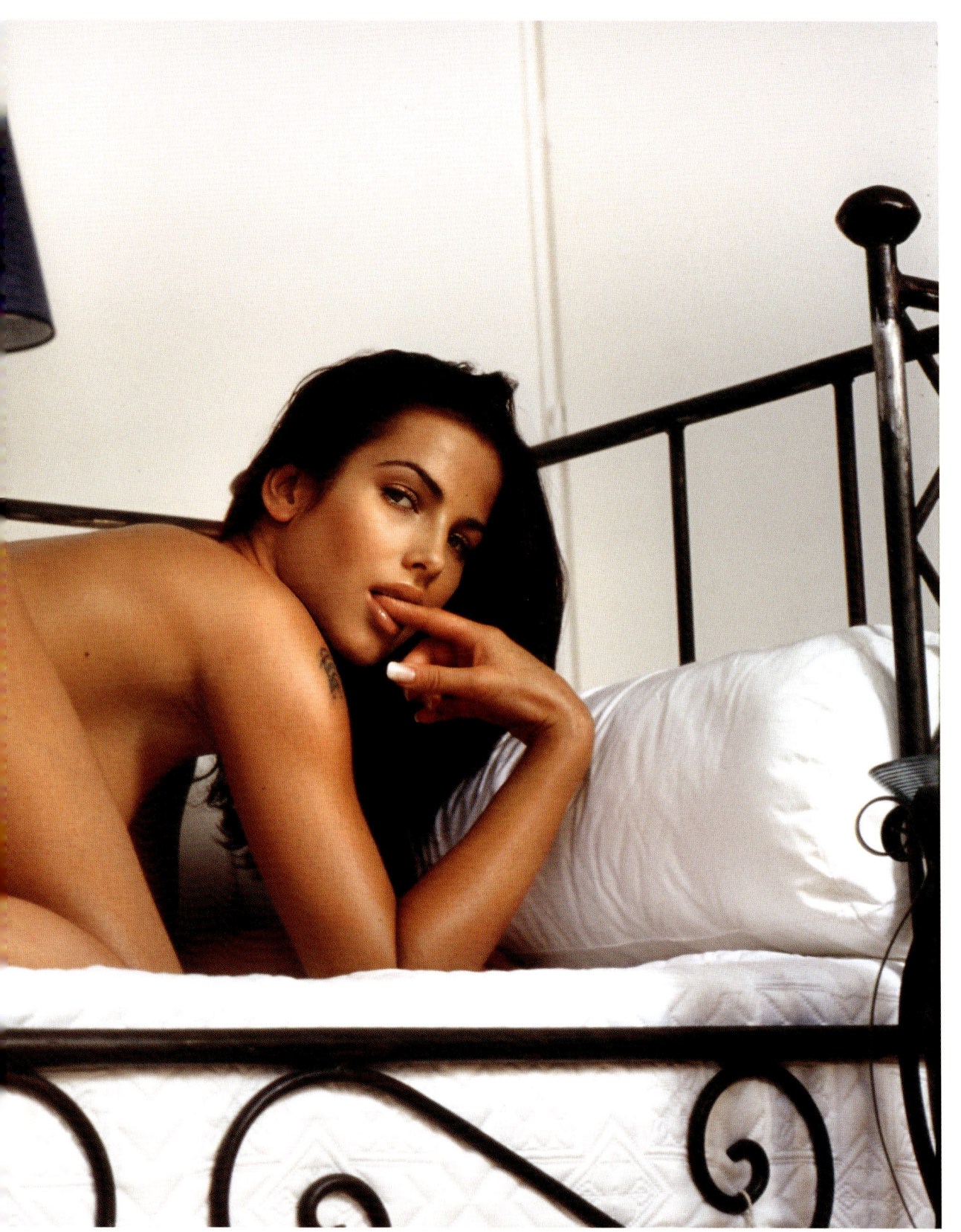

BARBARA

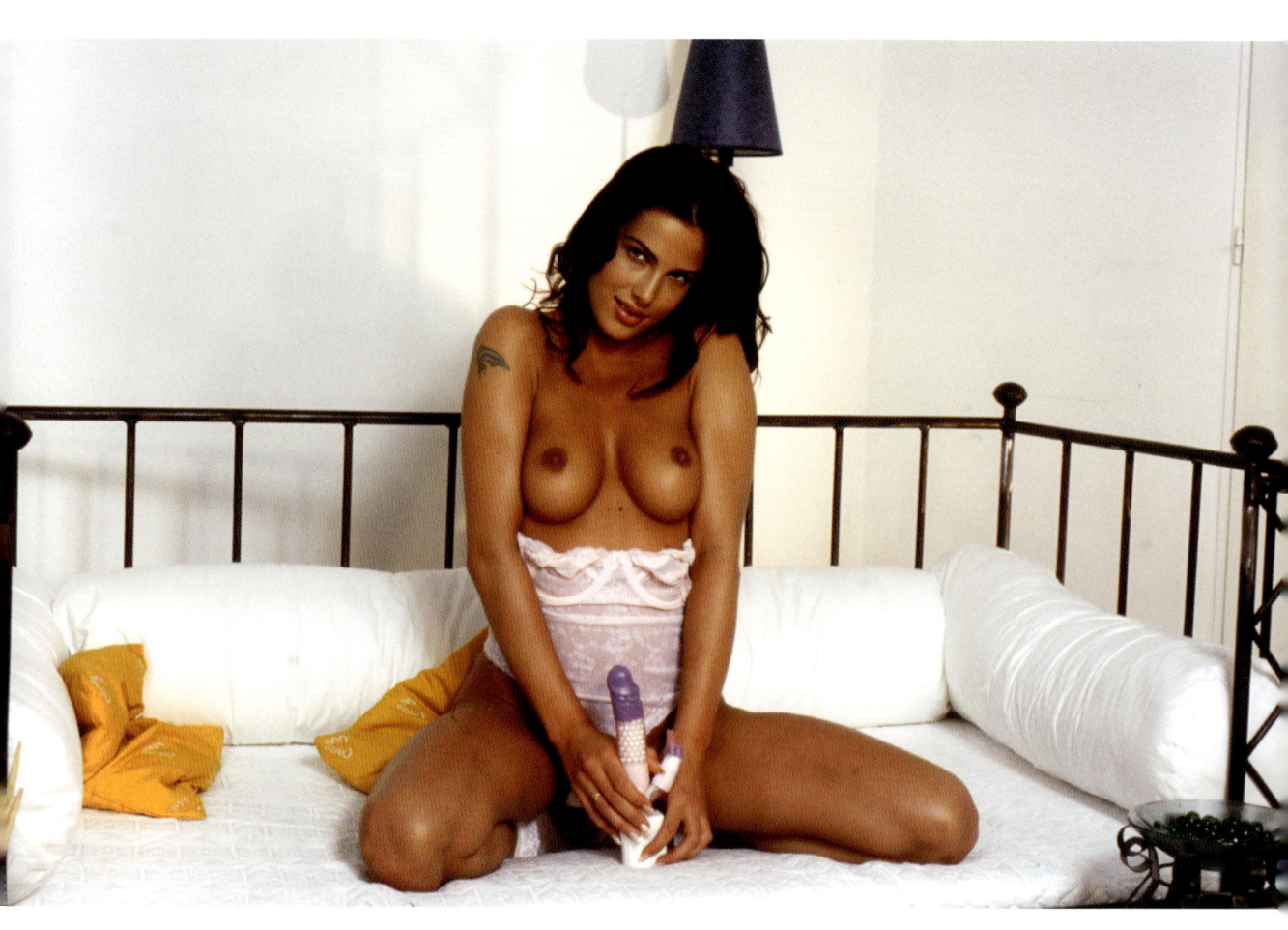

BARBARA

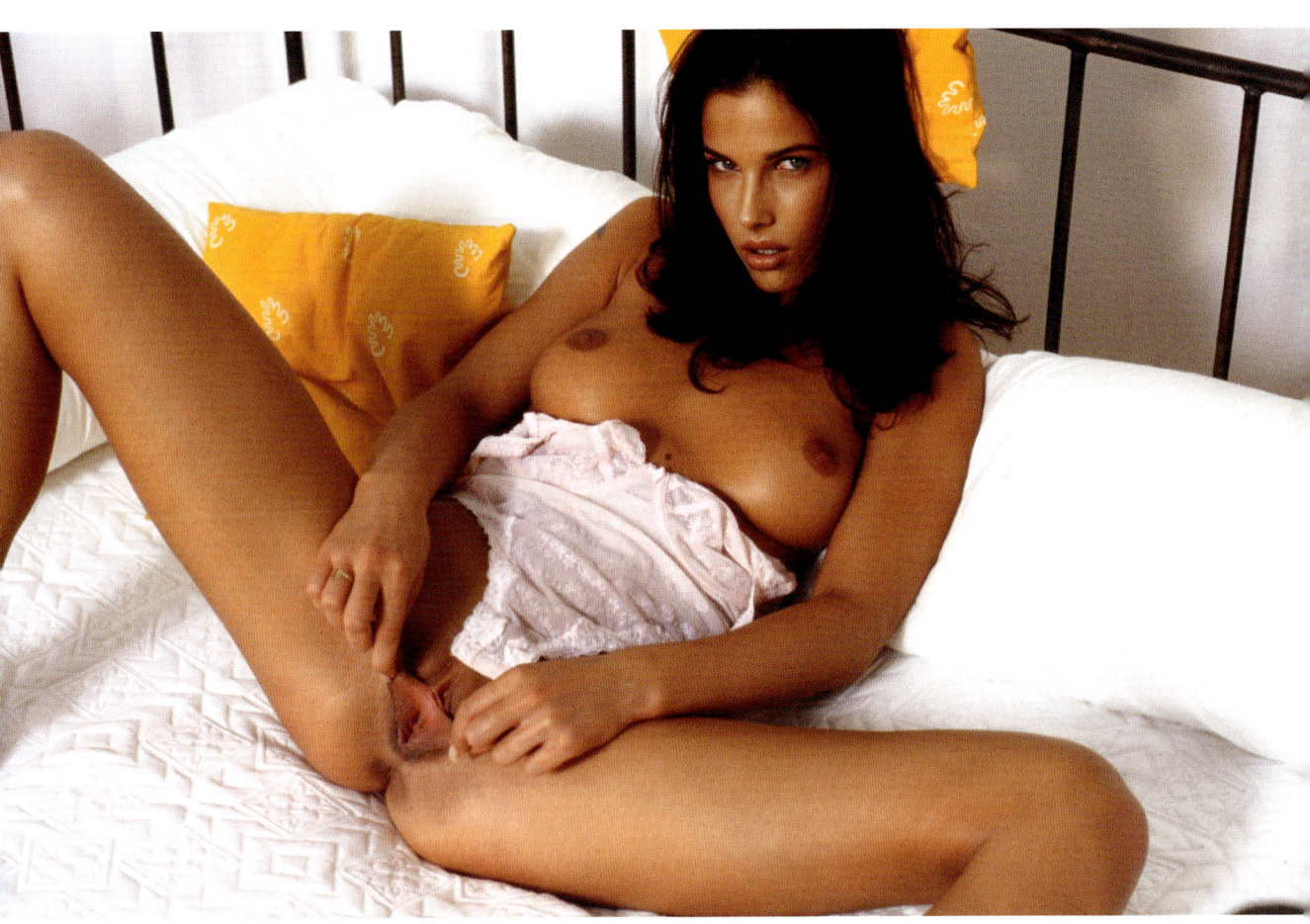

BARBARA

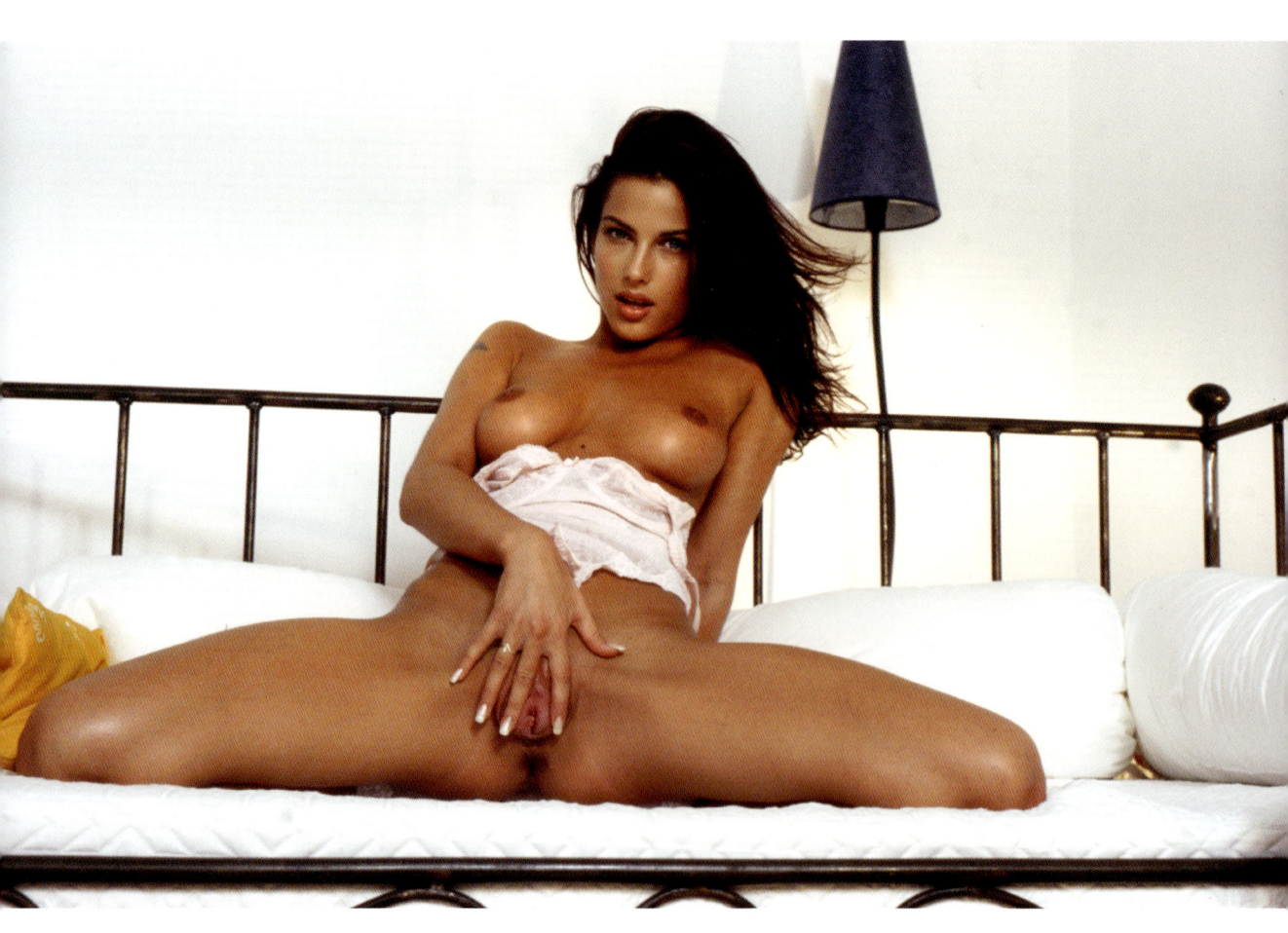

BARBARA

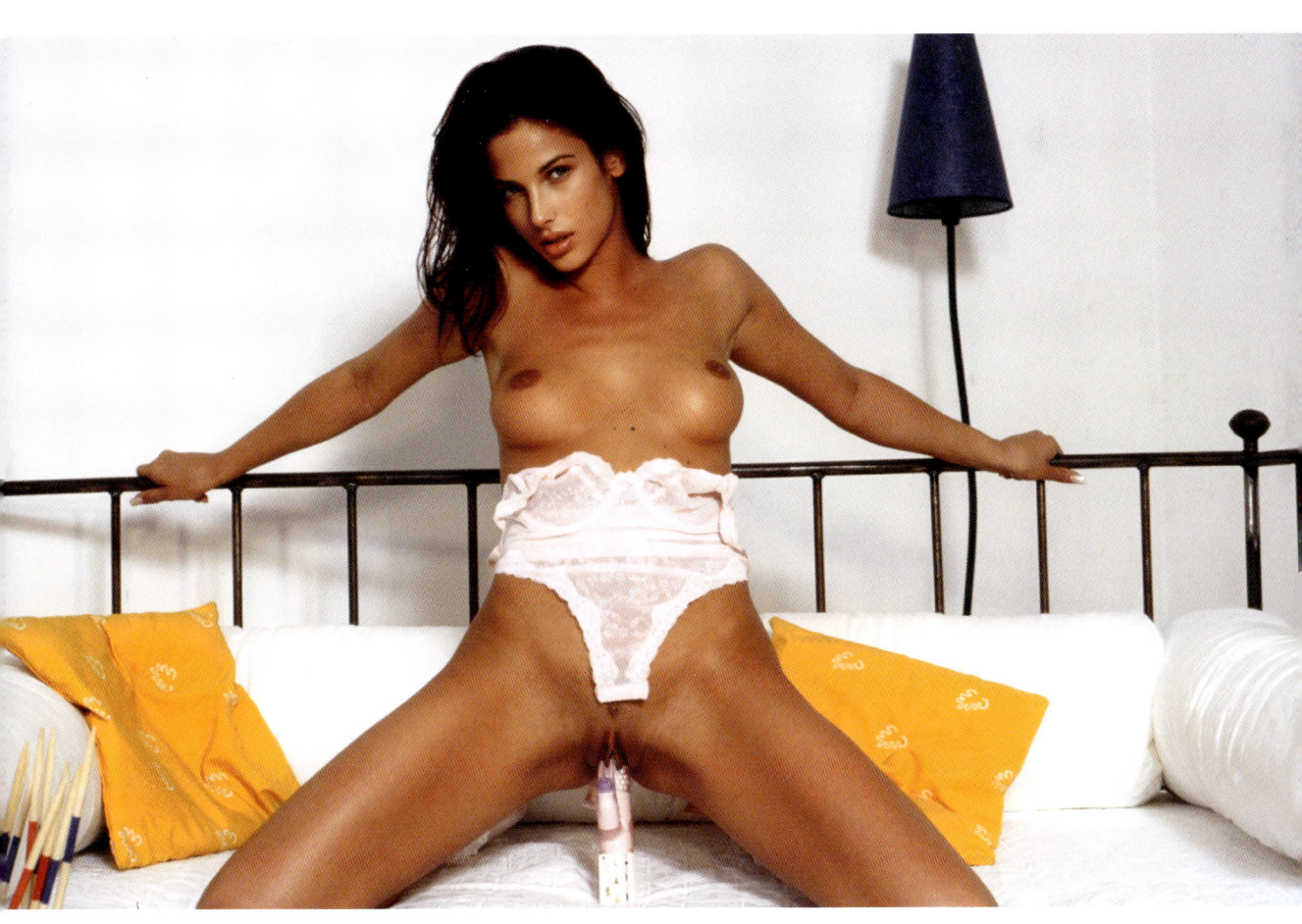

BARBARA

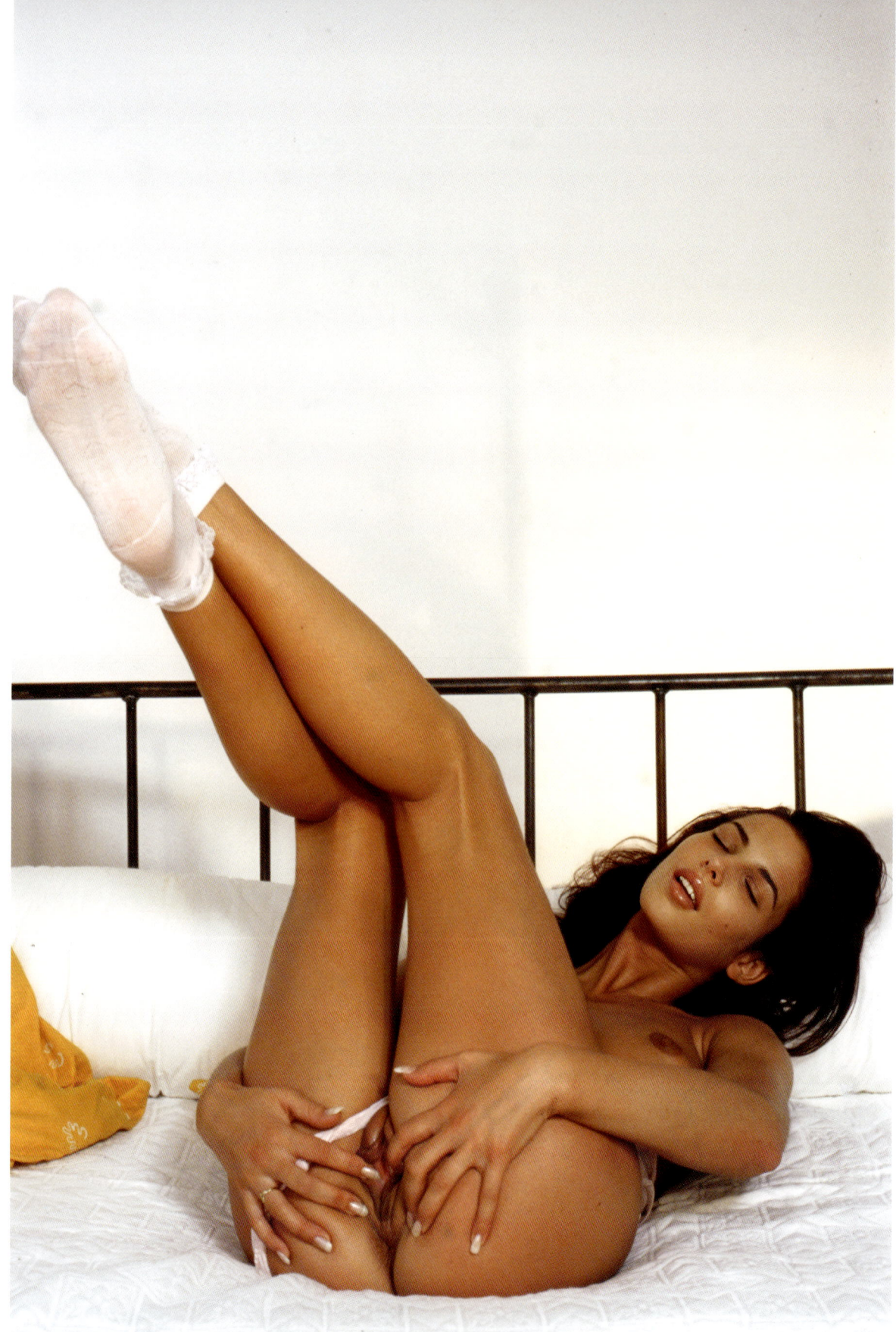

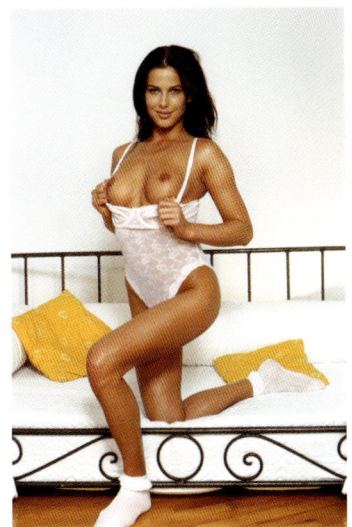

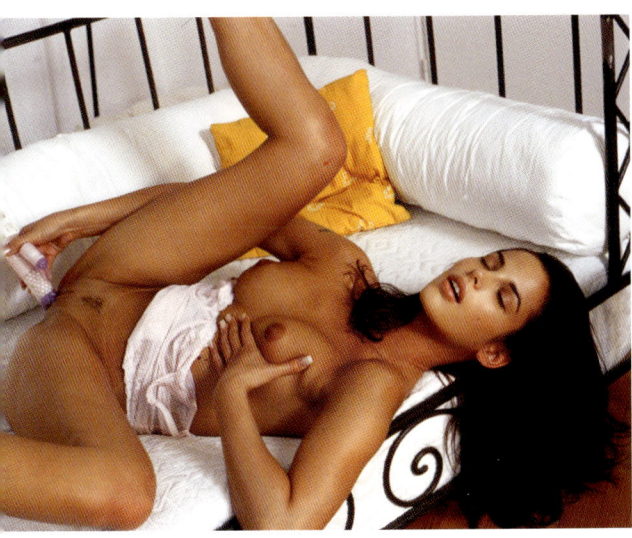

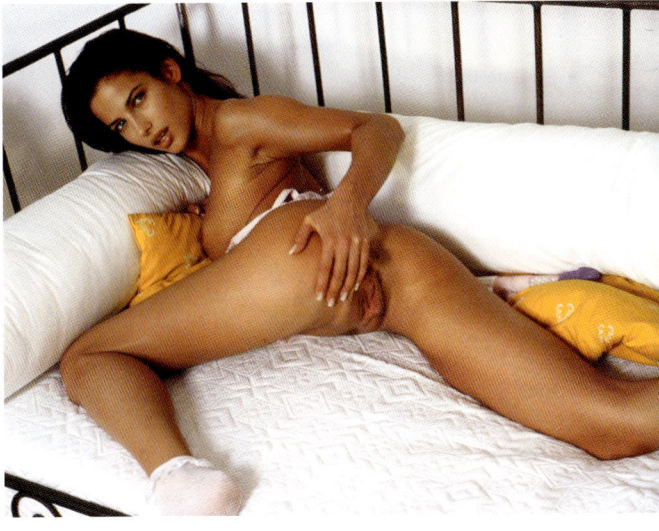

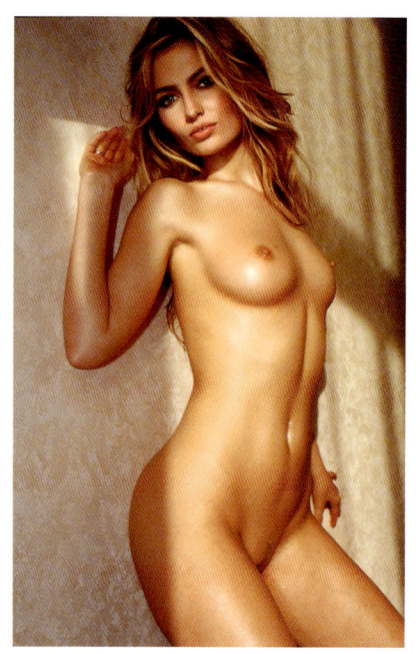
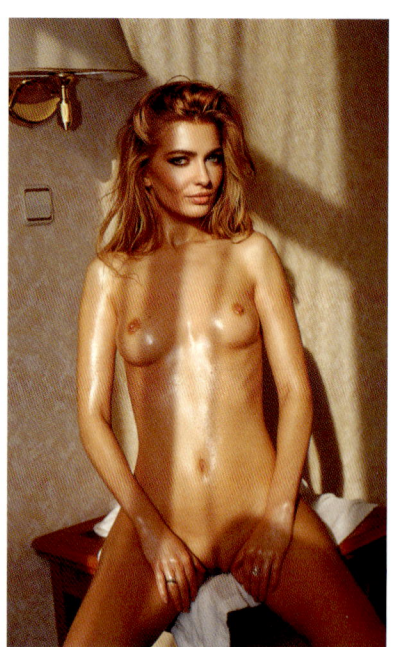
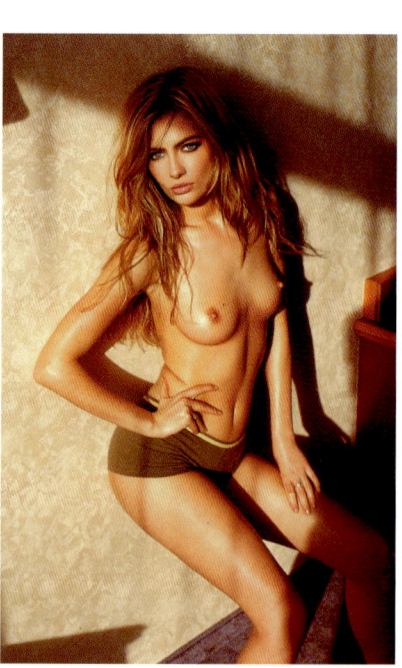

BERNADETT C

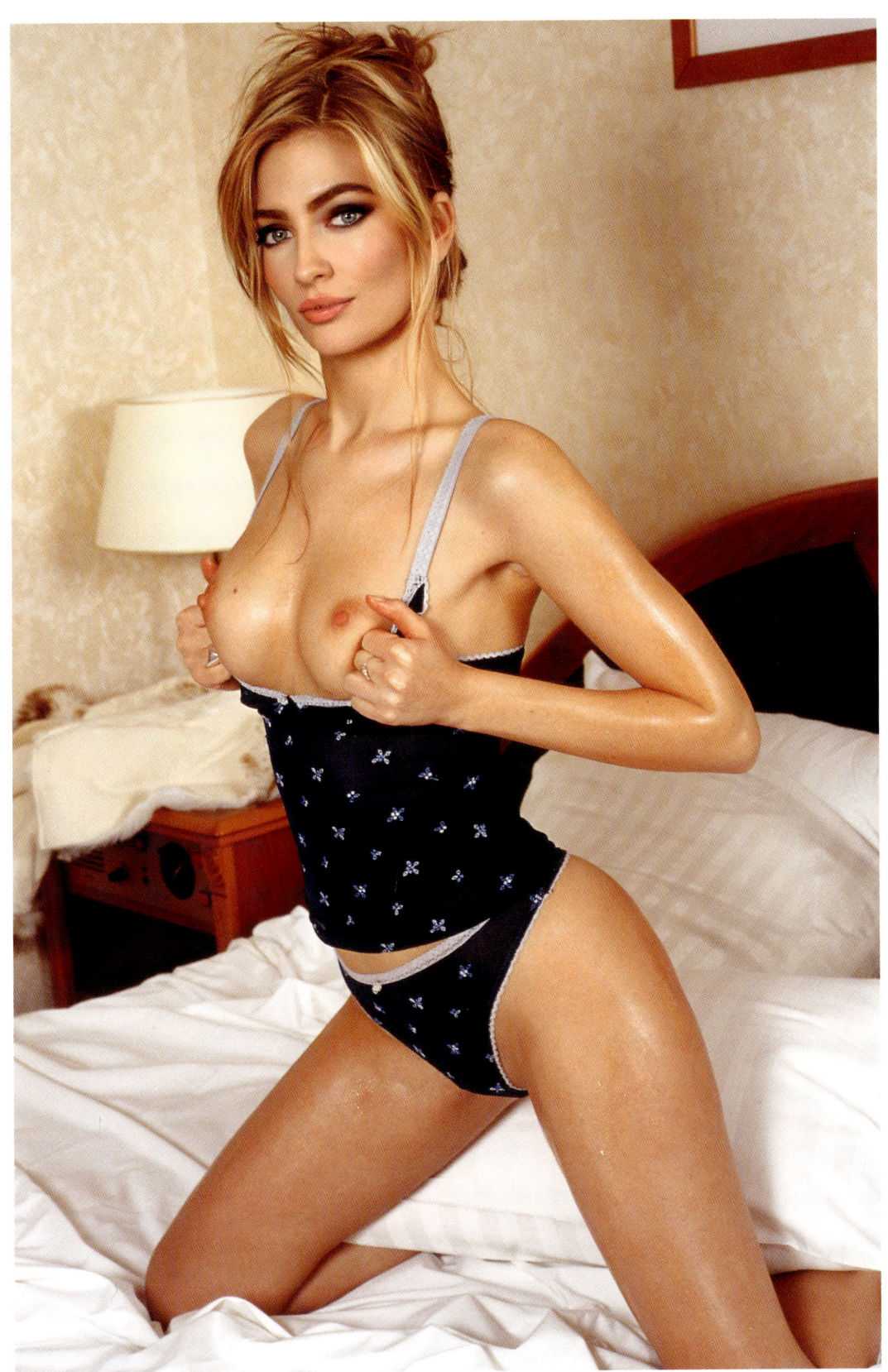

BERNADETT C

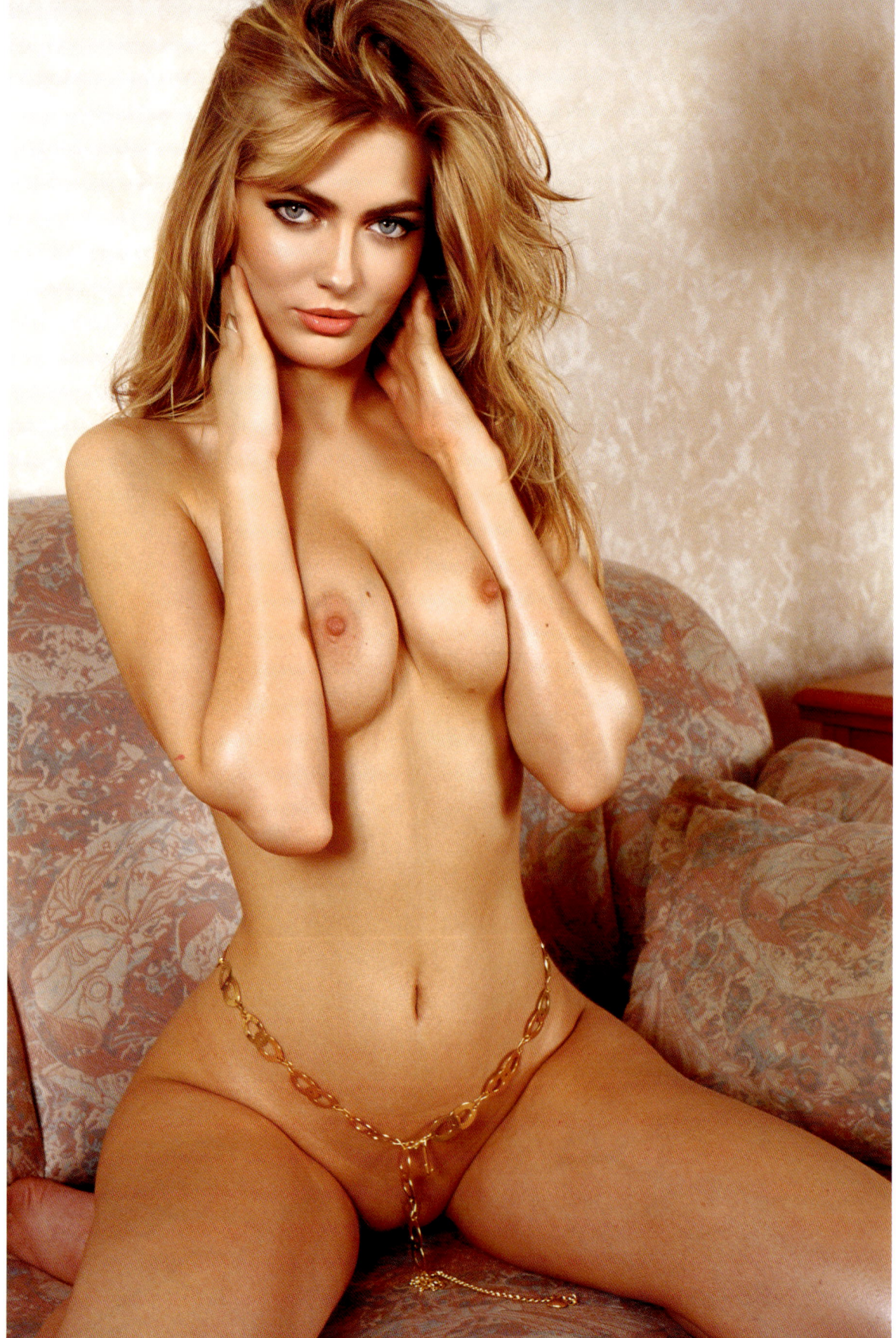

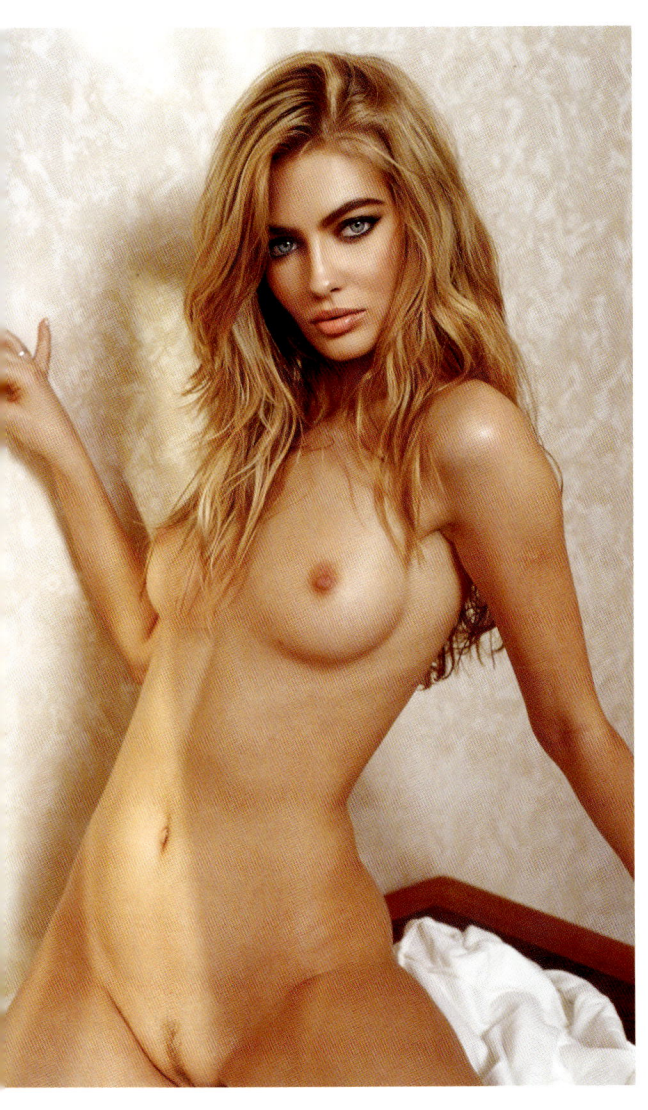
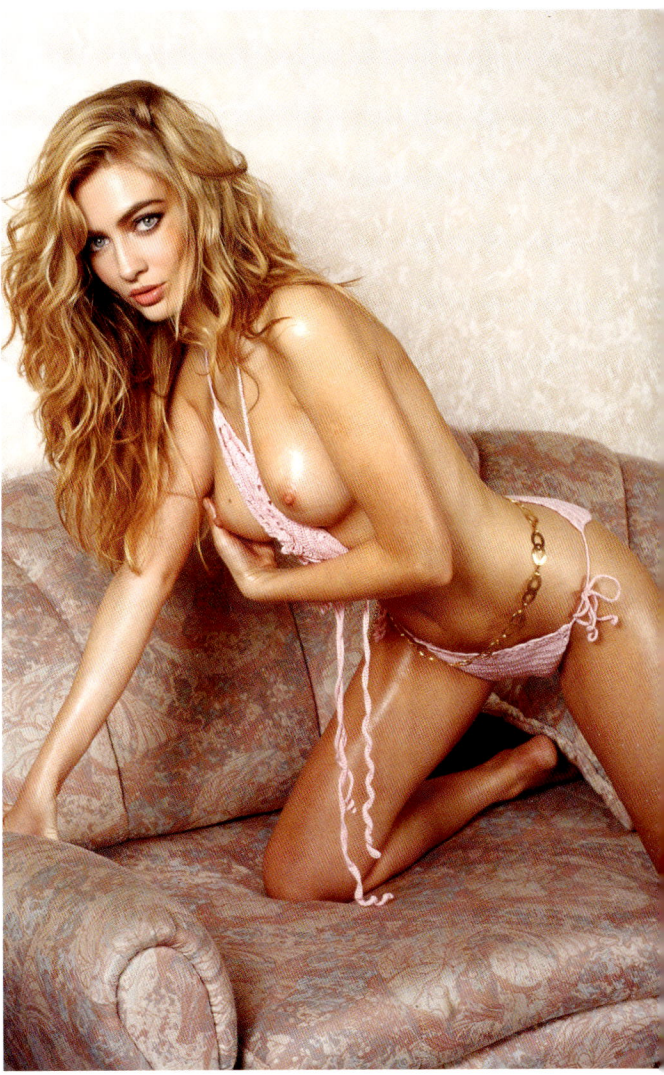

BERNADETT C

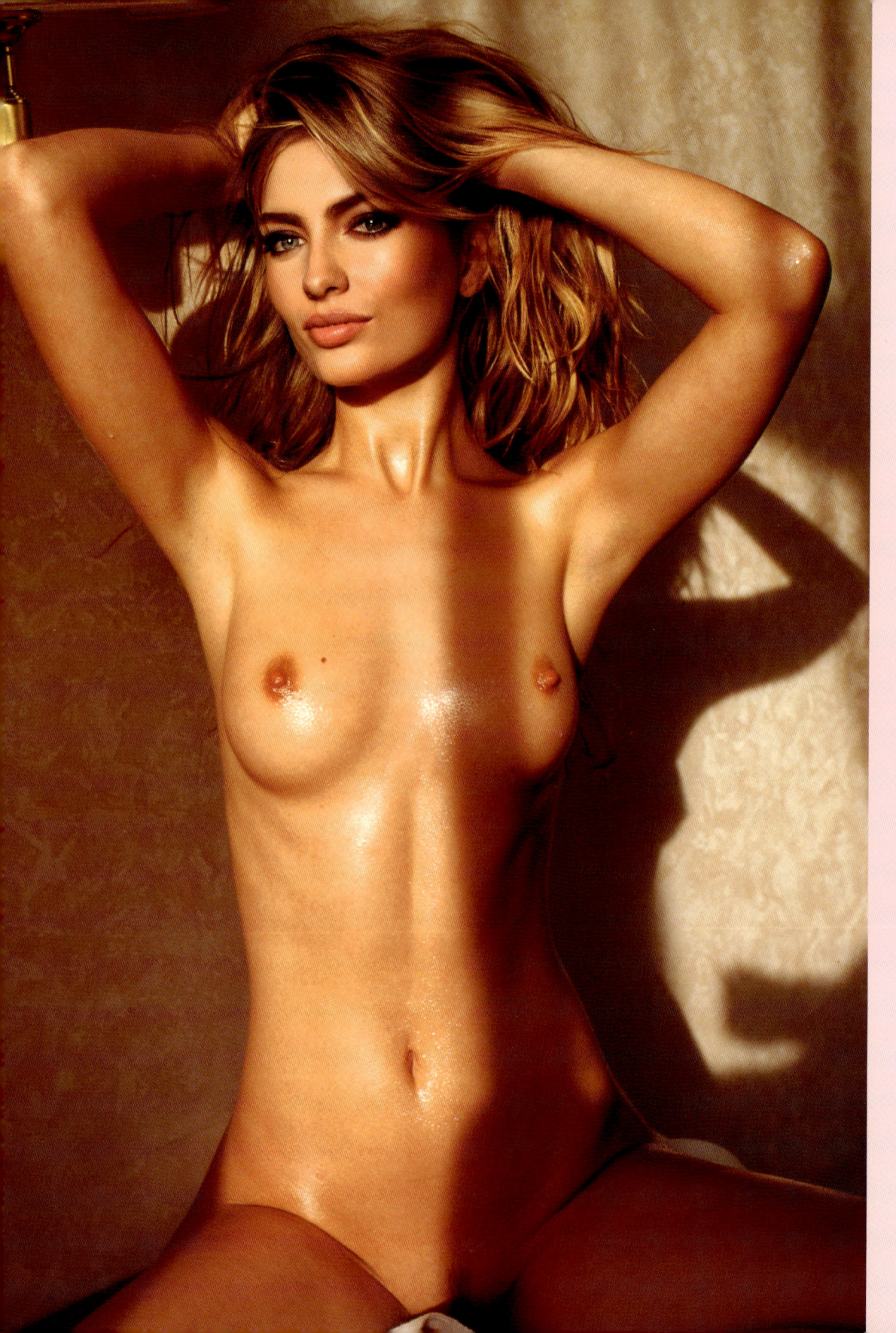

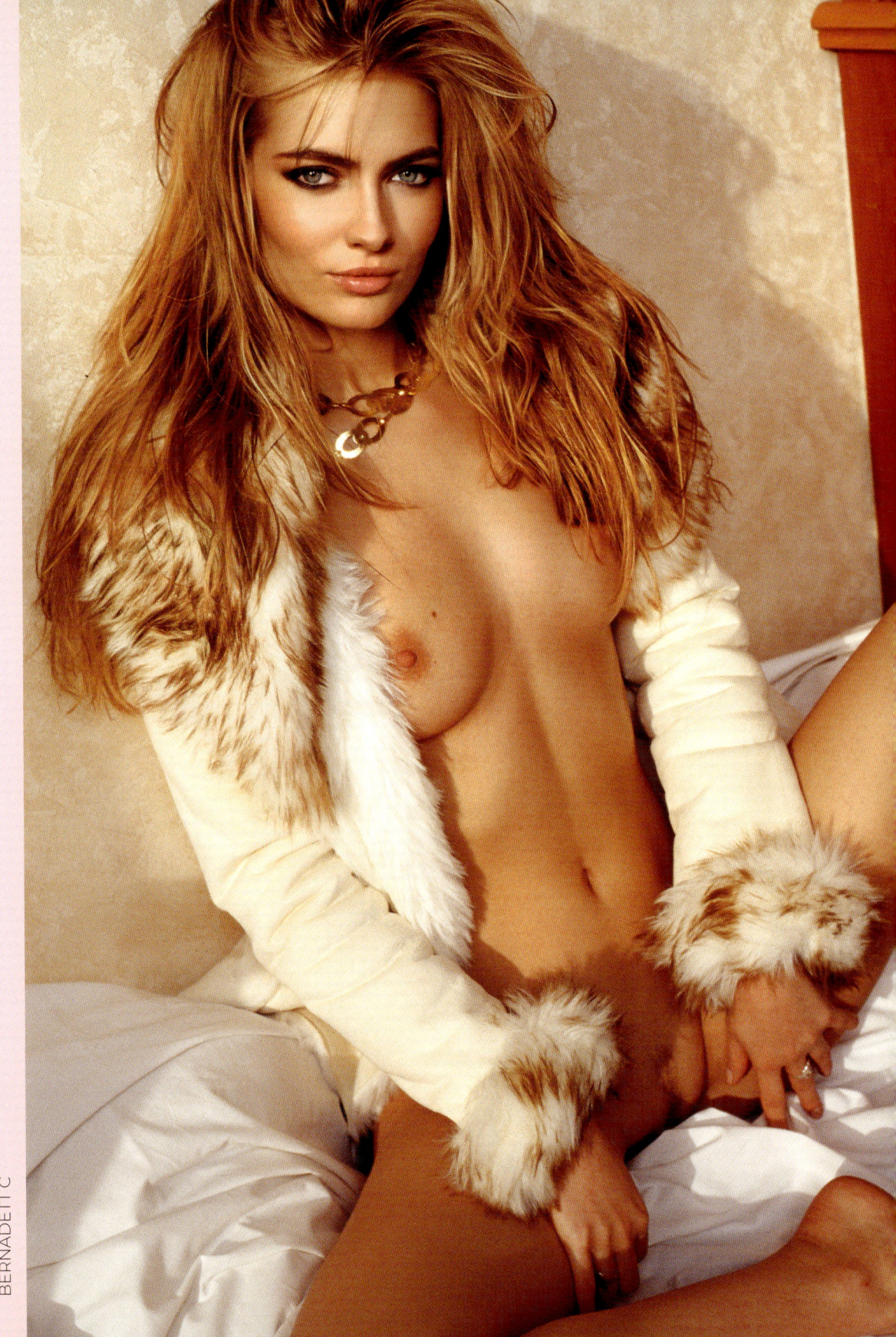

BERNADETT C

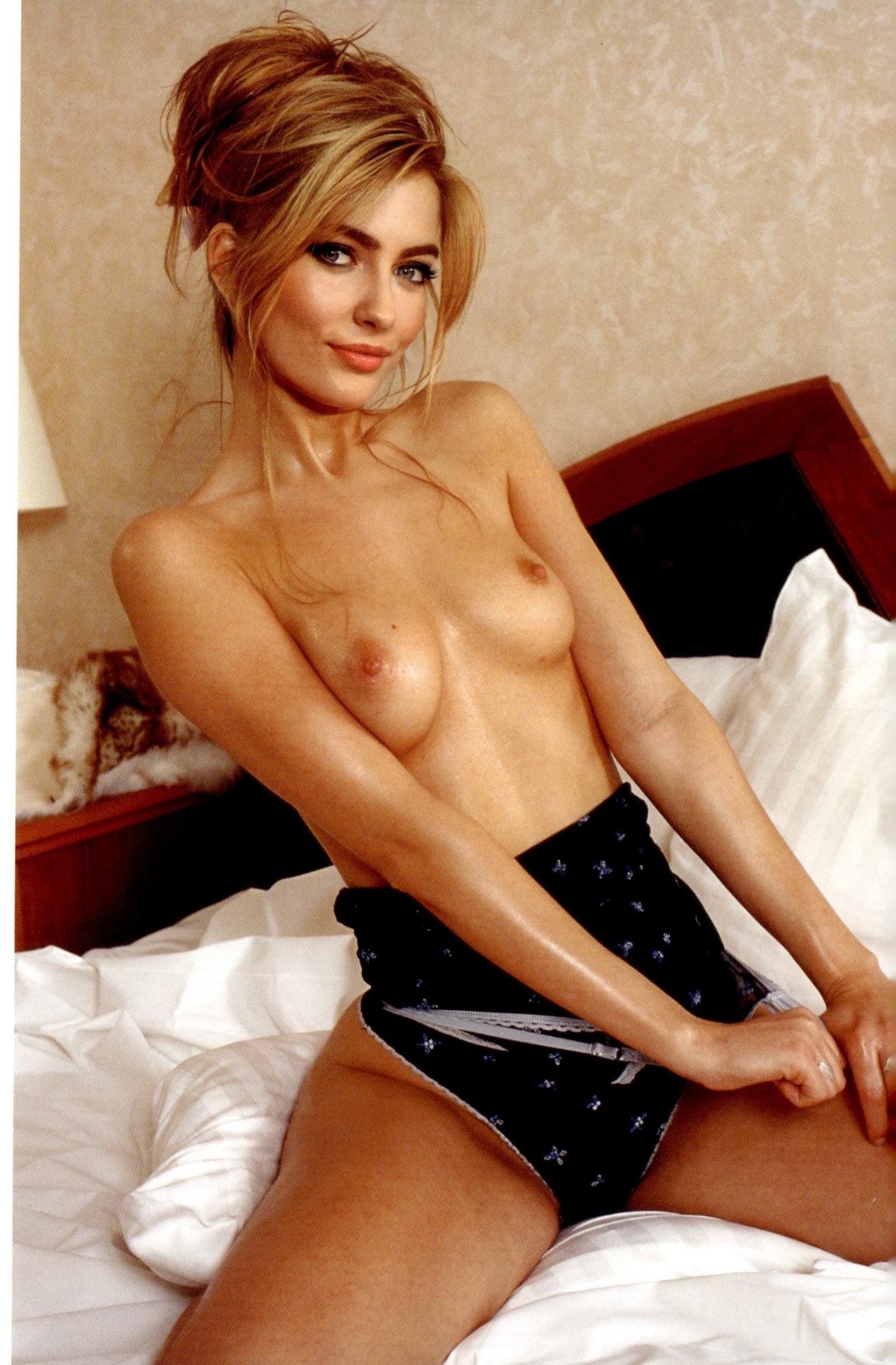

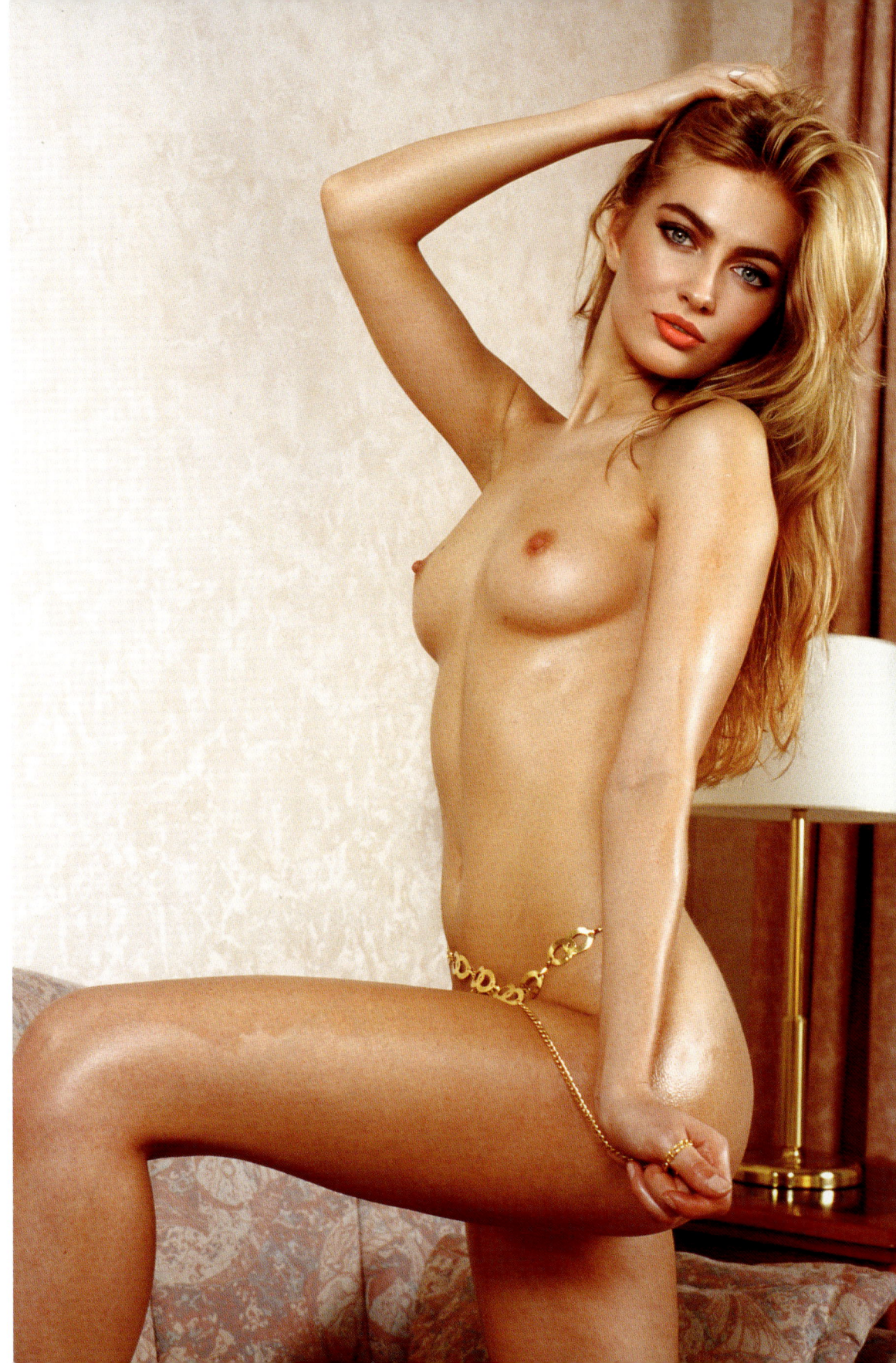

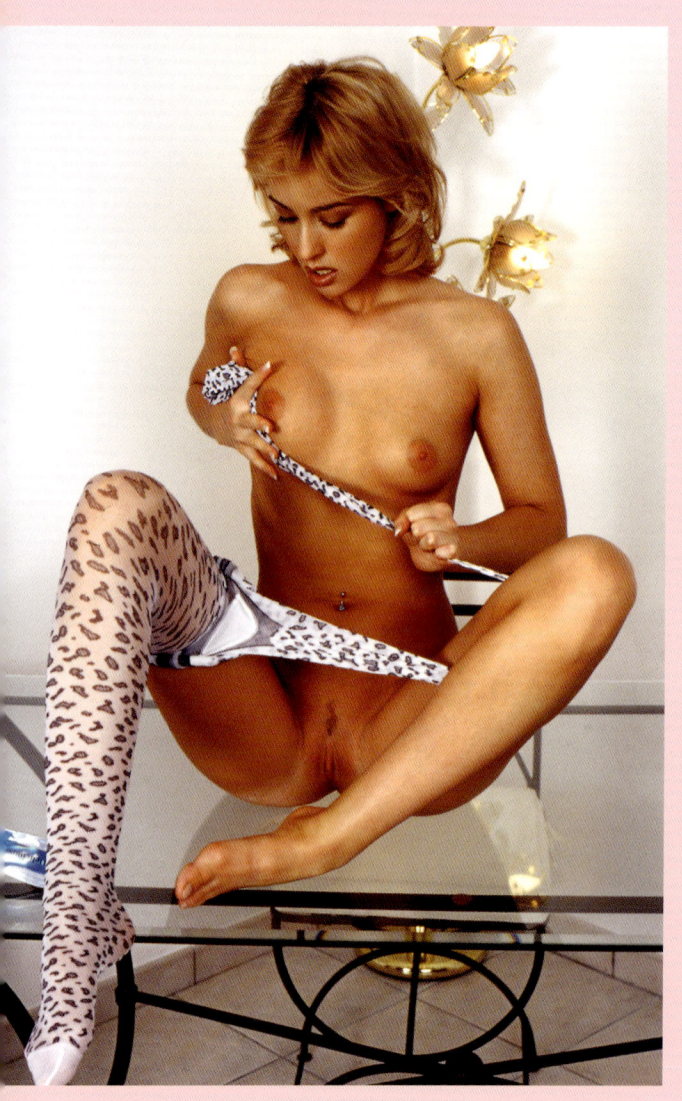
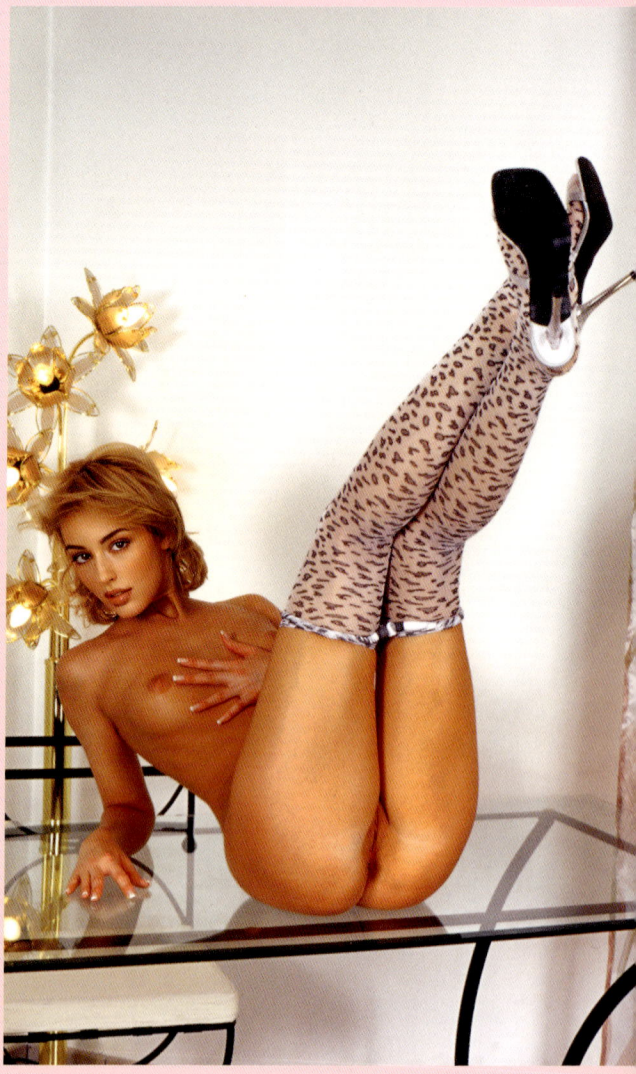

BERNADETTE

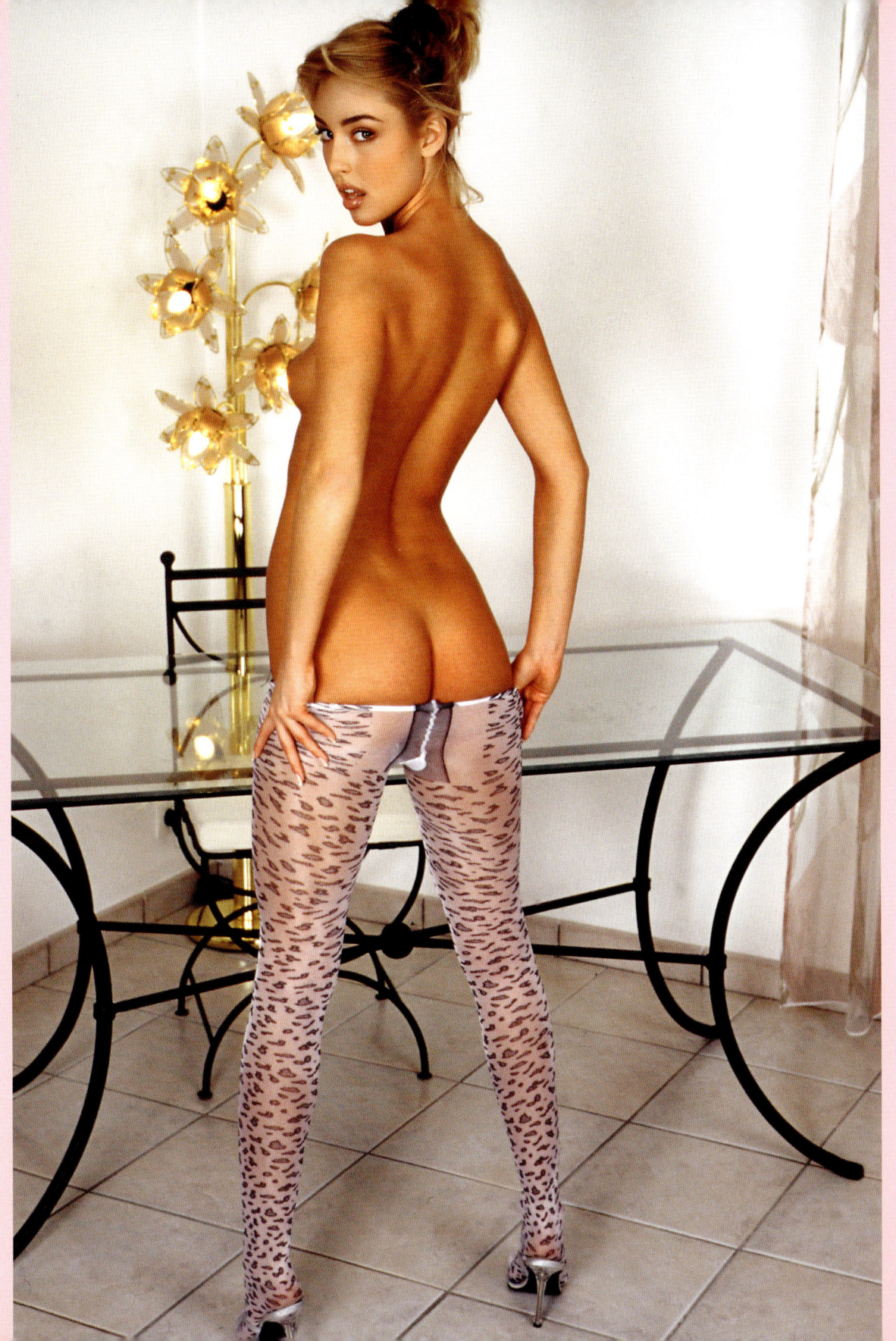

37

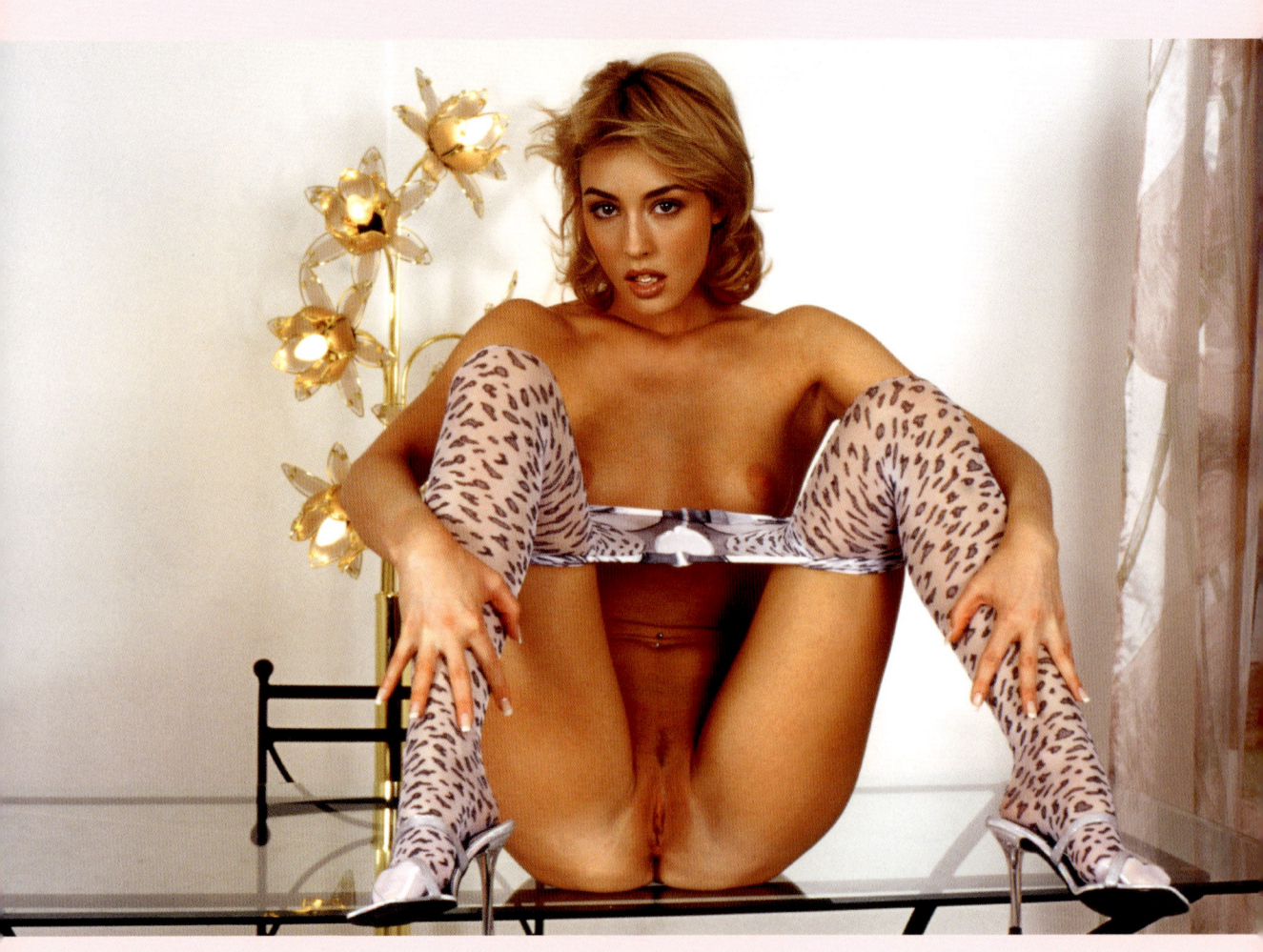

BERNADETTE

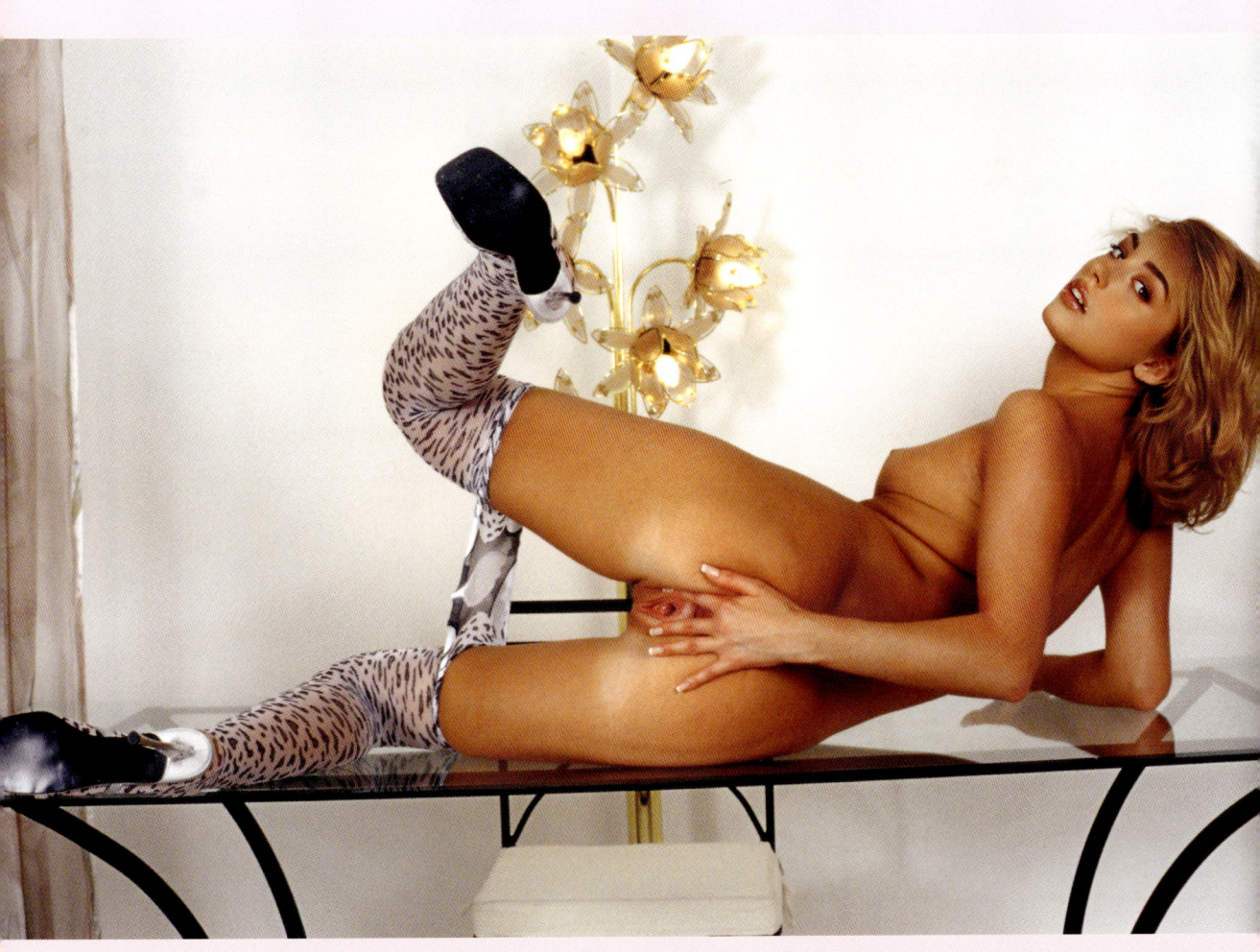

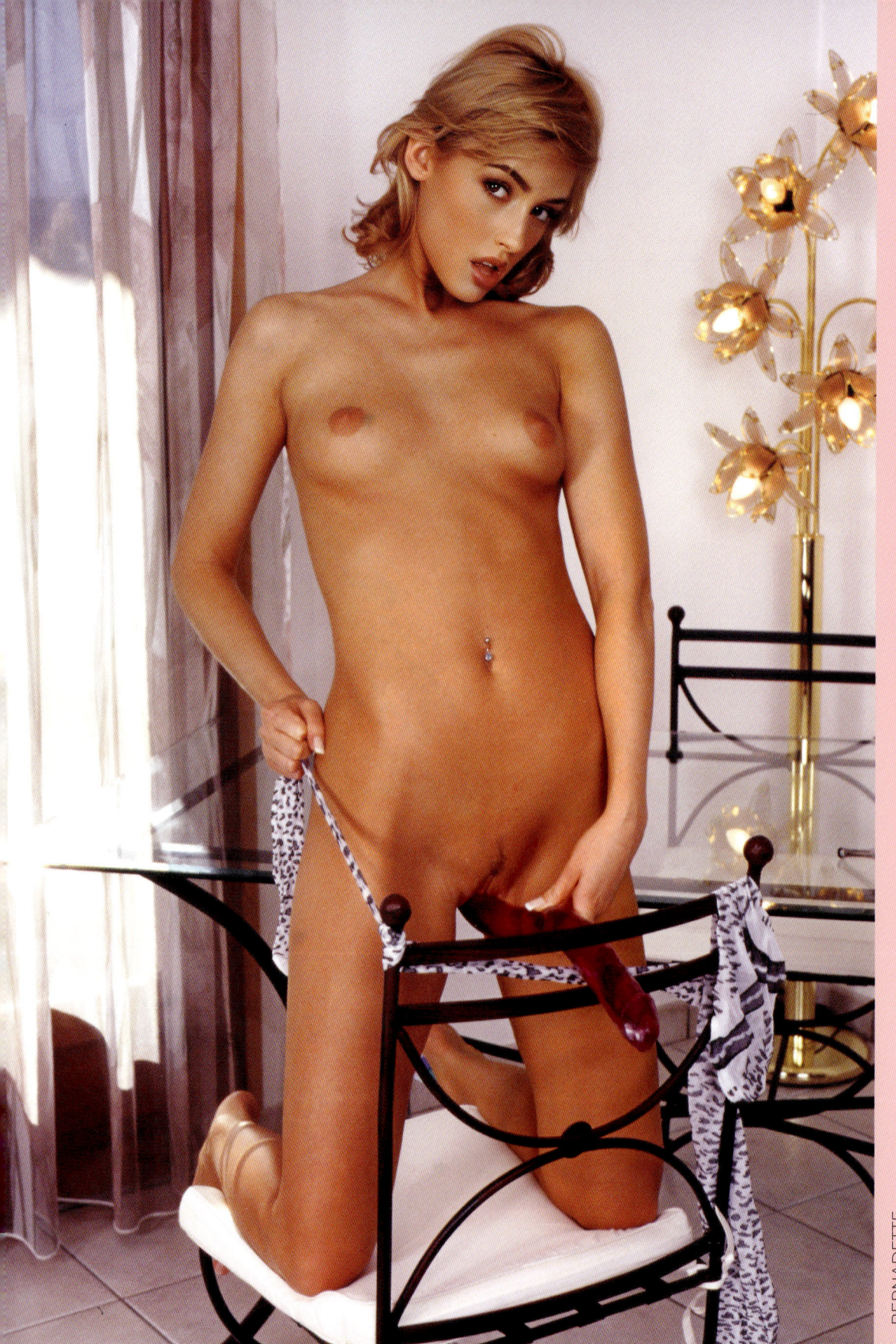

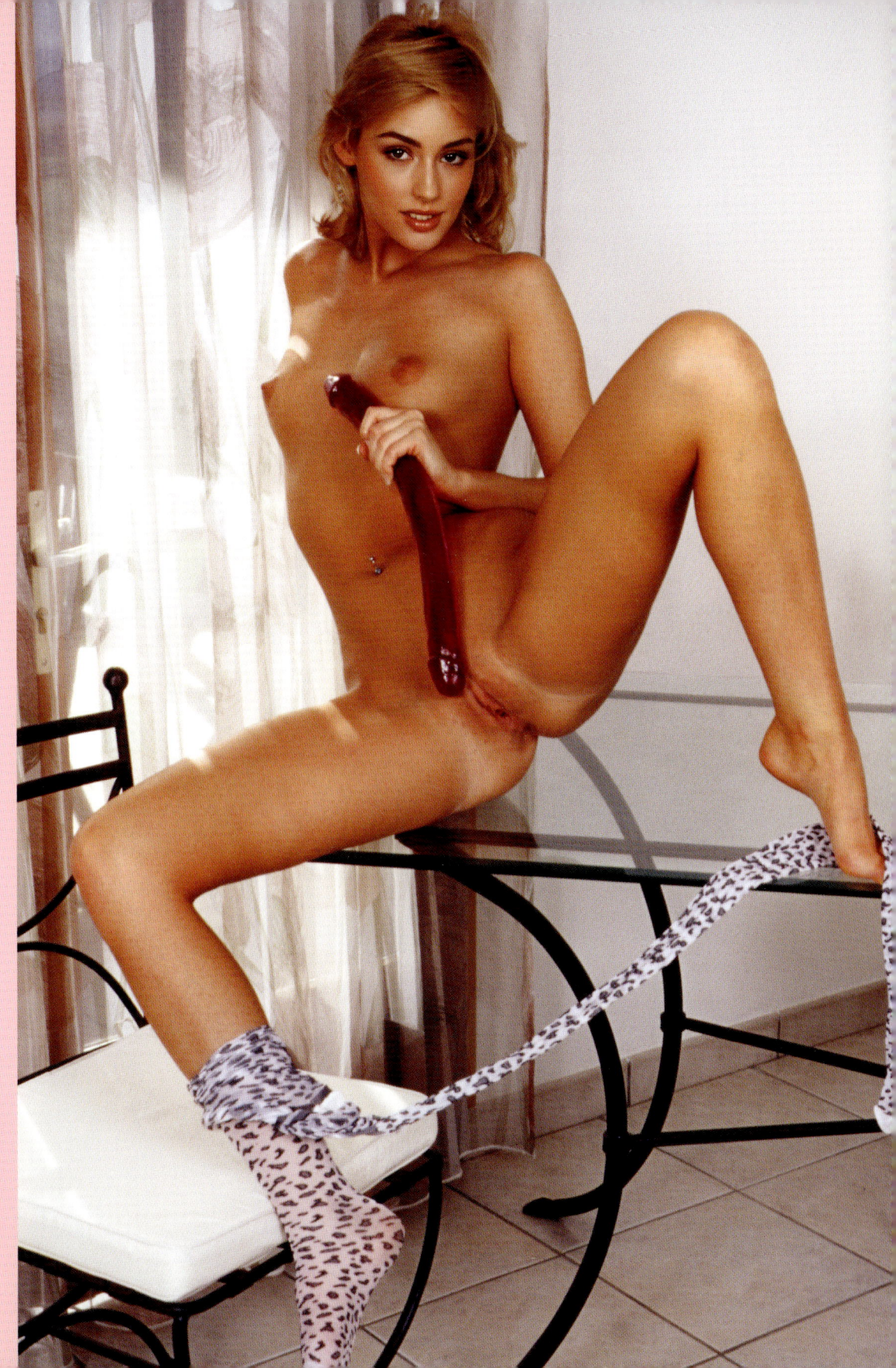

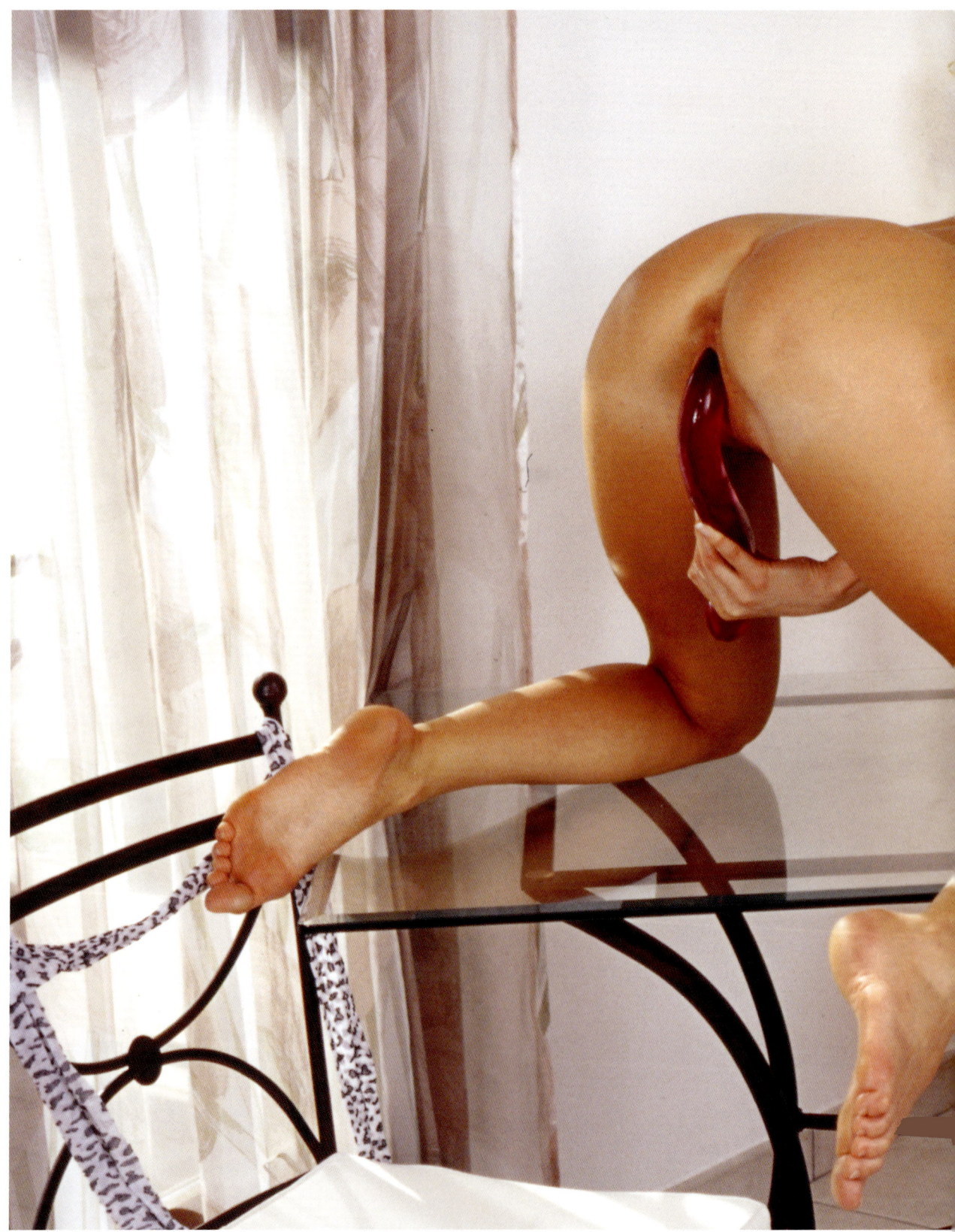

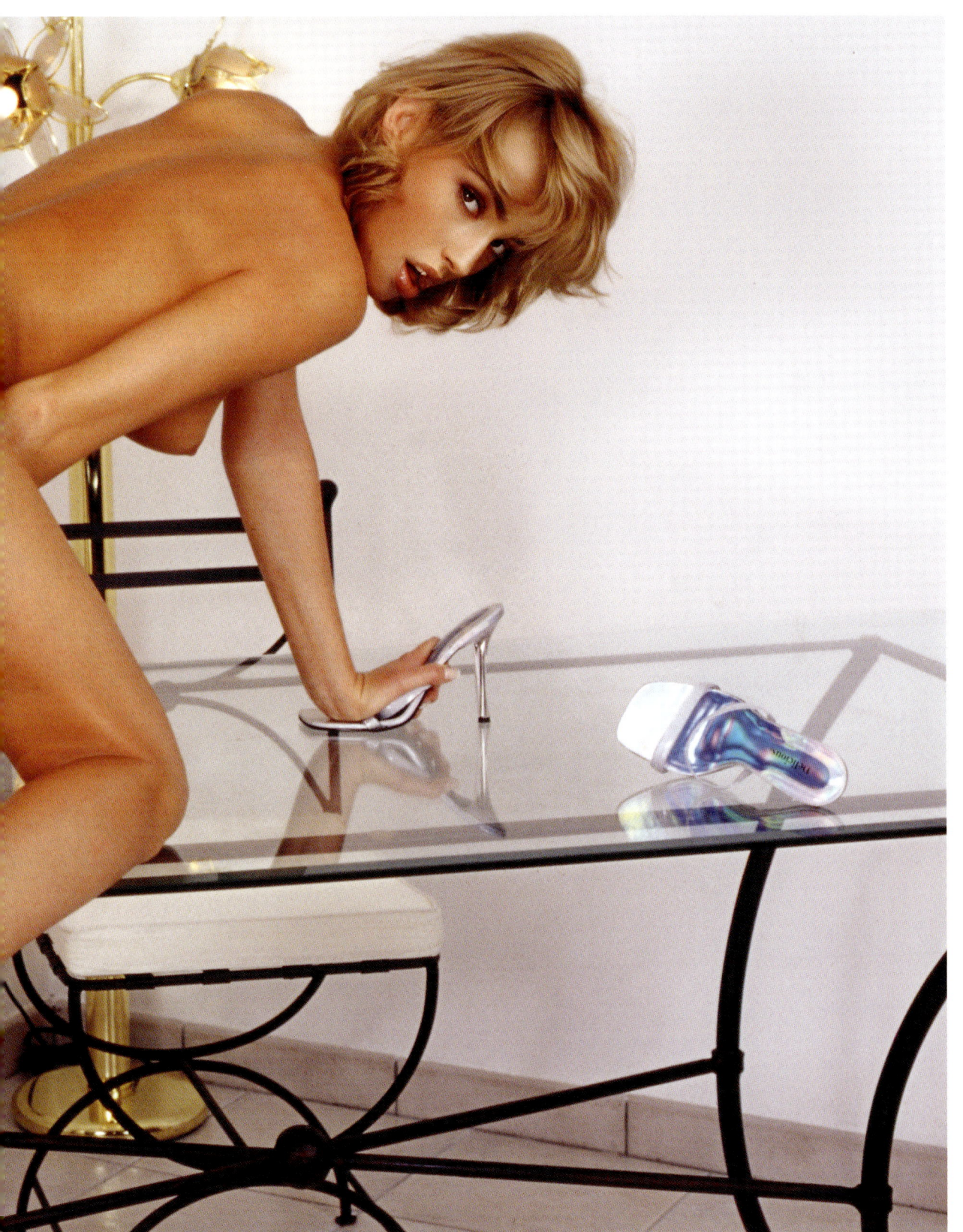

BERNADETTE

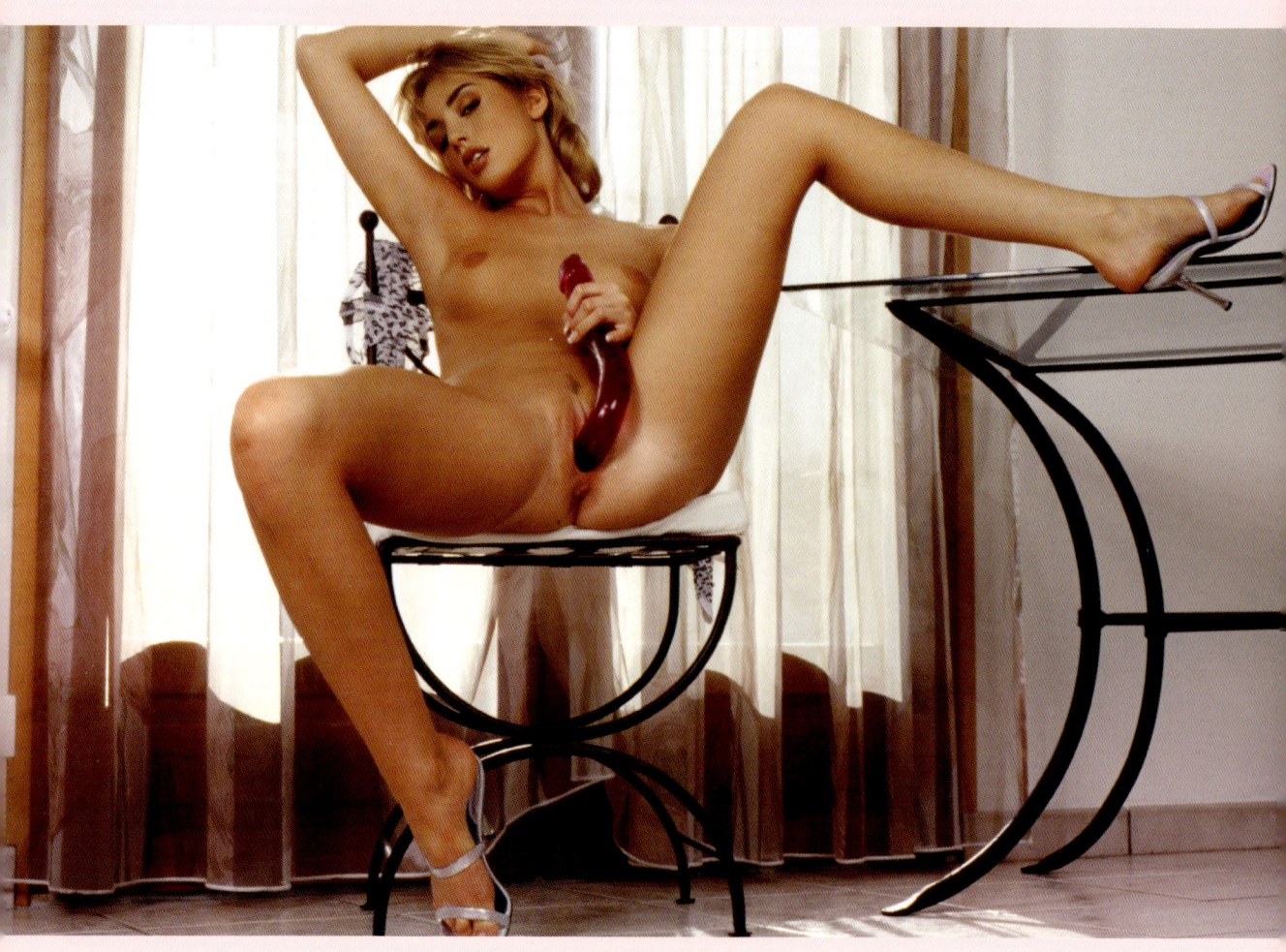

BERNADETTE

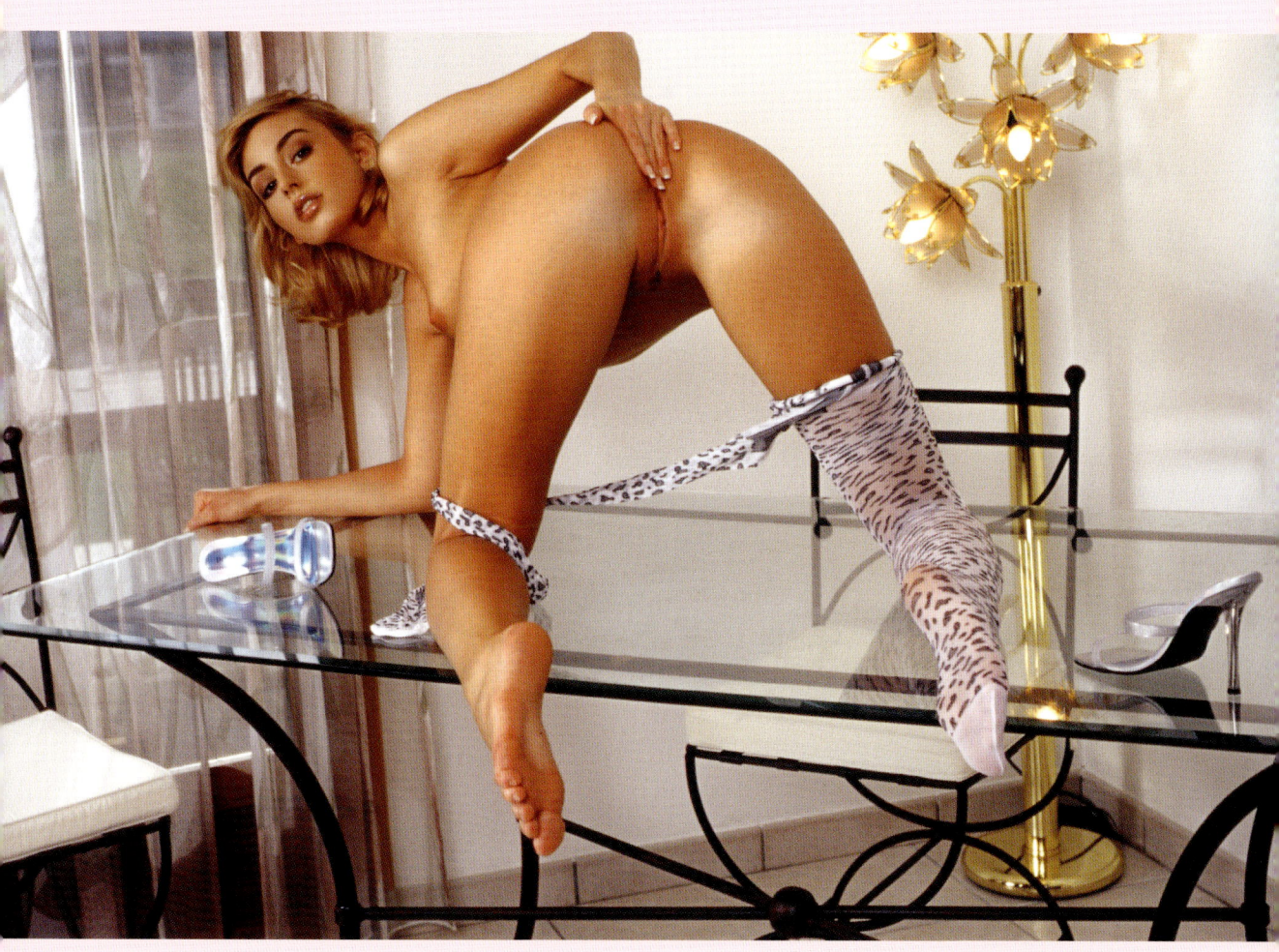

BERNADETTE

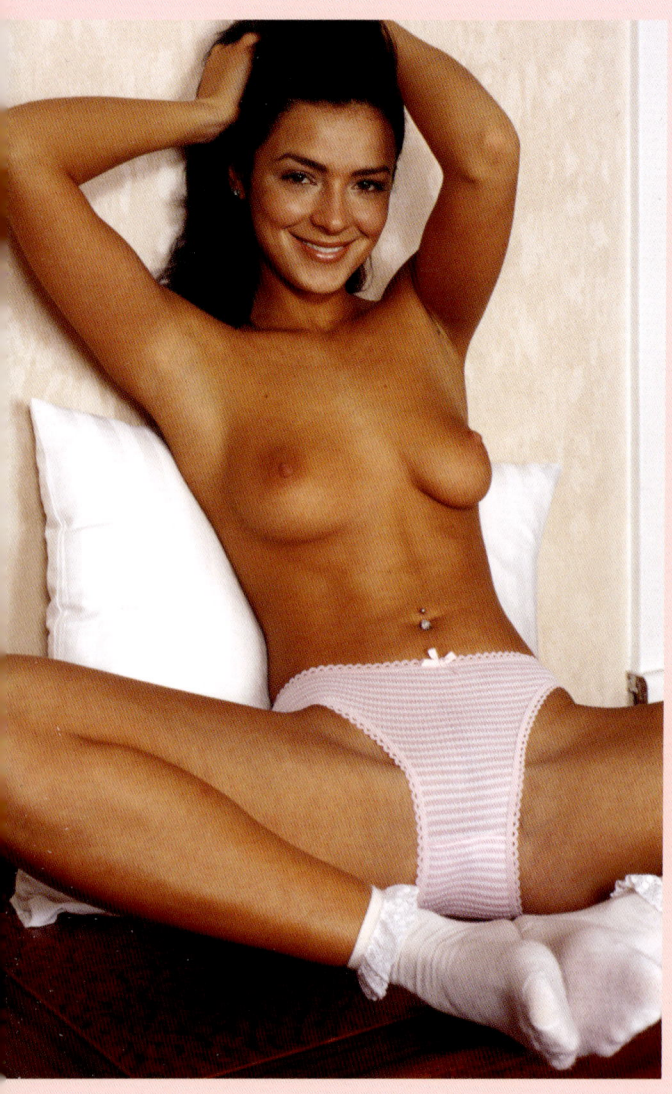
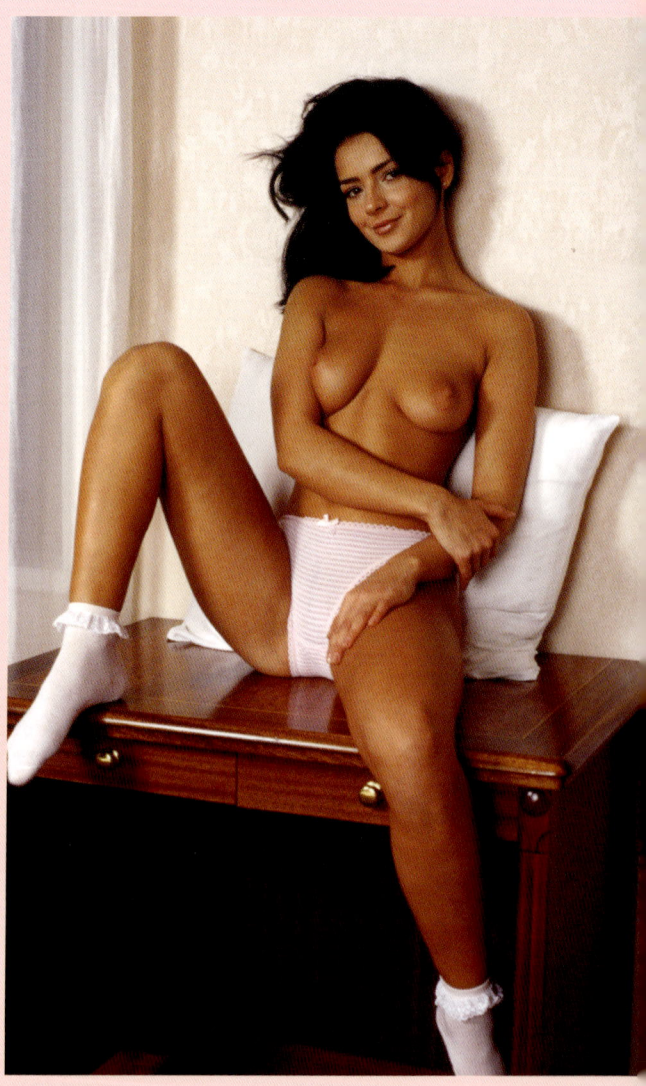

CATHY

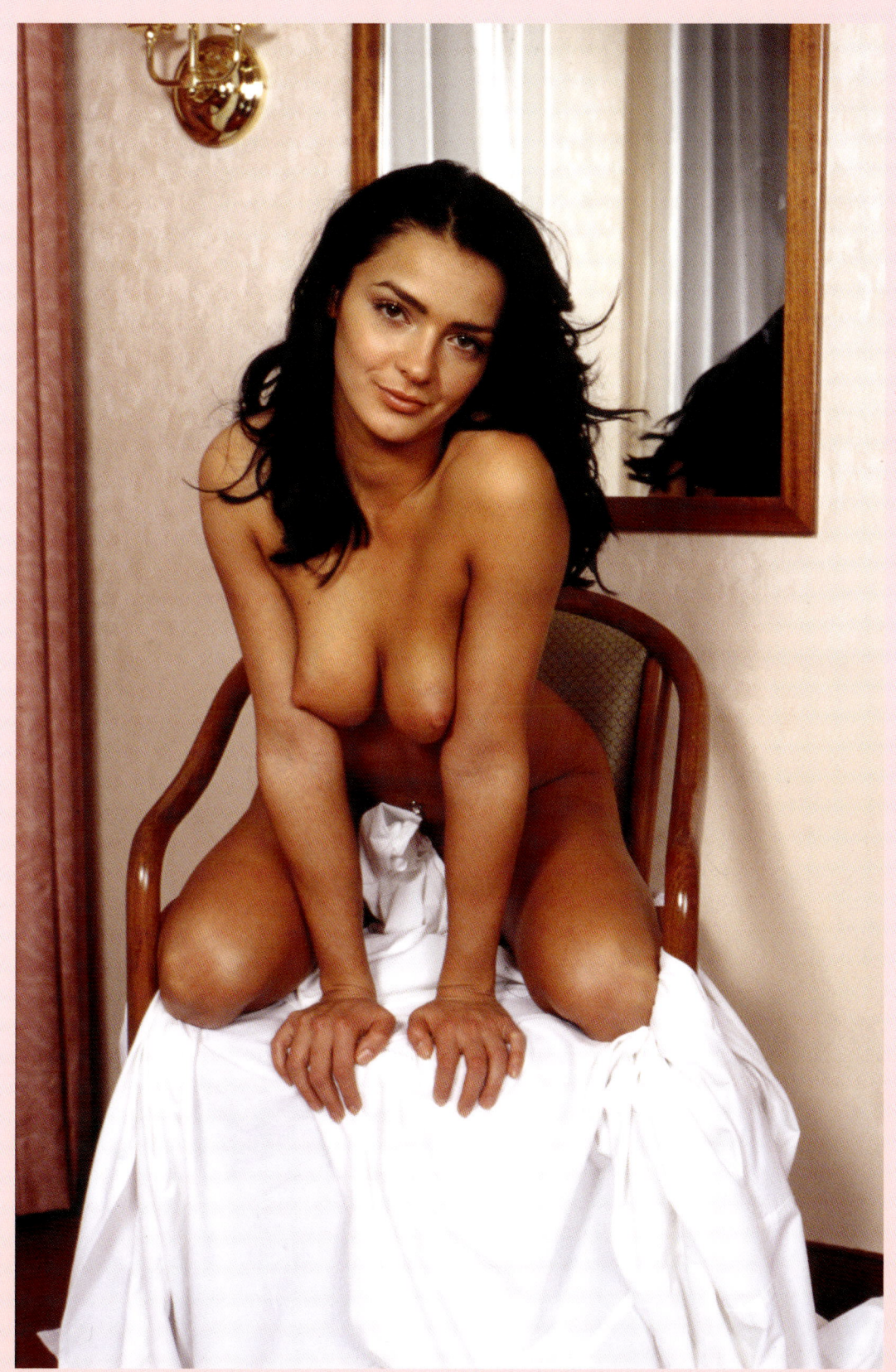

CATHY

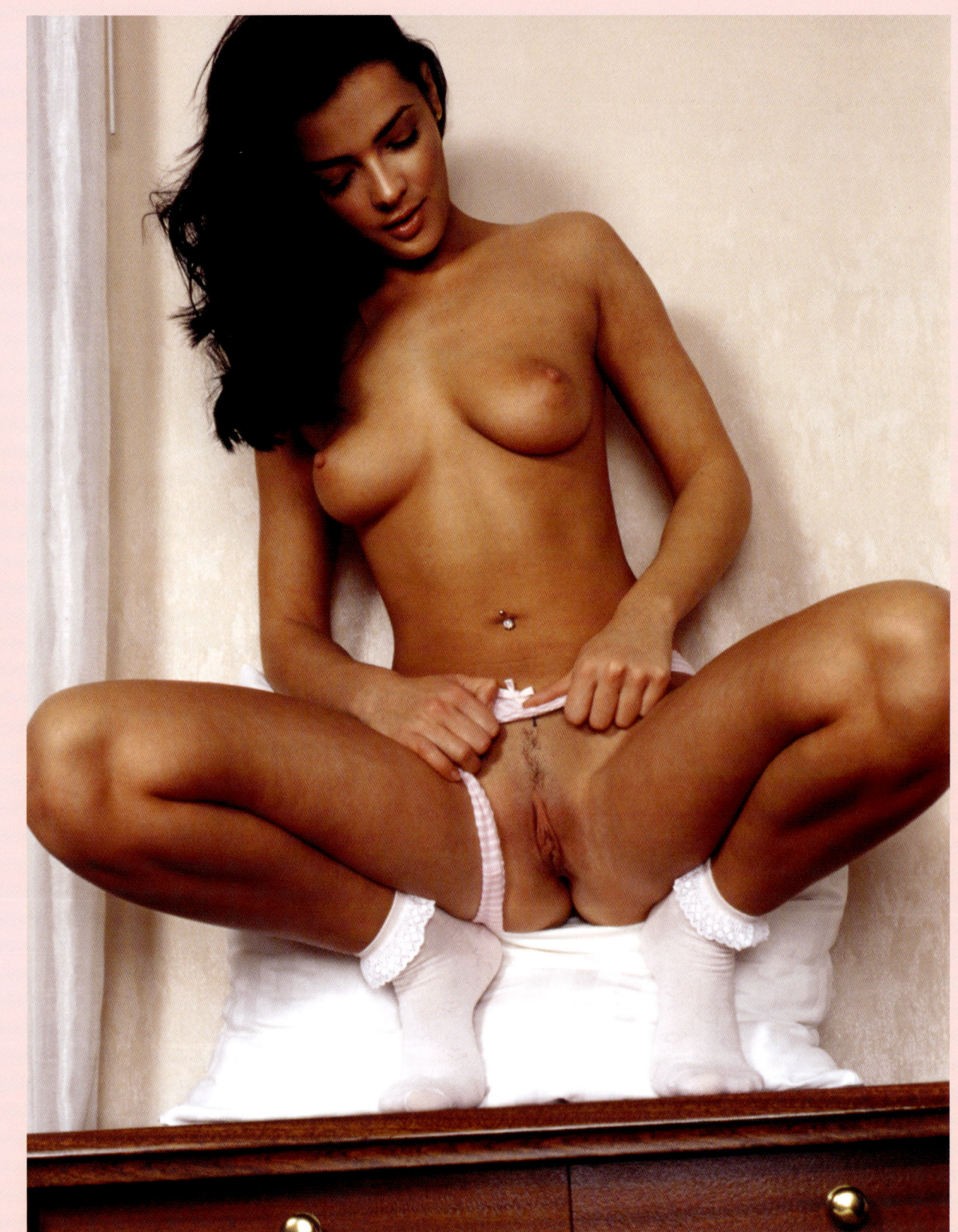

CATHY

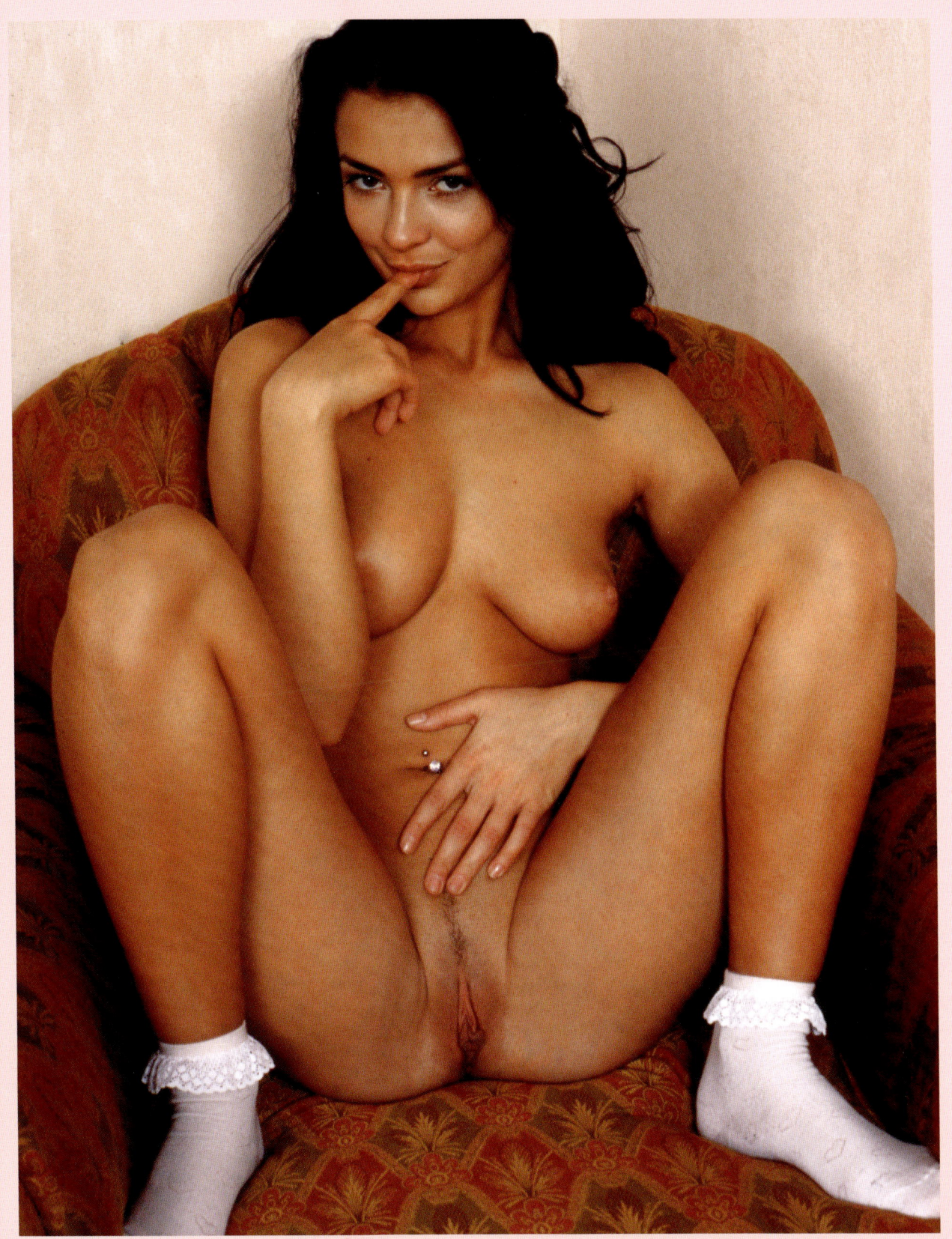

CATHY

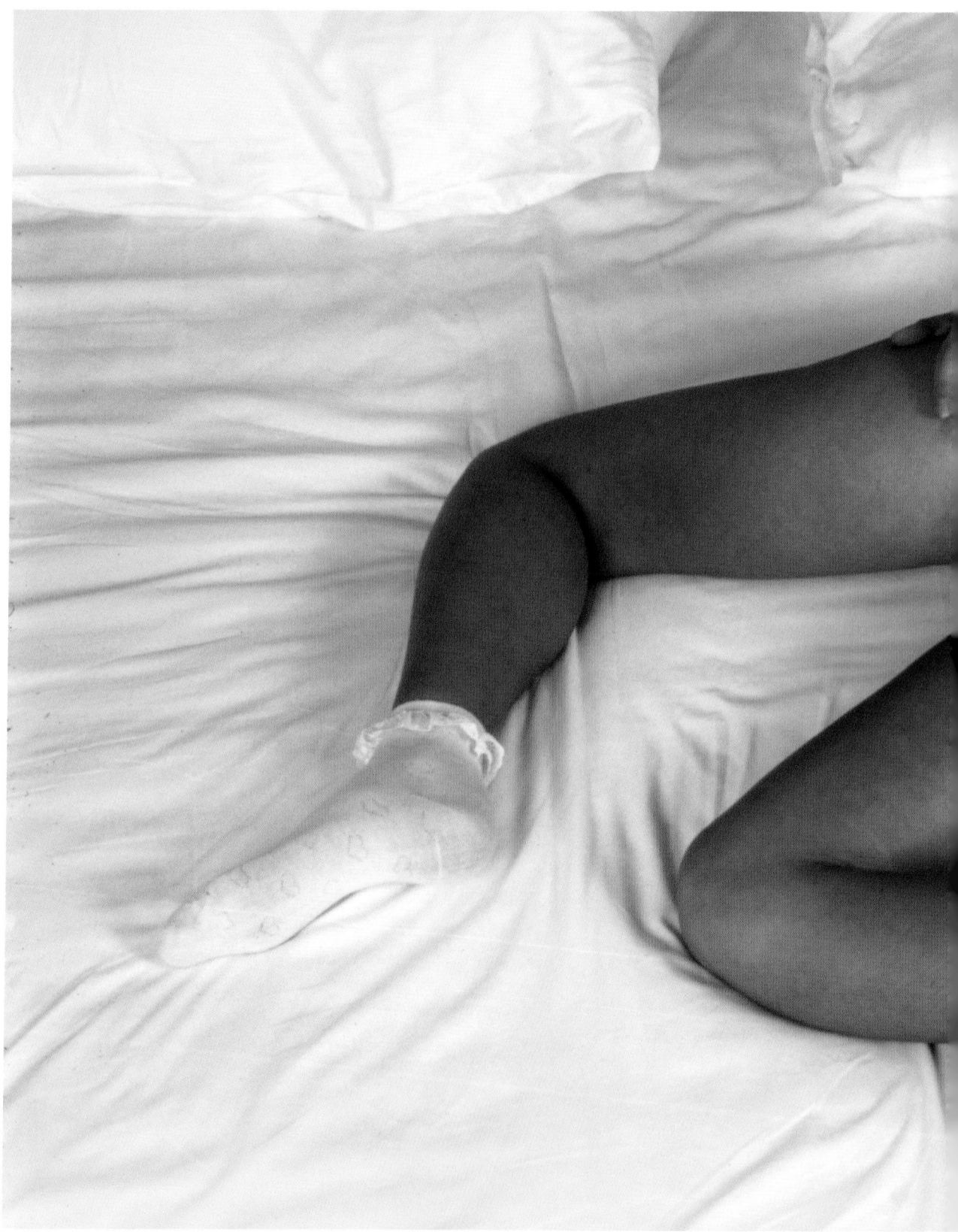

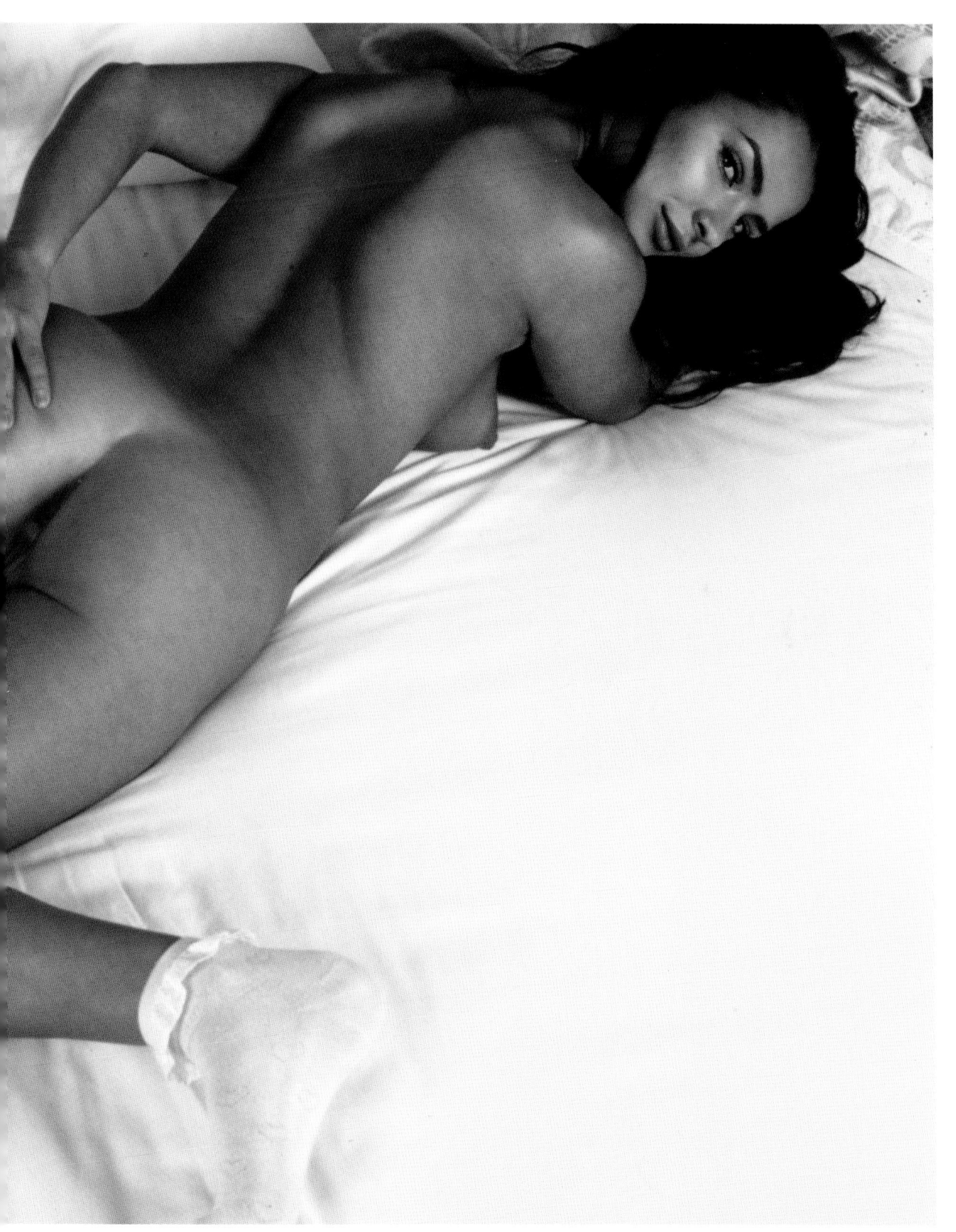

CATHY

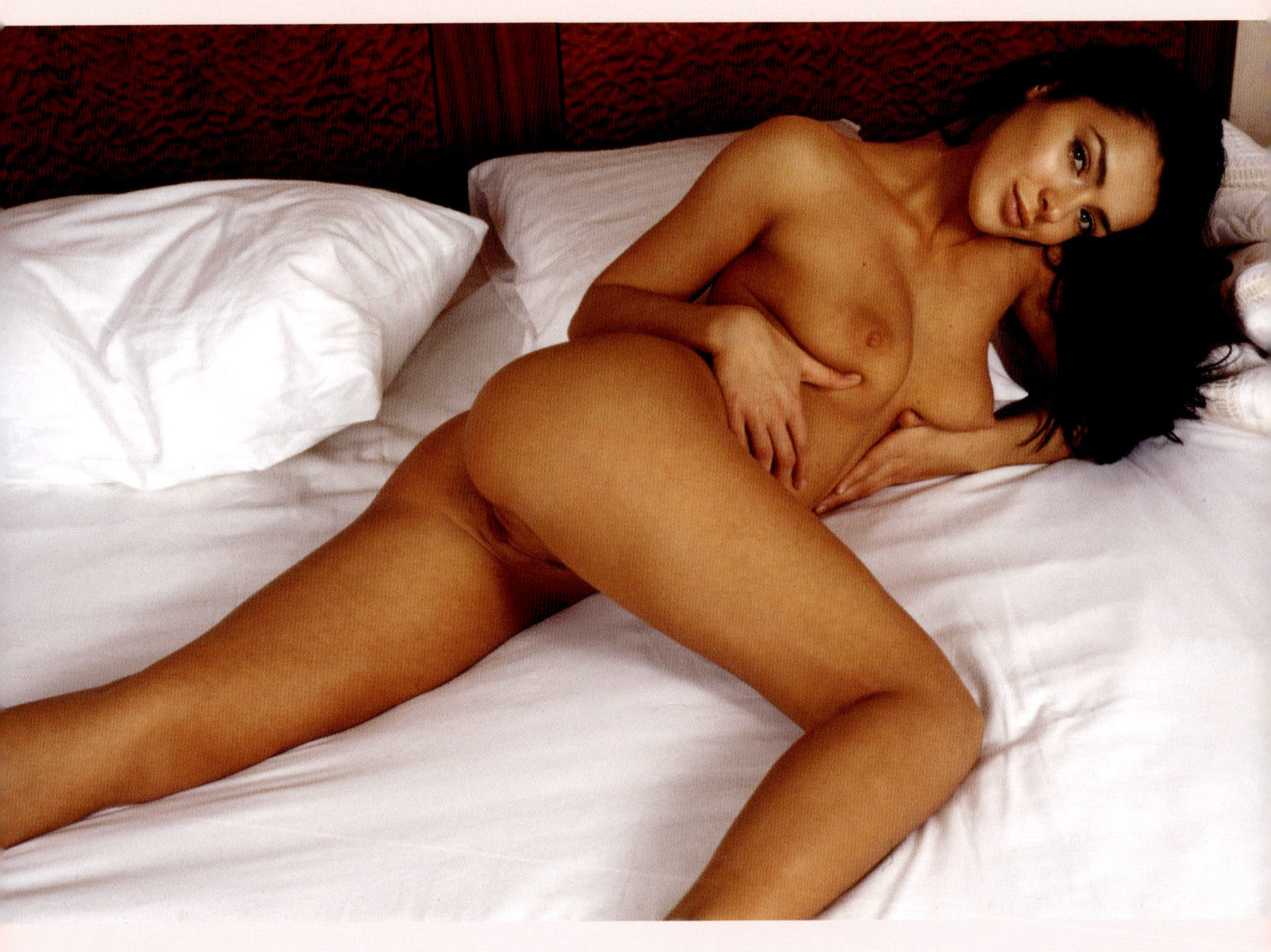

CATHY

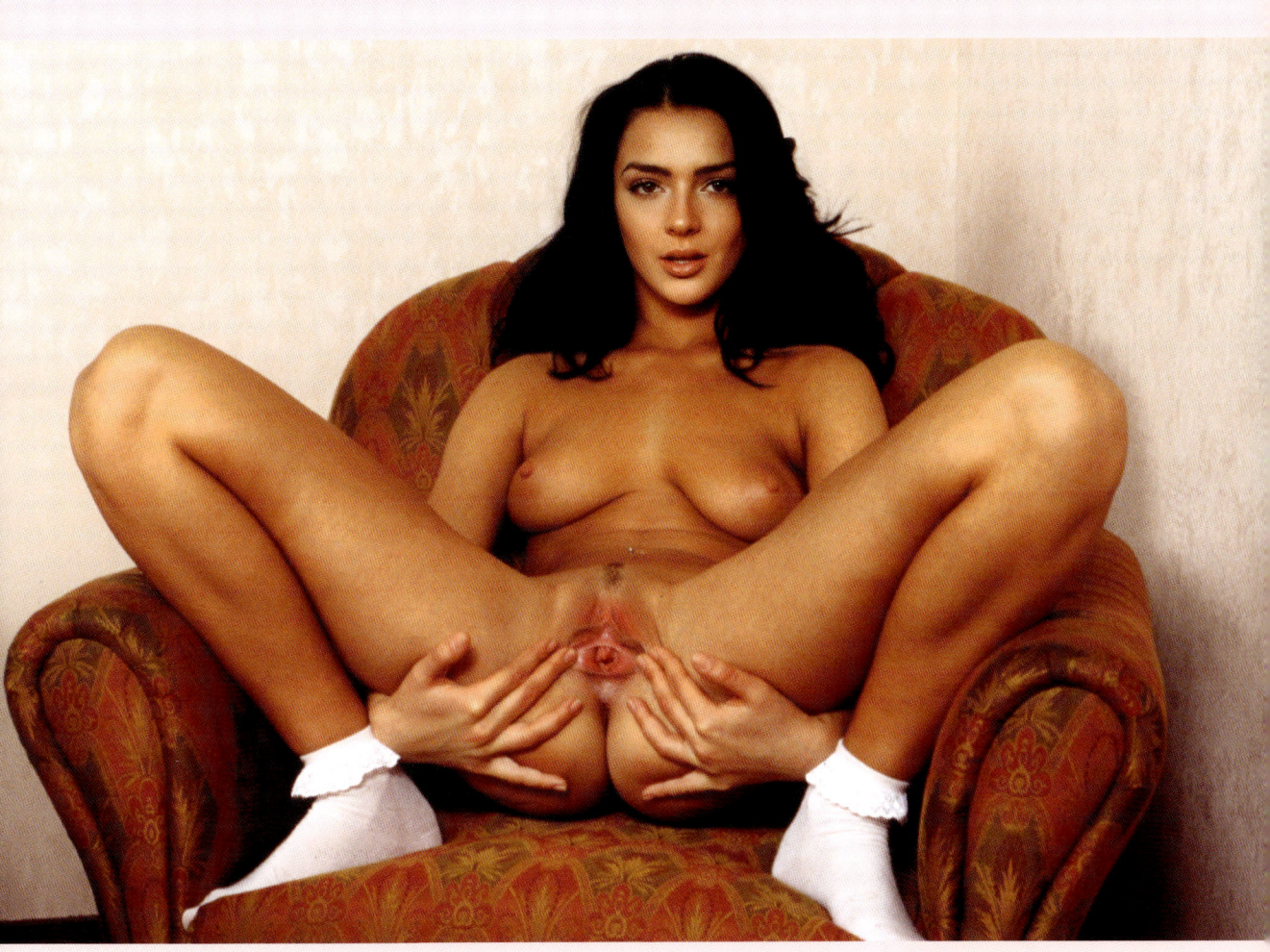

CATHY

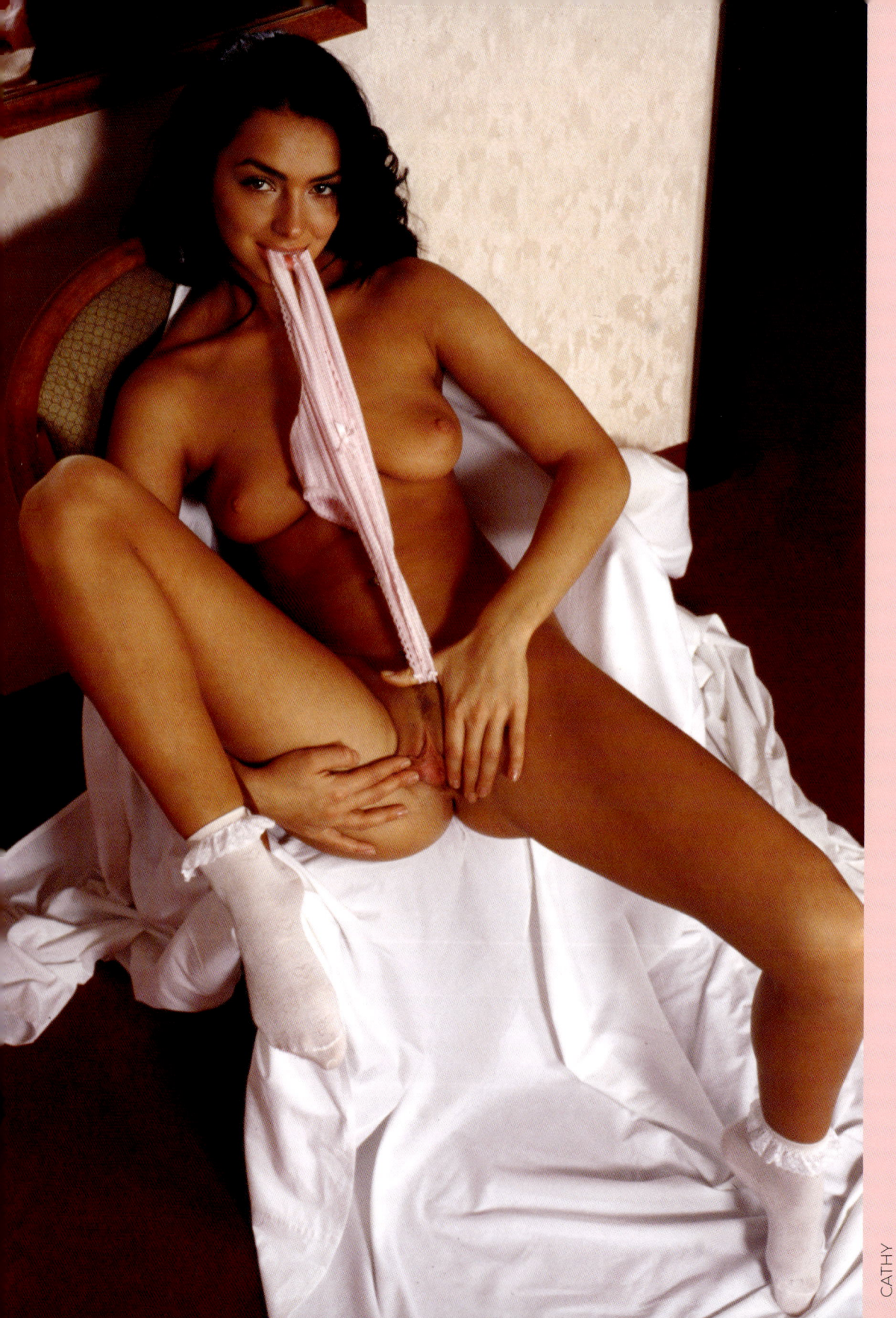

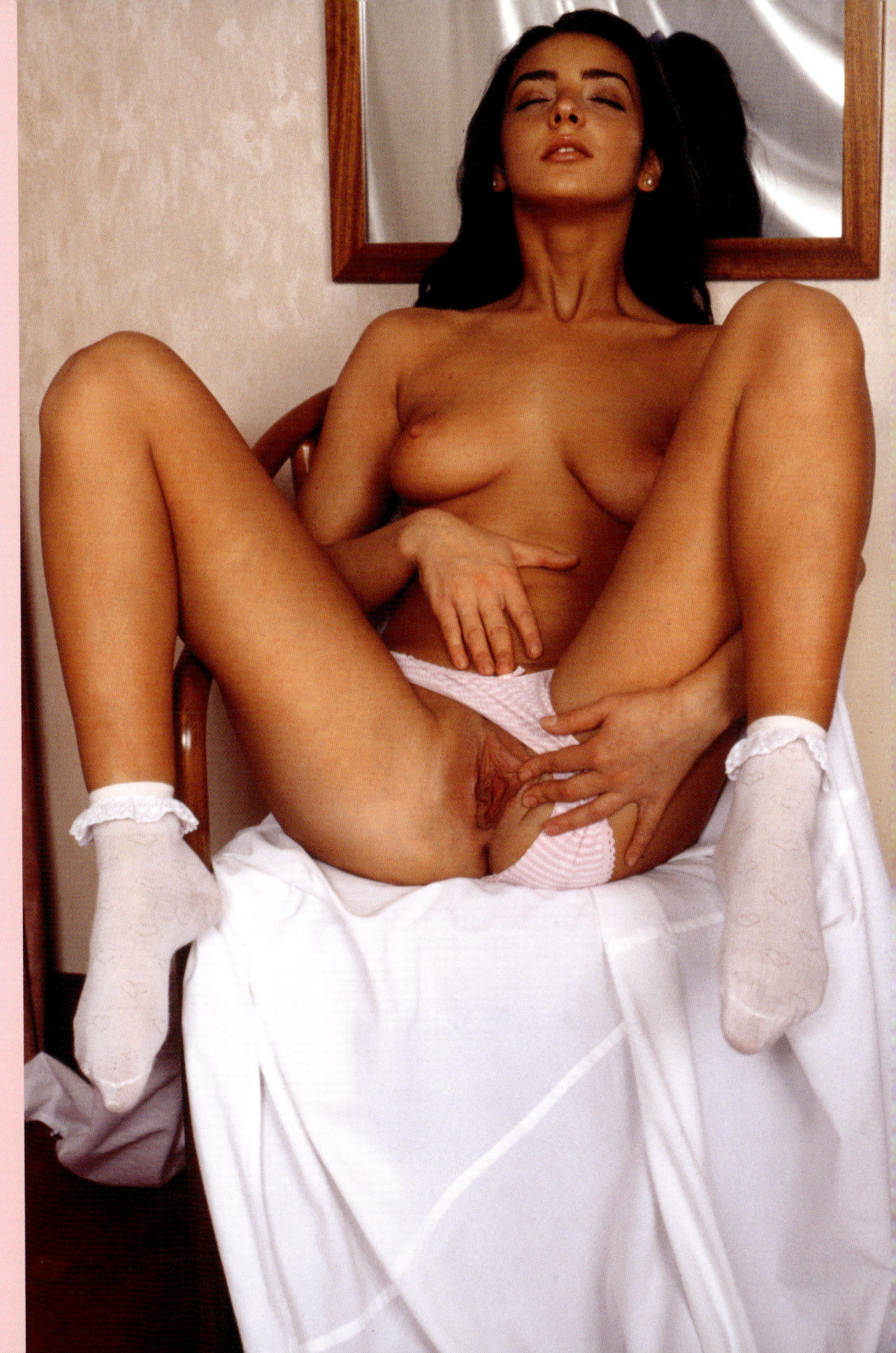

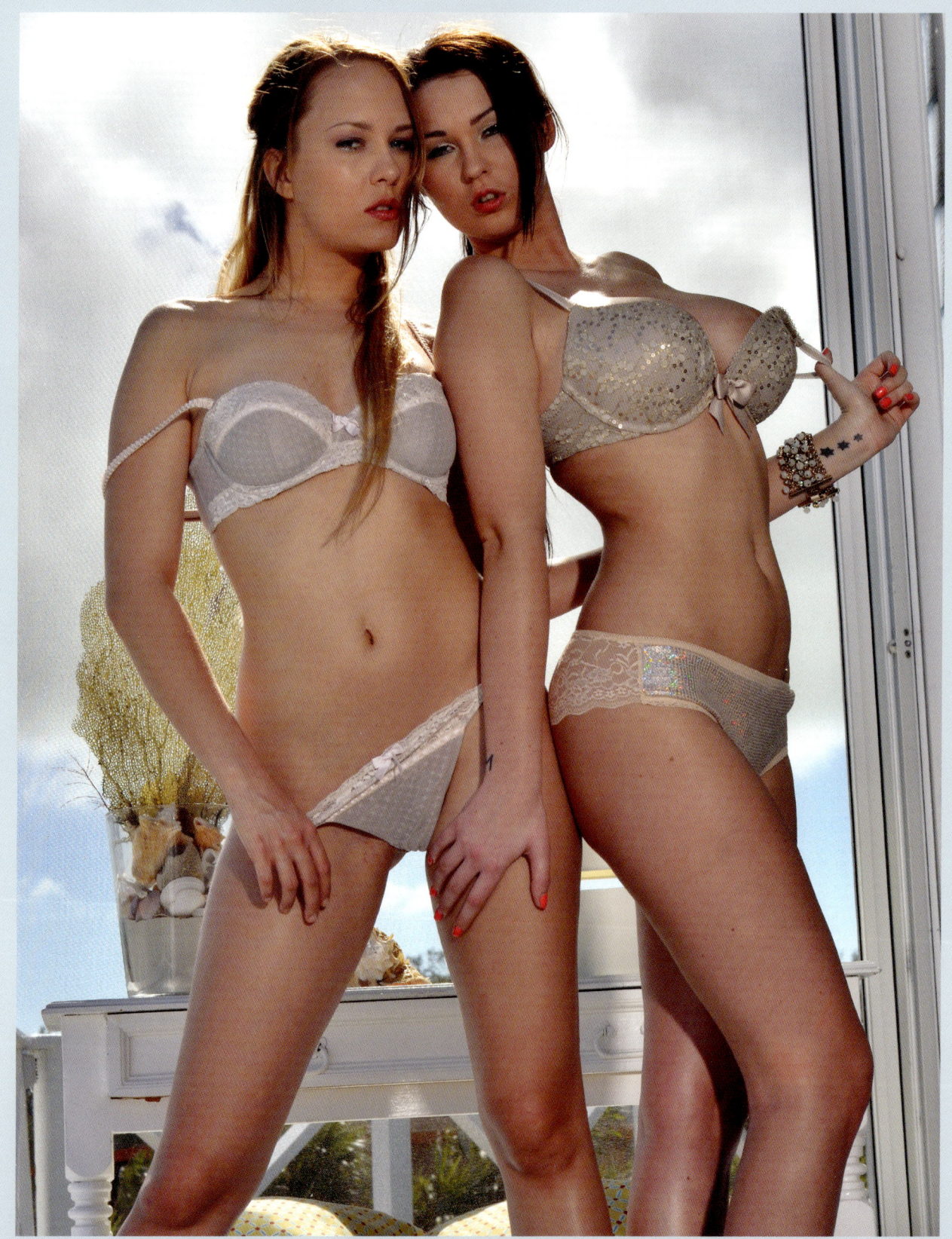

EVA & VIVIEN

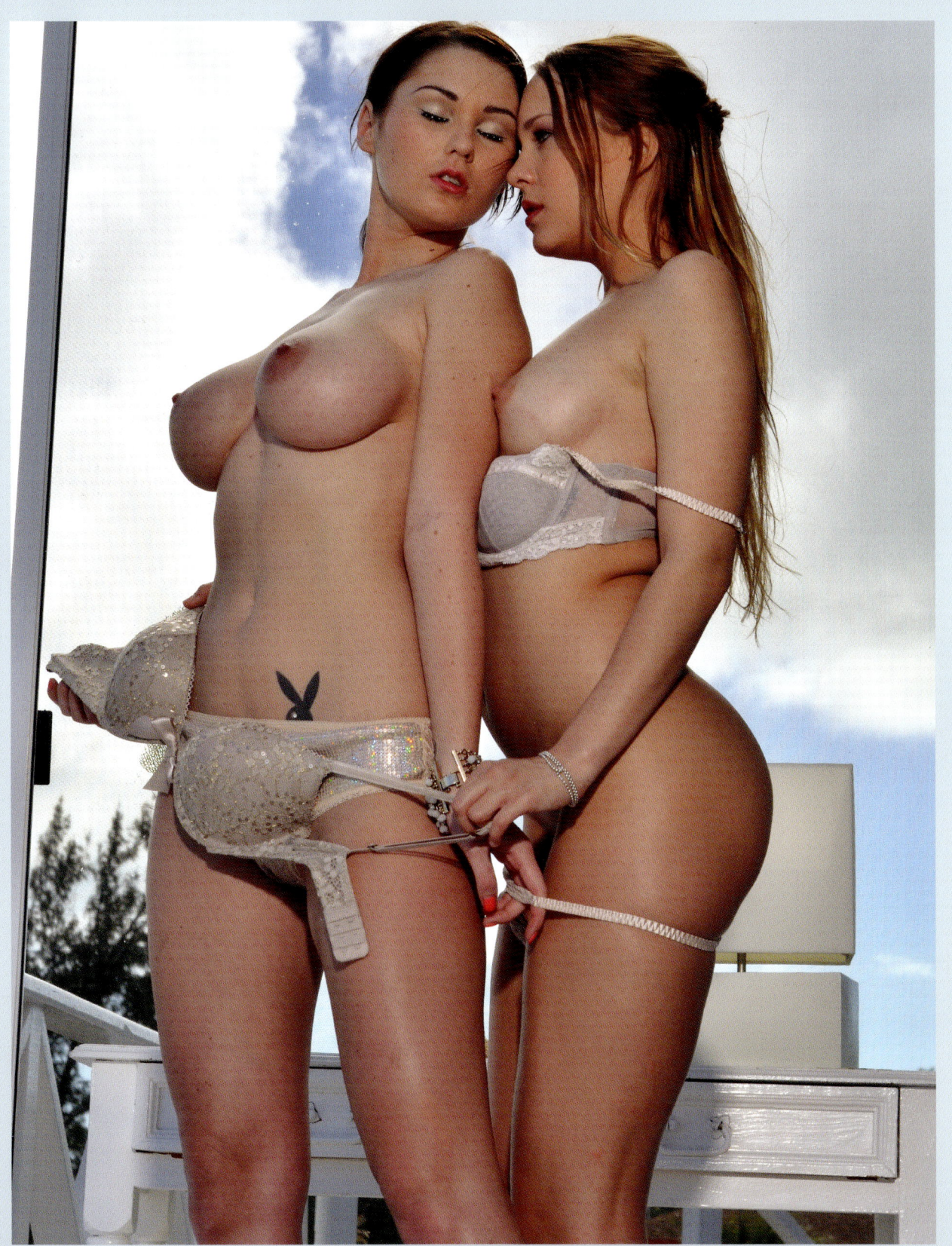

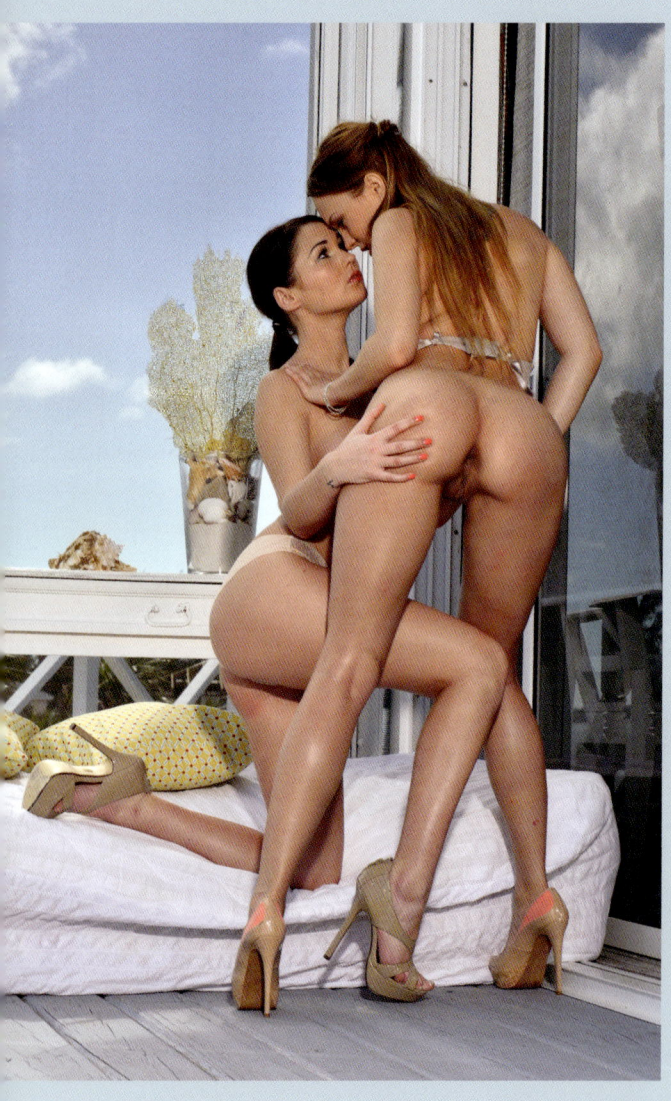
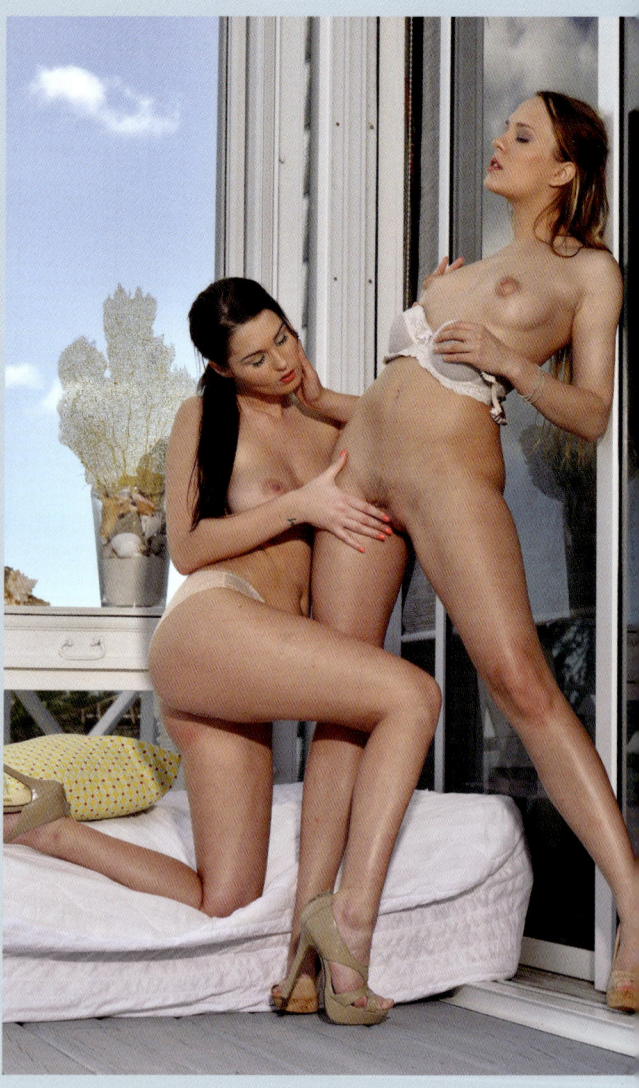

EVA & VIVIEN

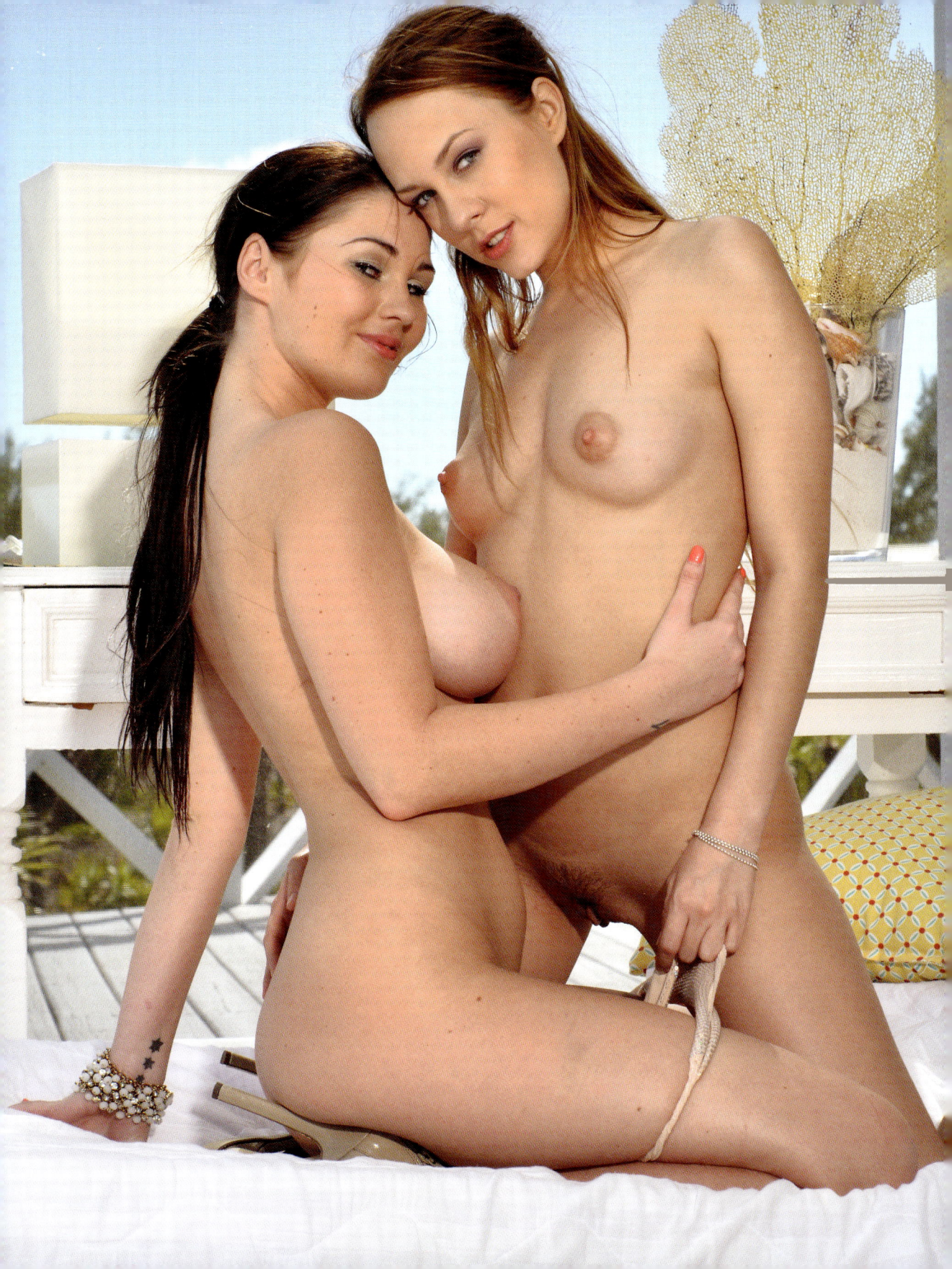

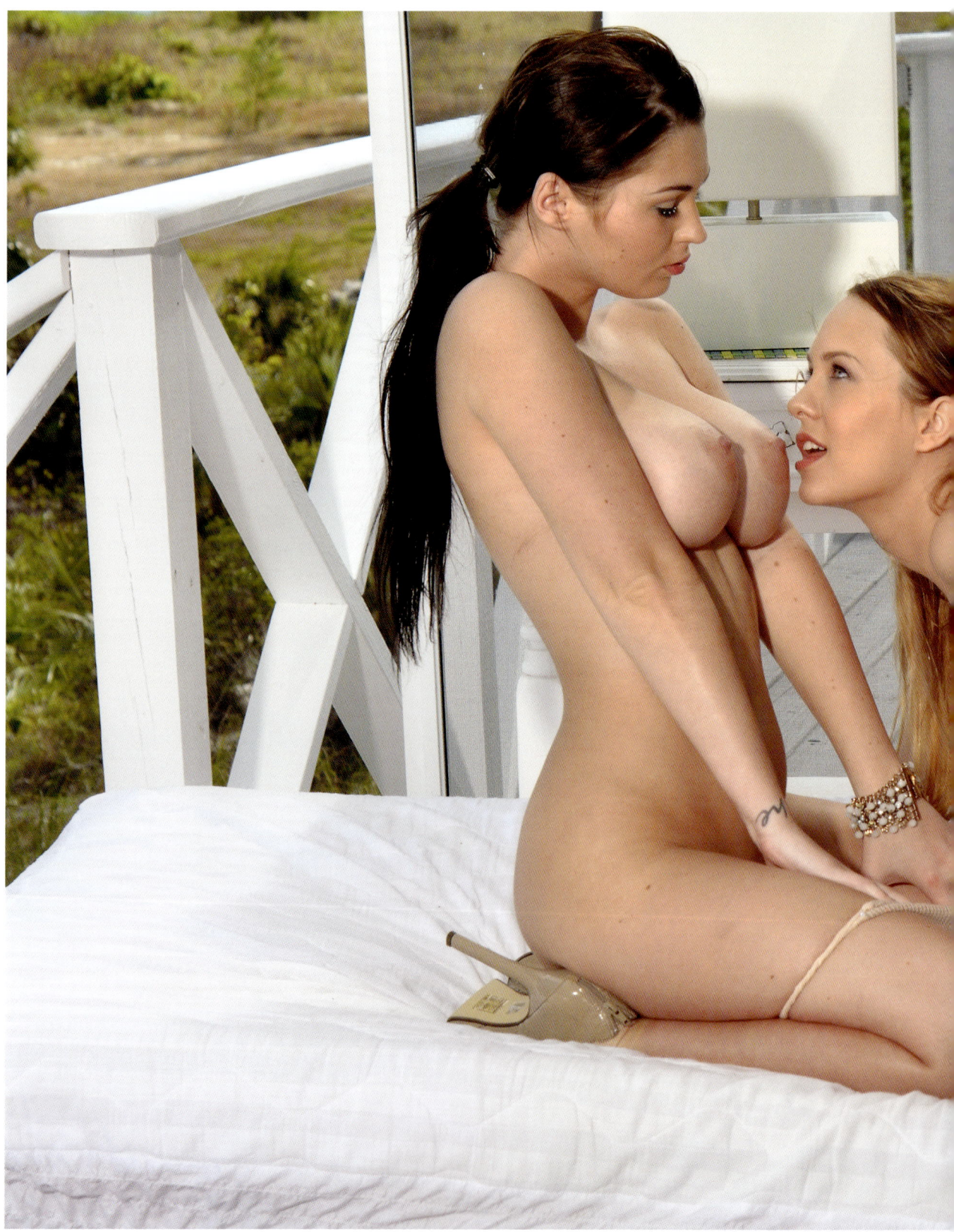

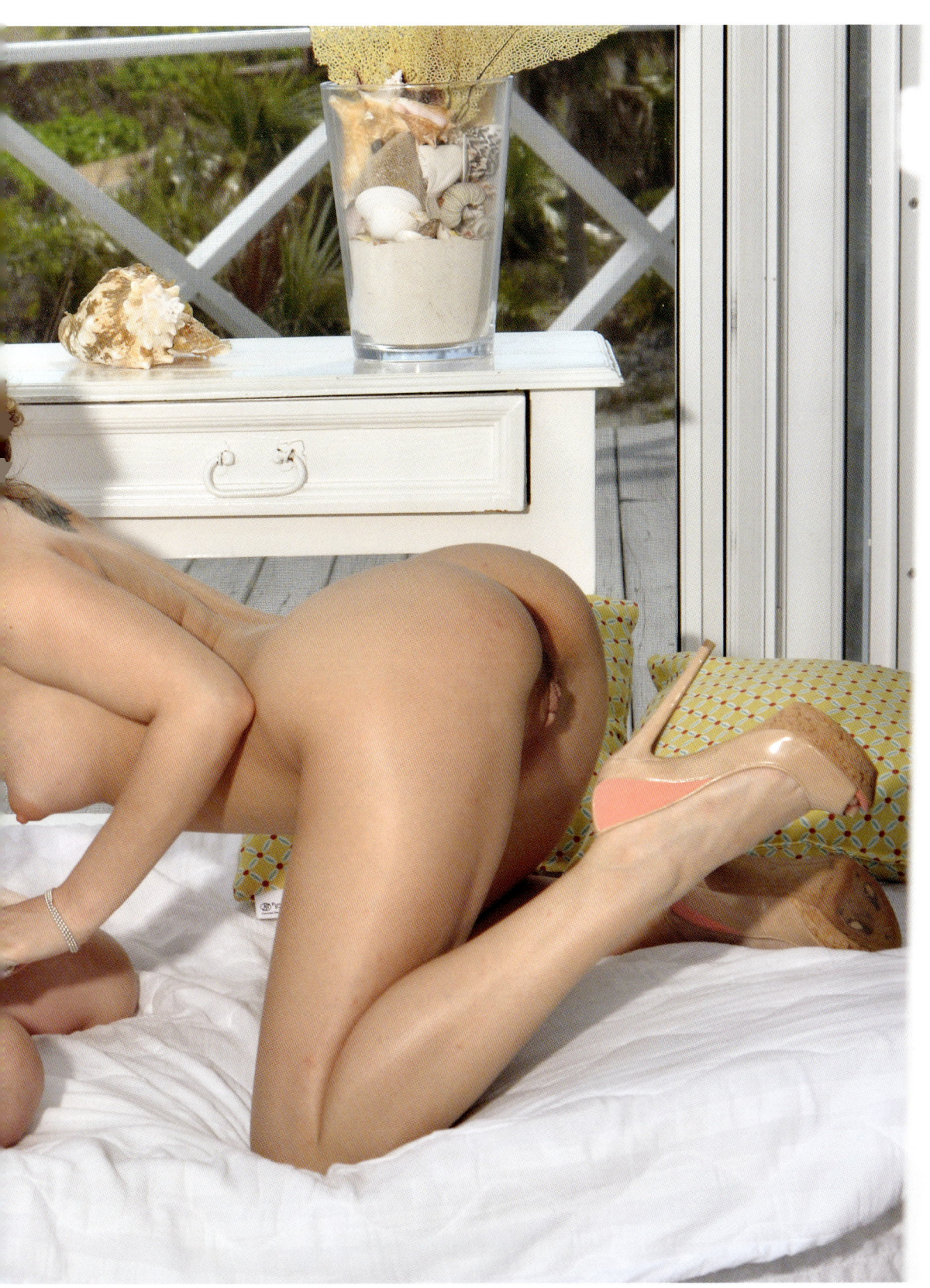

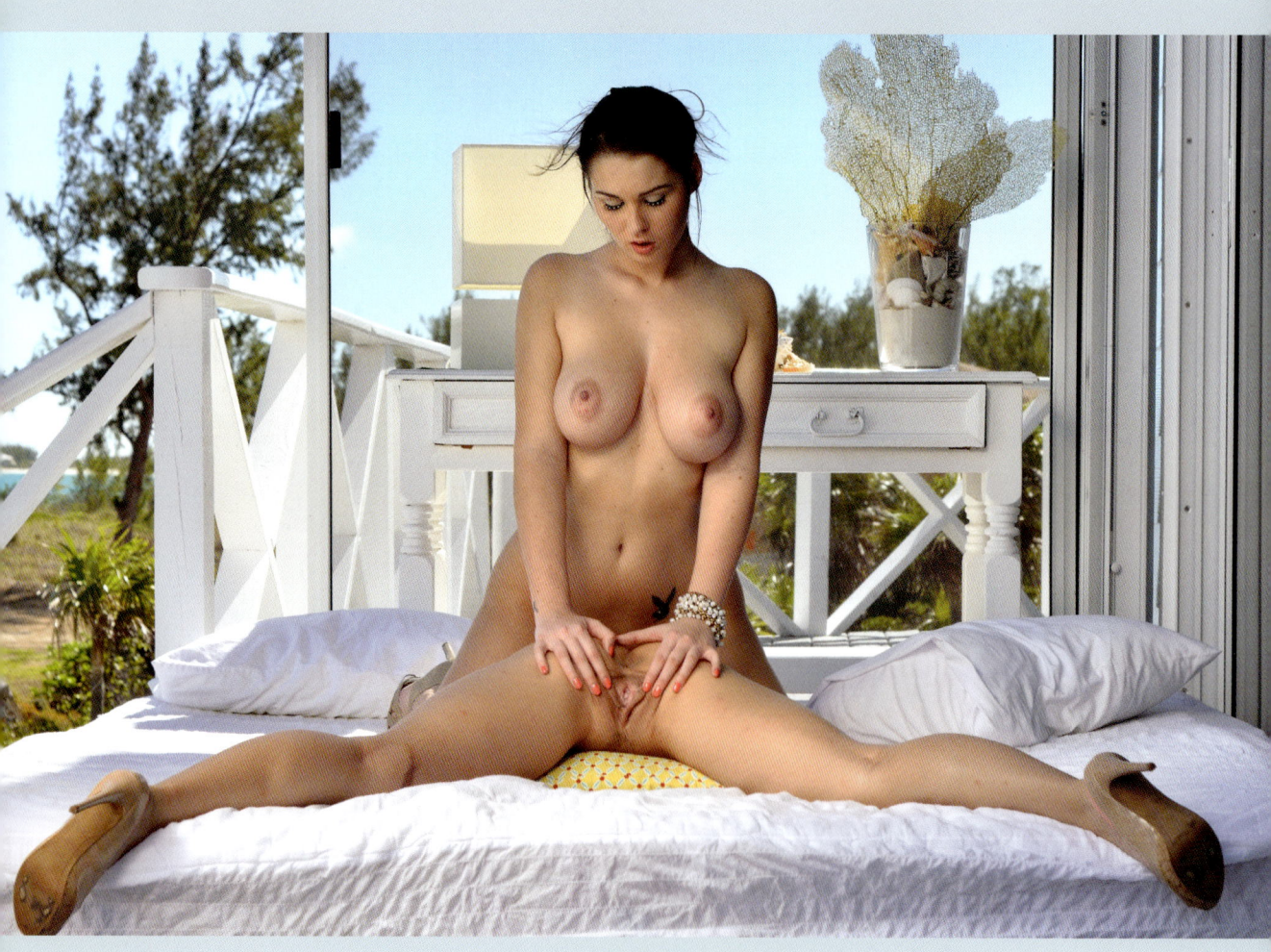

EVA & VIVIEN

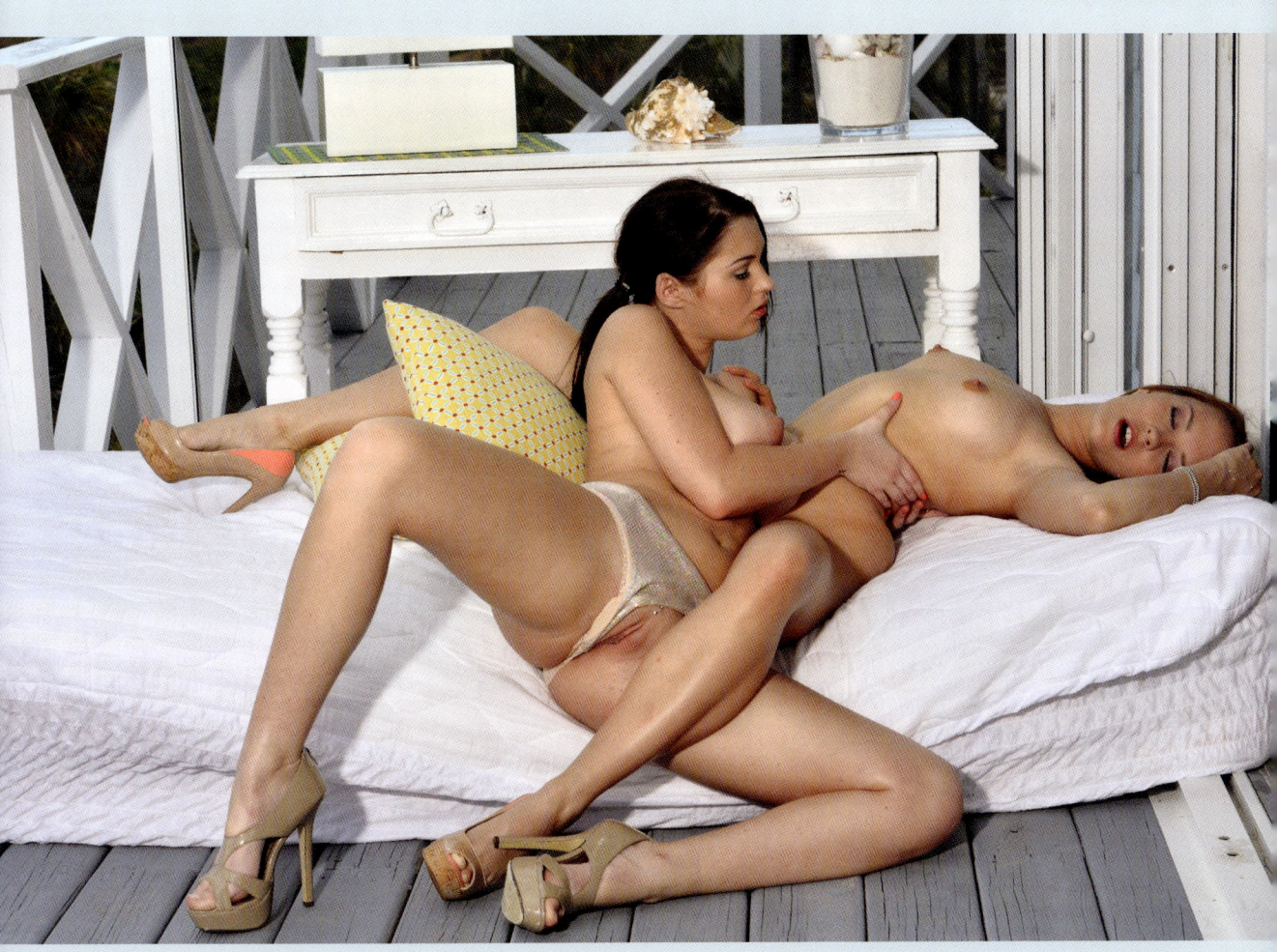

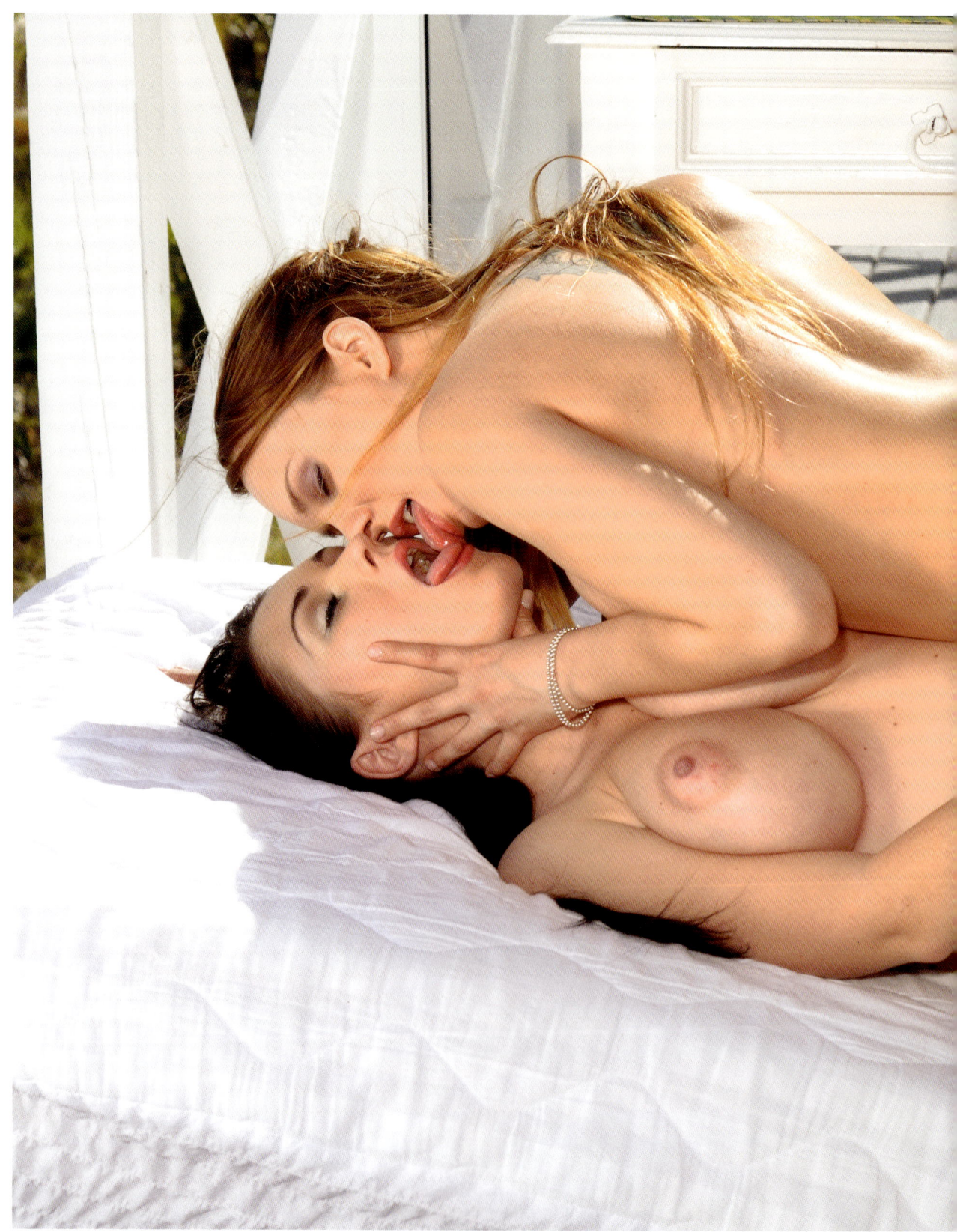

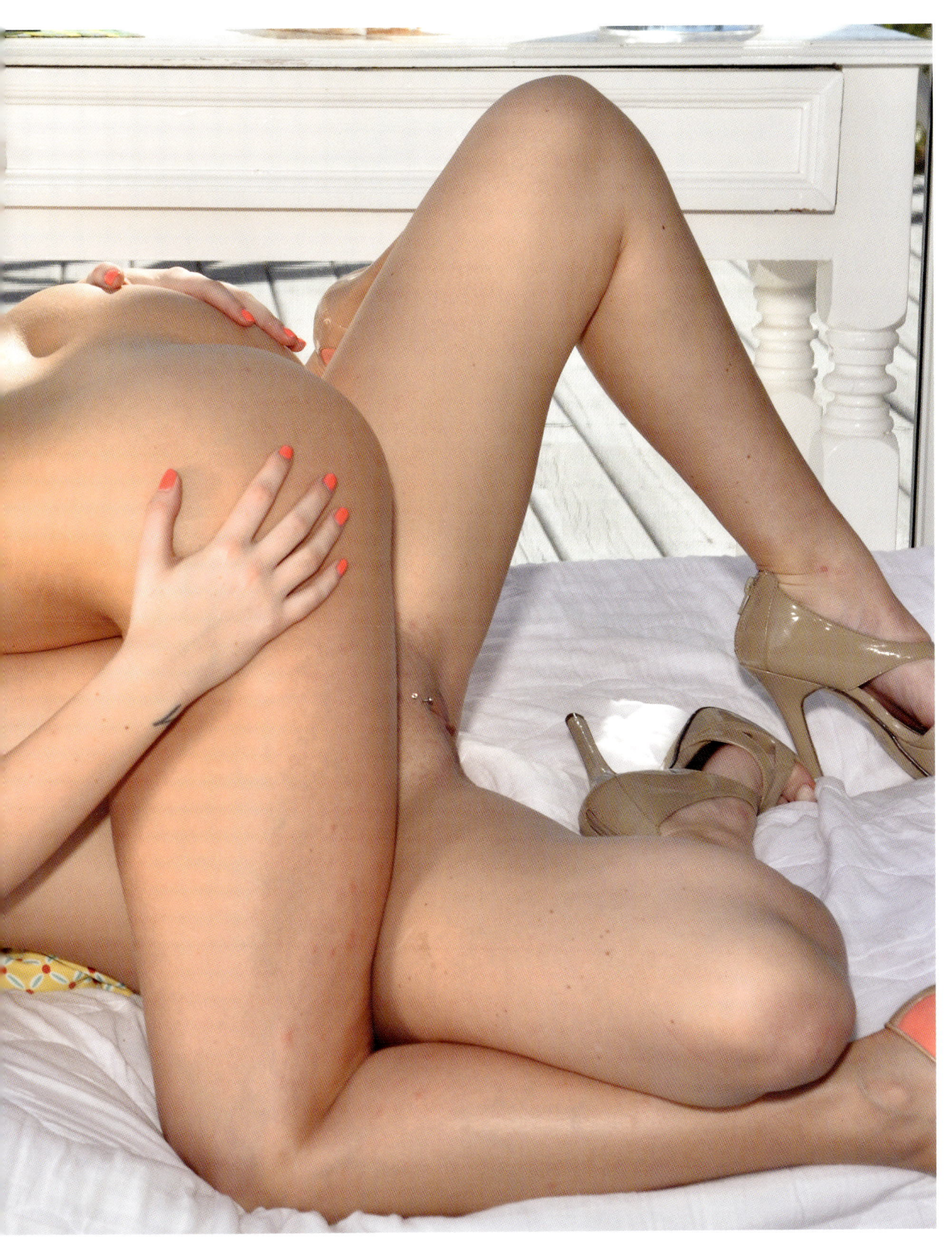

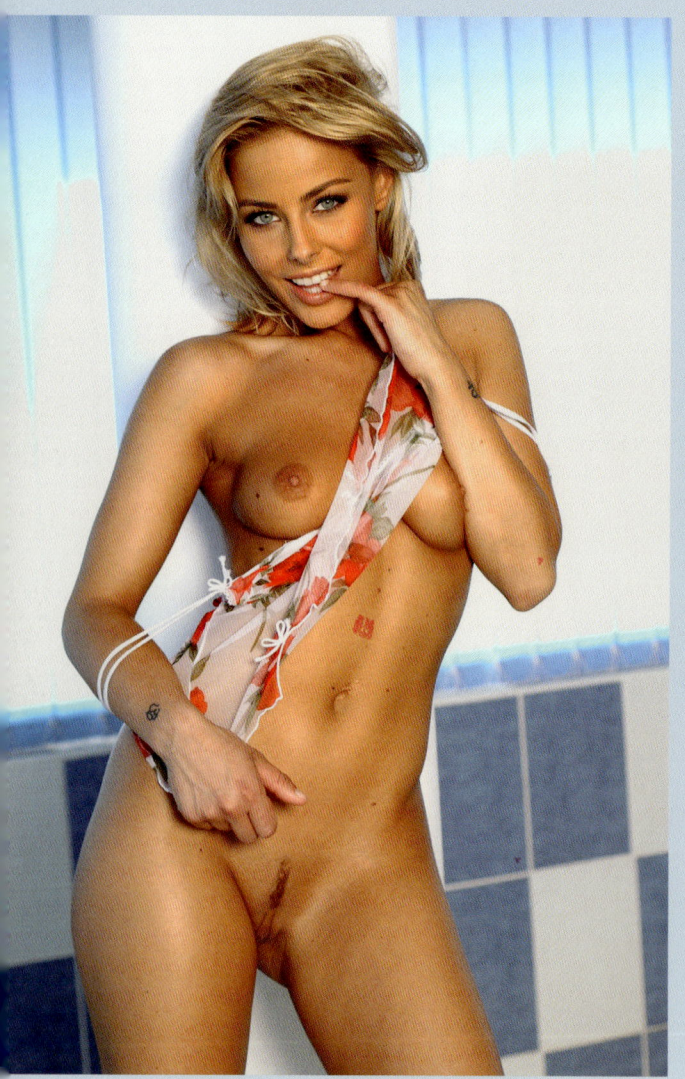
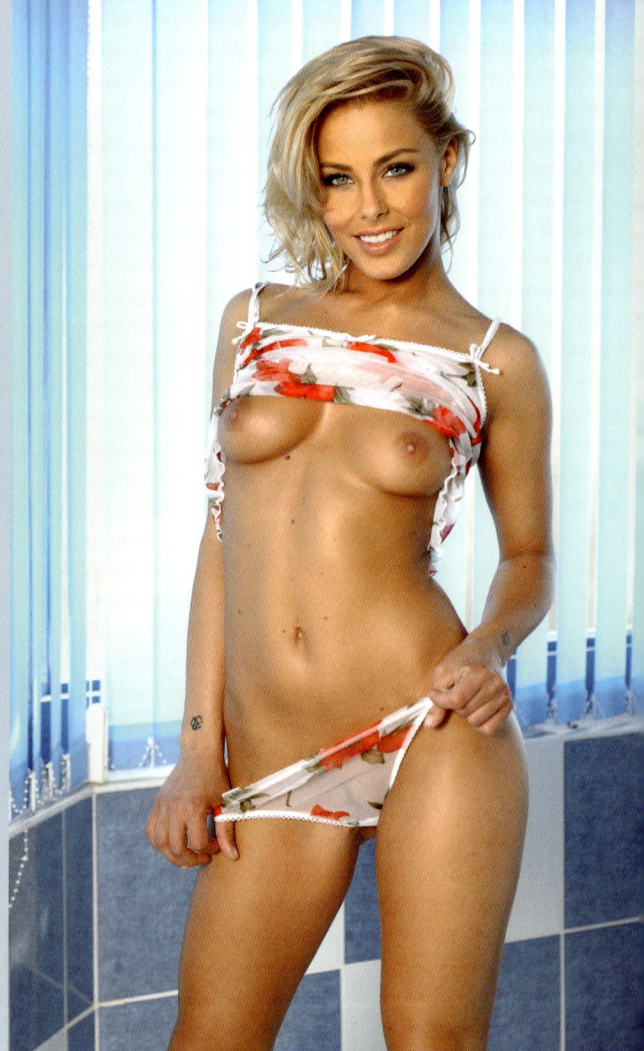

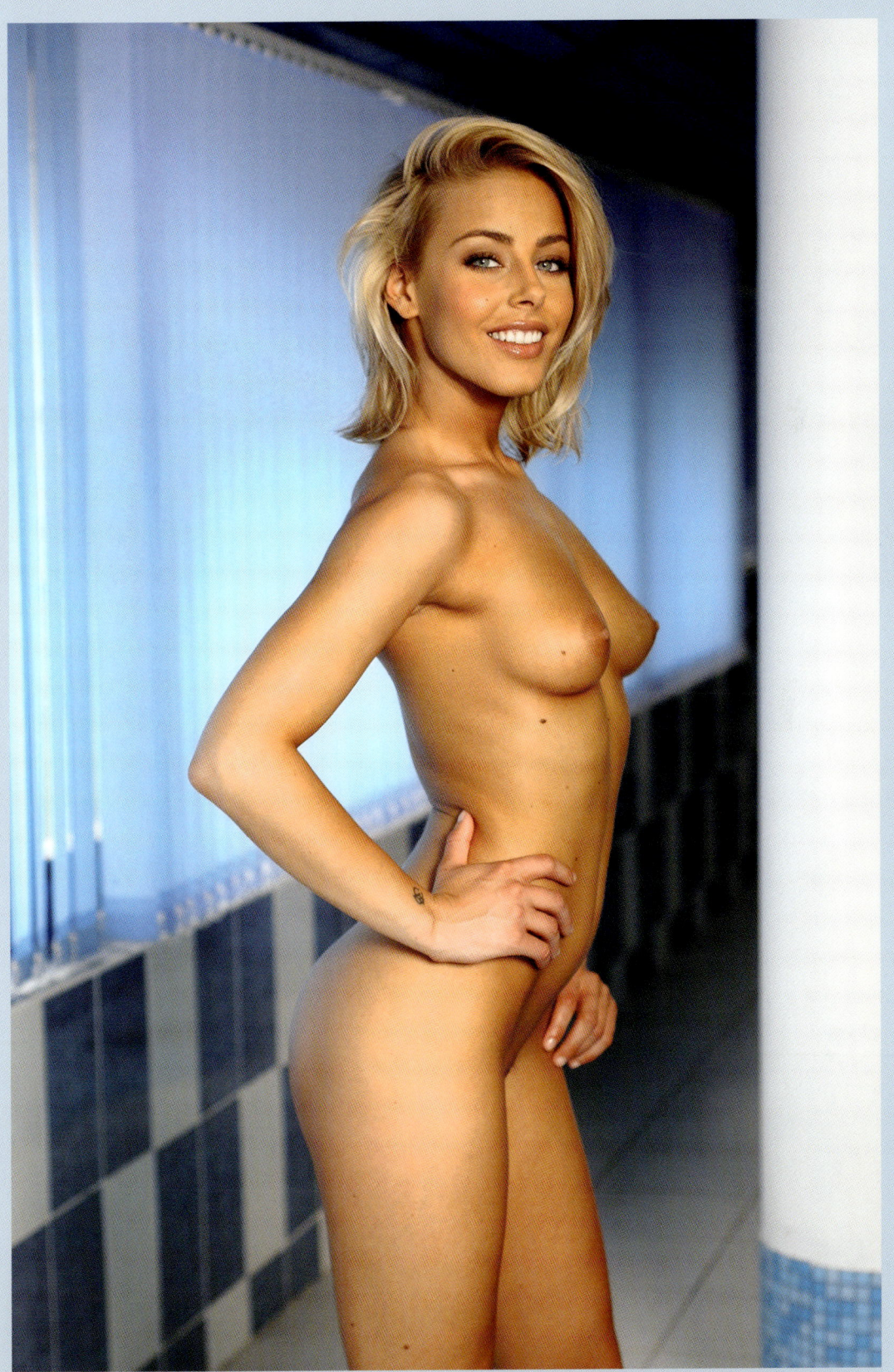

MIA

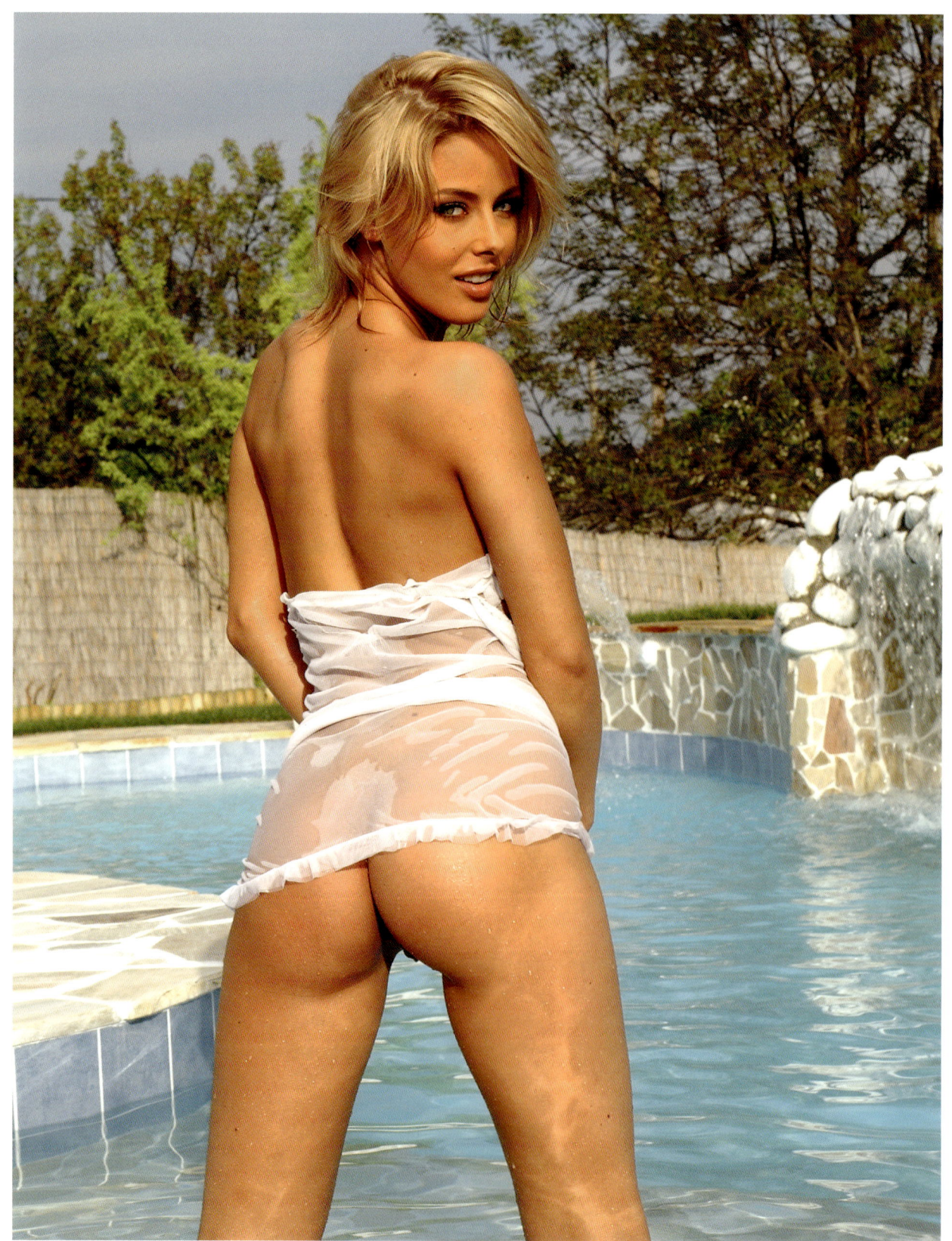

MIA

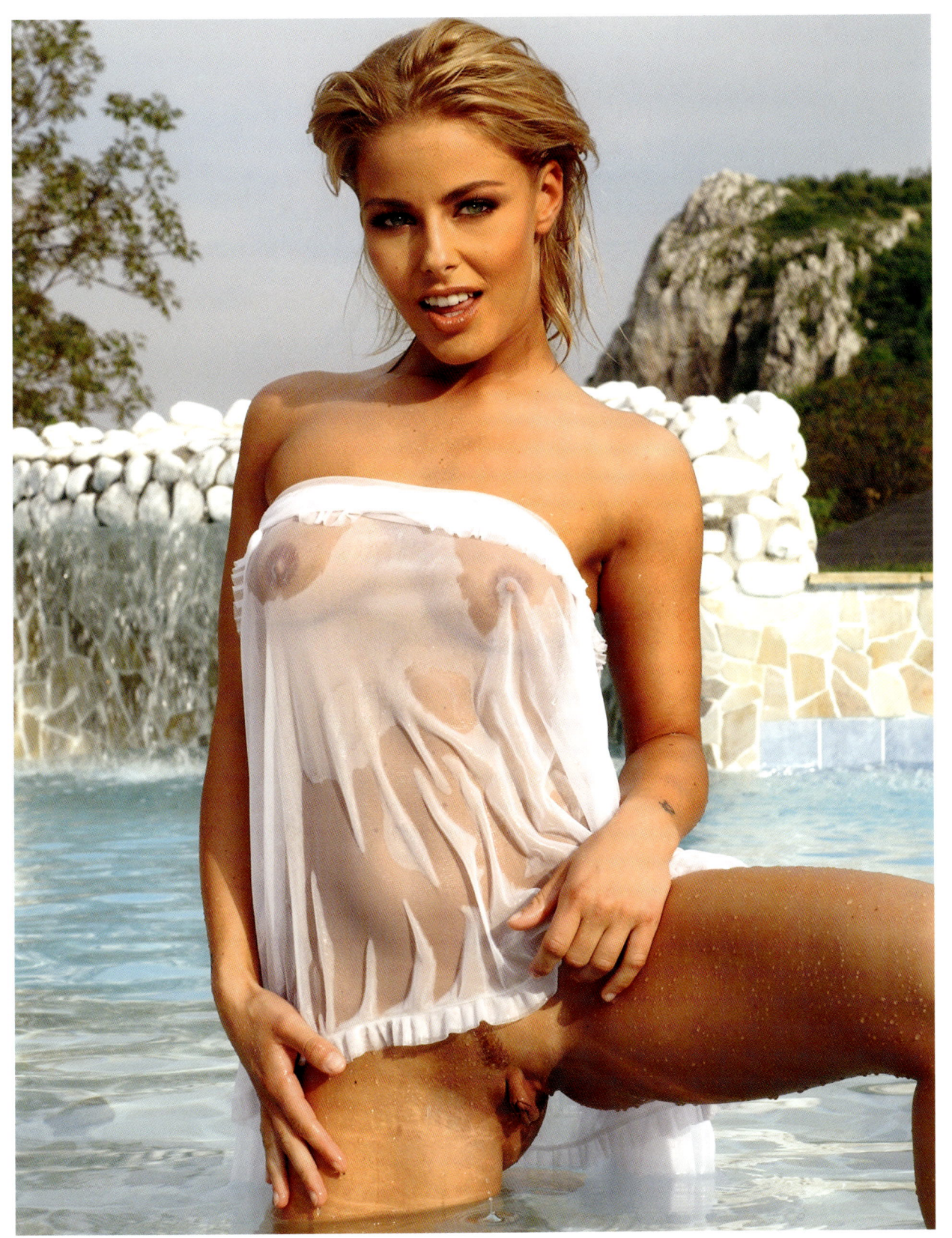

MIA

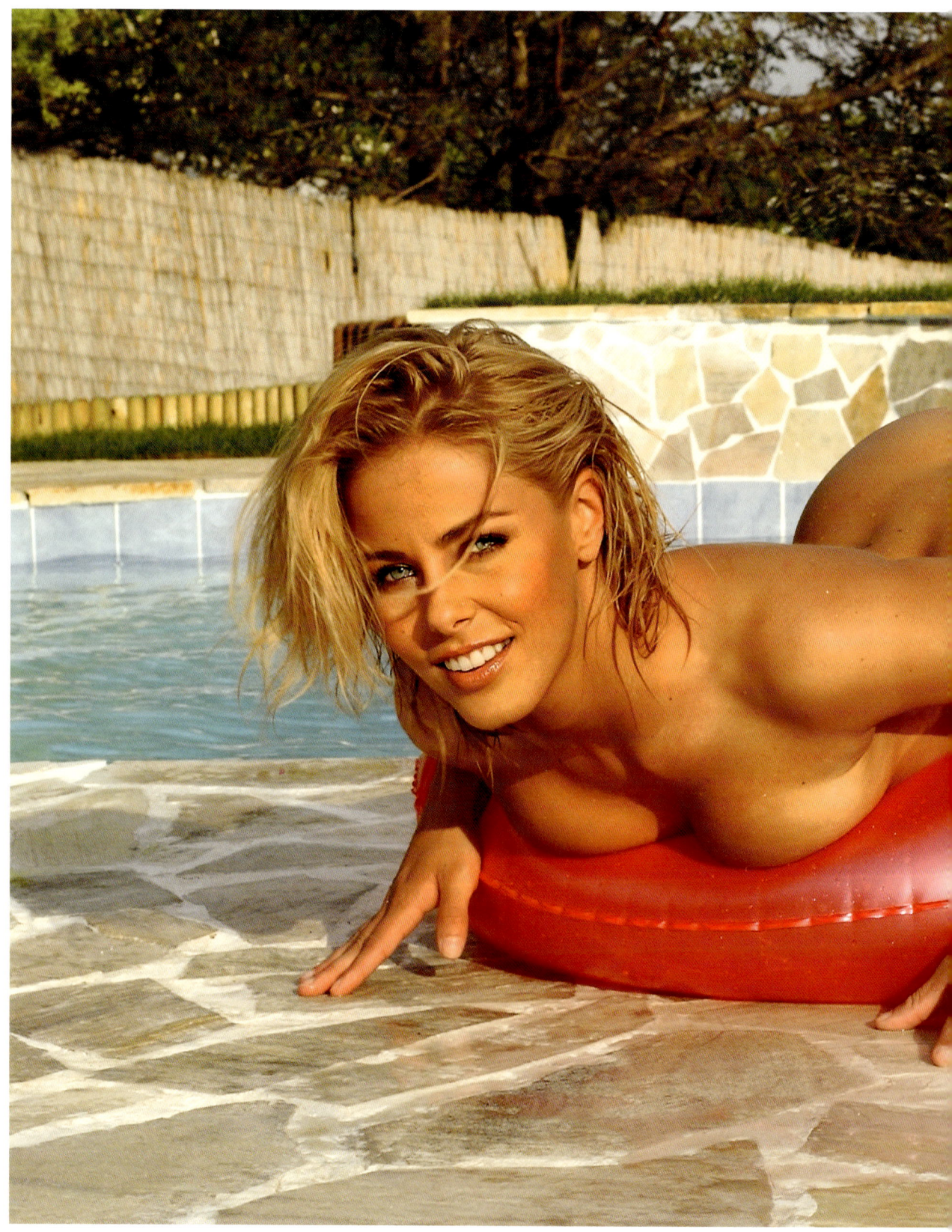

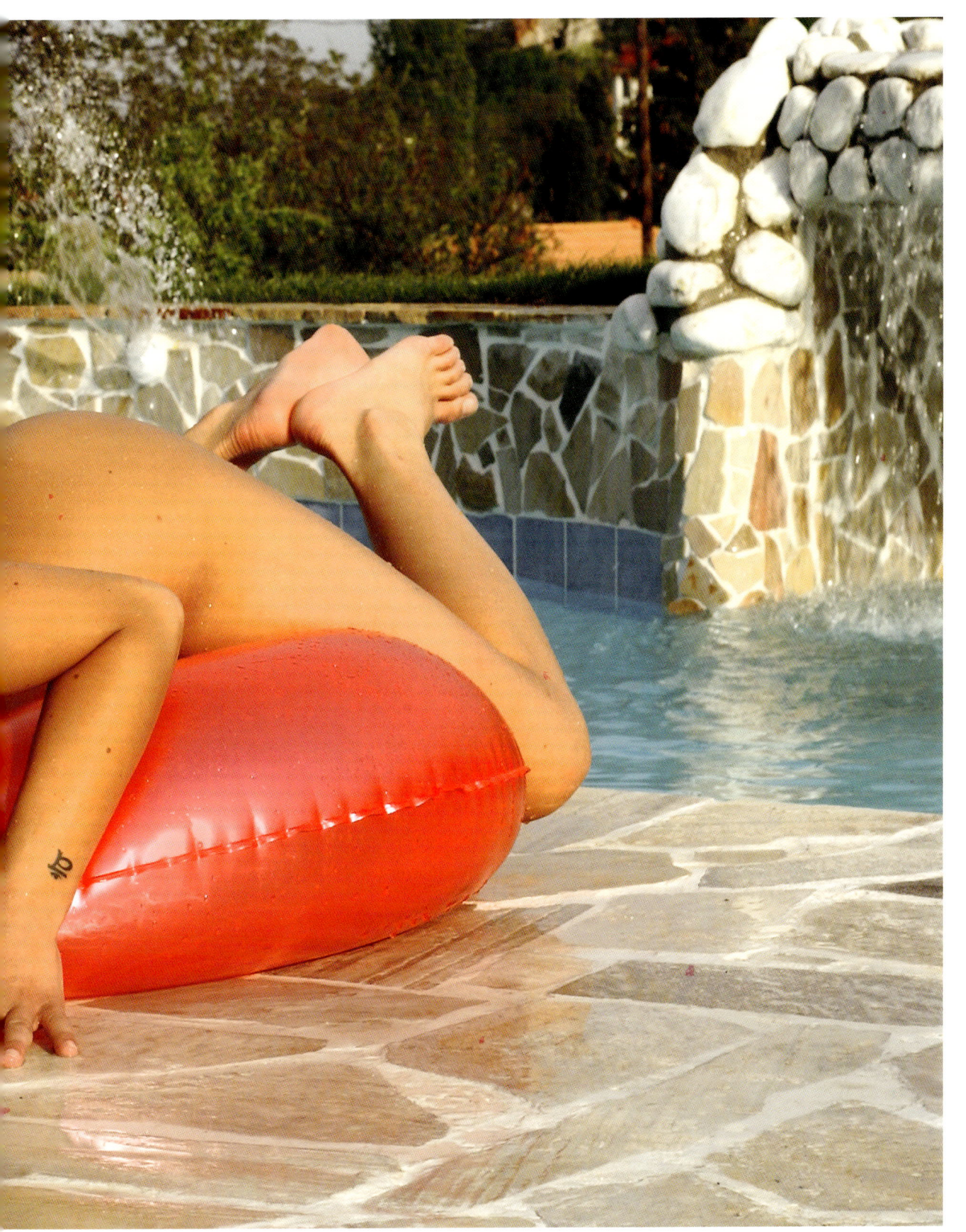

MIA

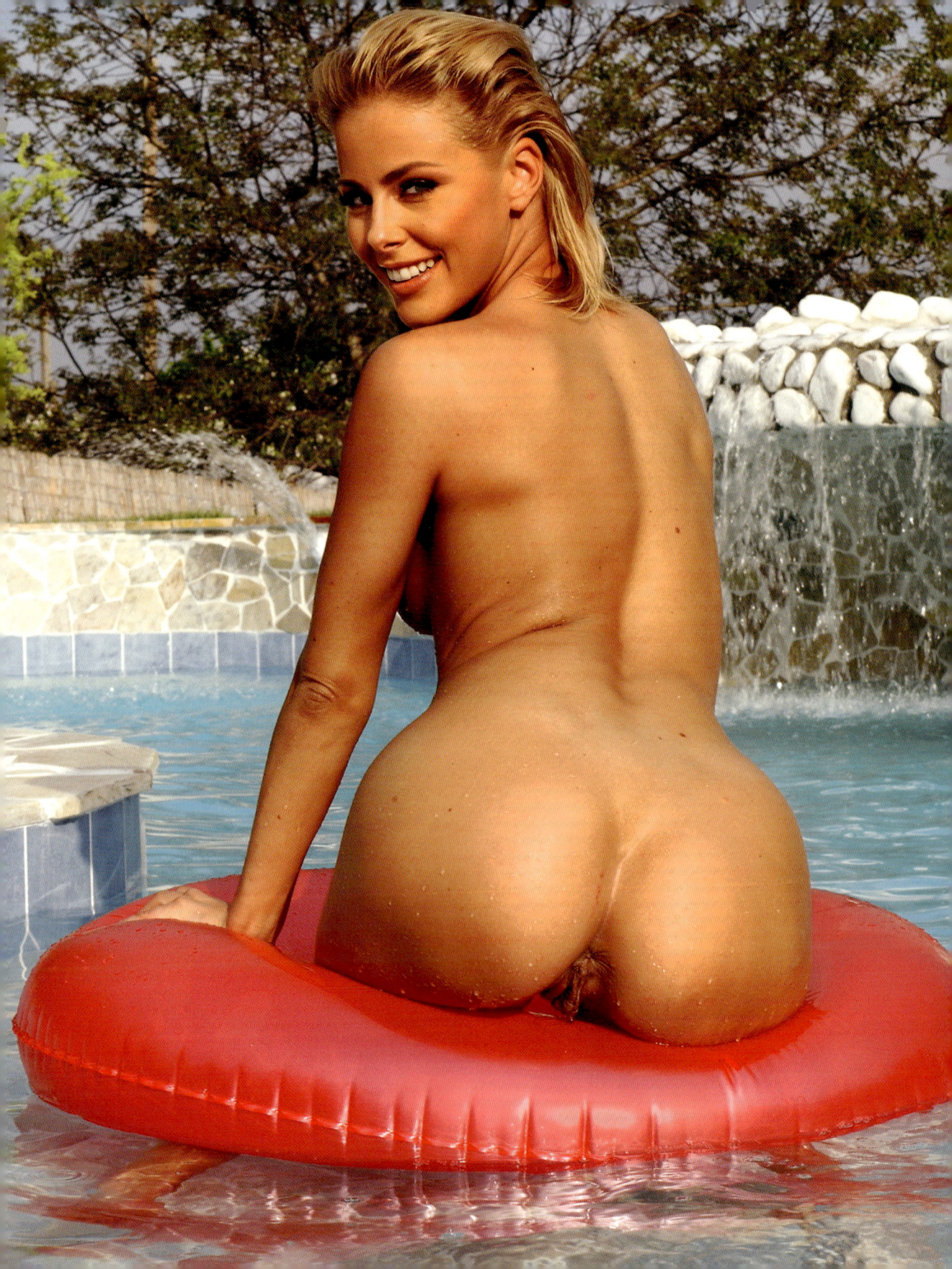

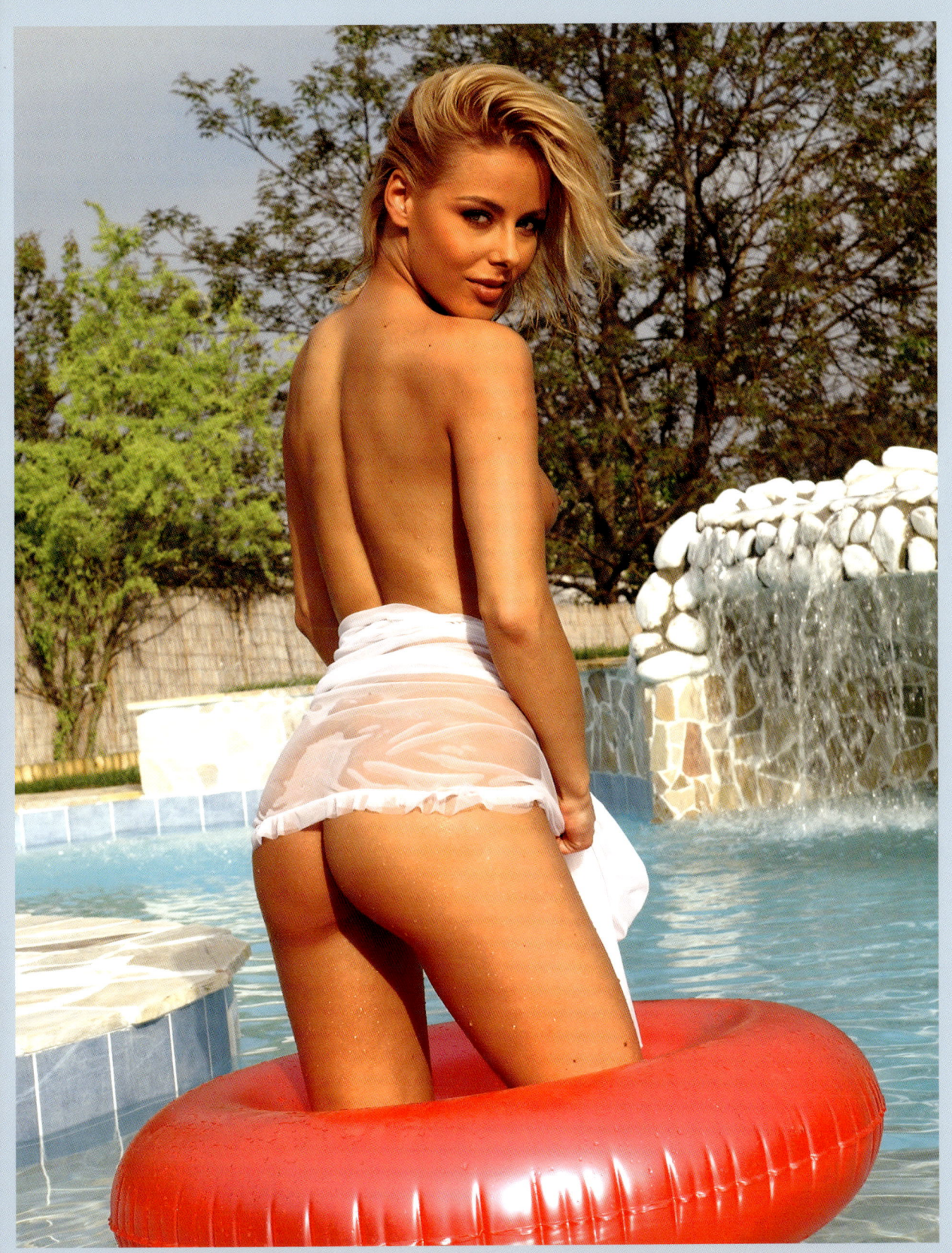

MIA

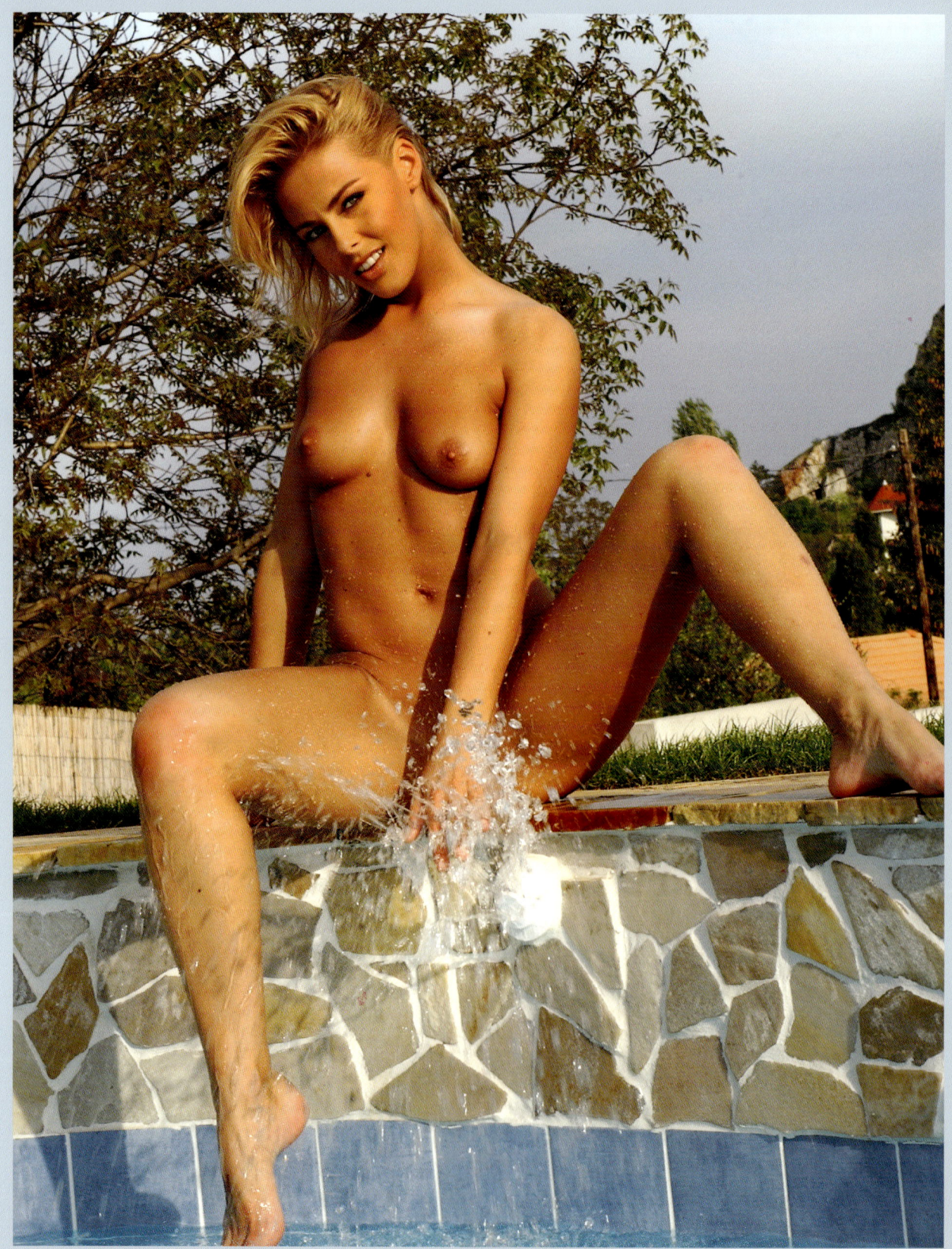

MIA

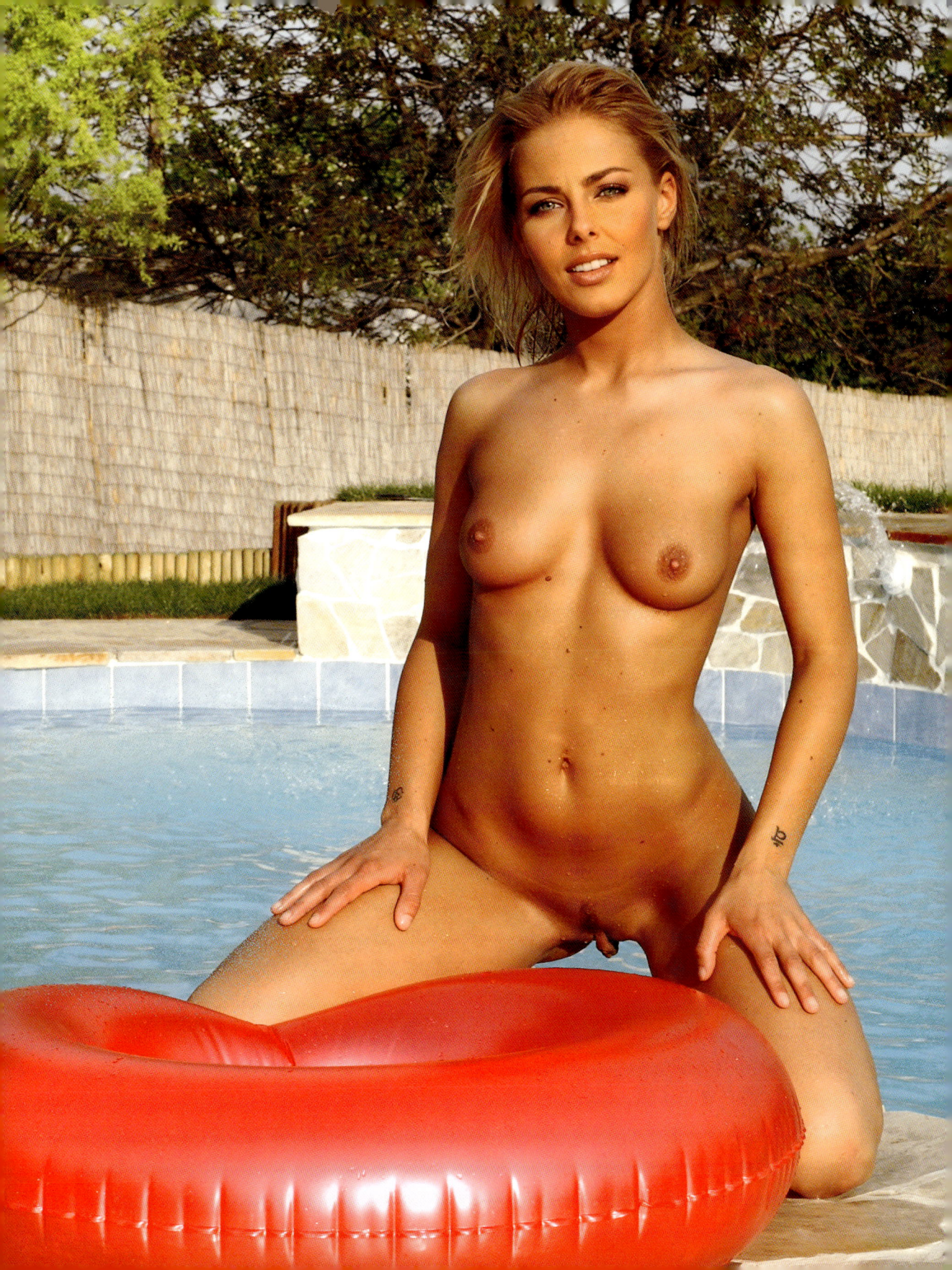

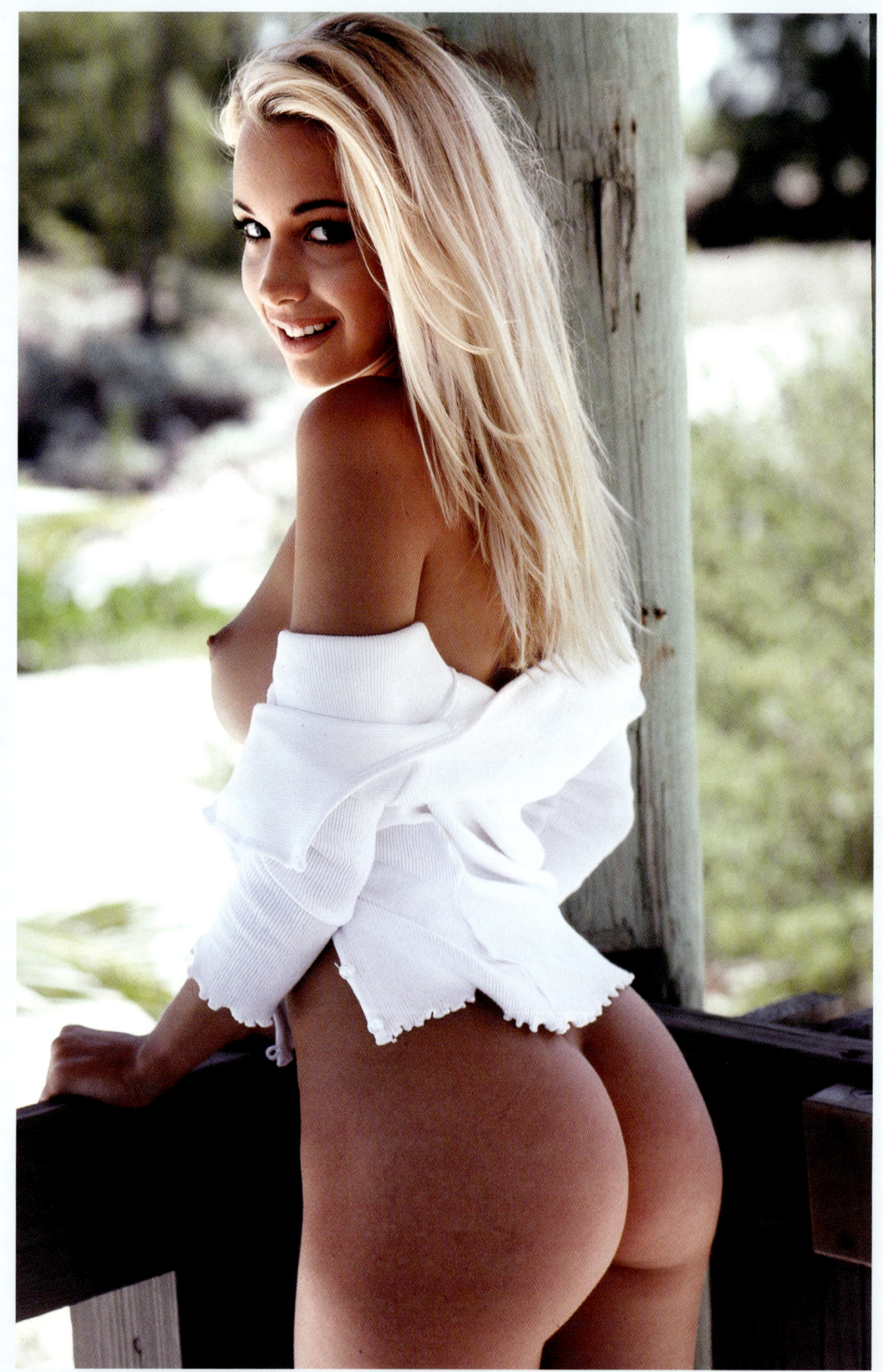

JANA

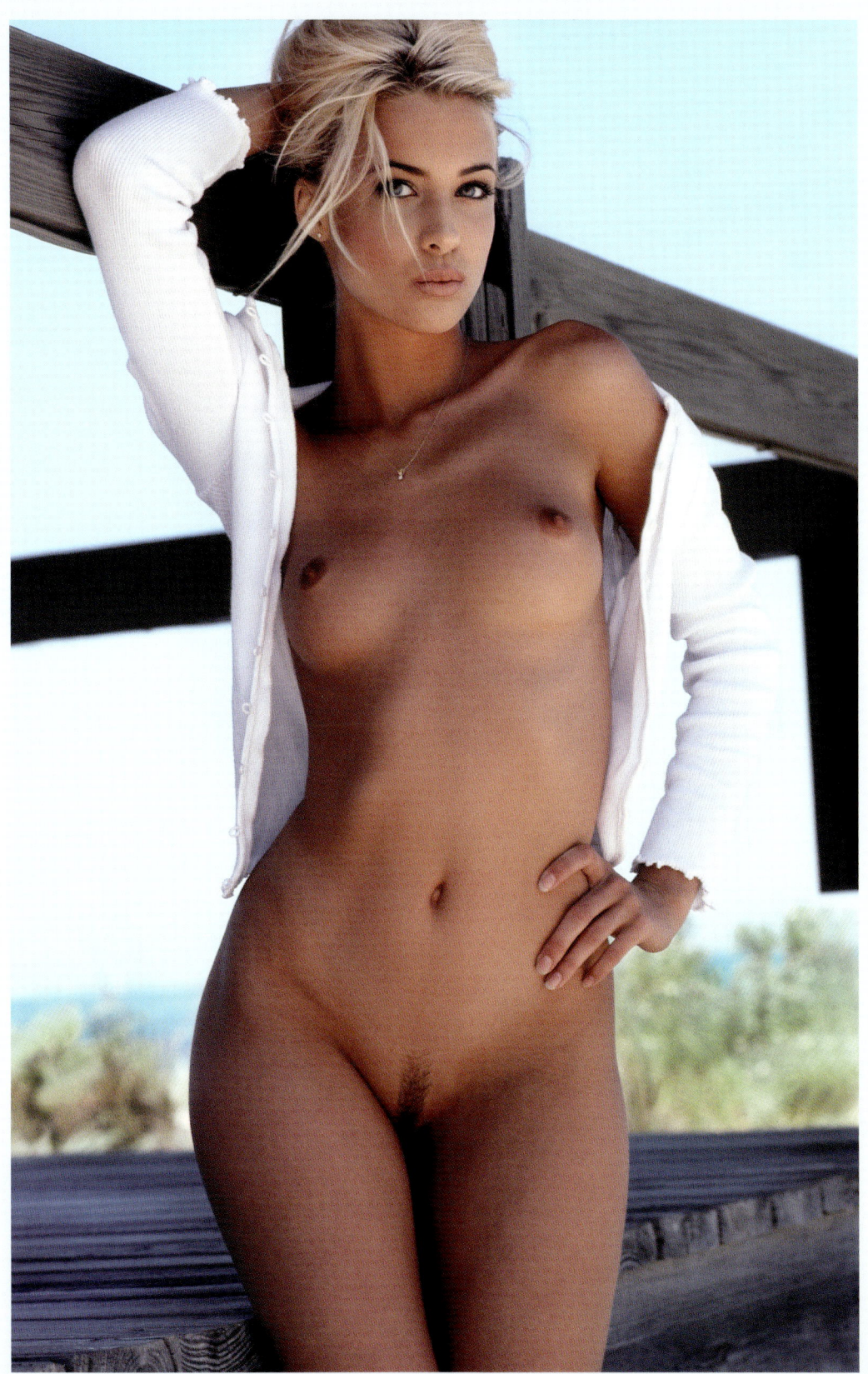

JANA

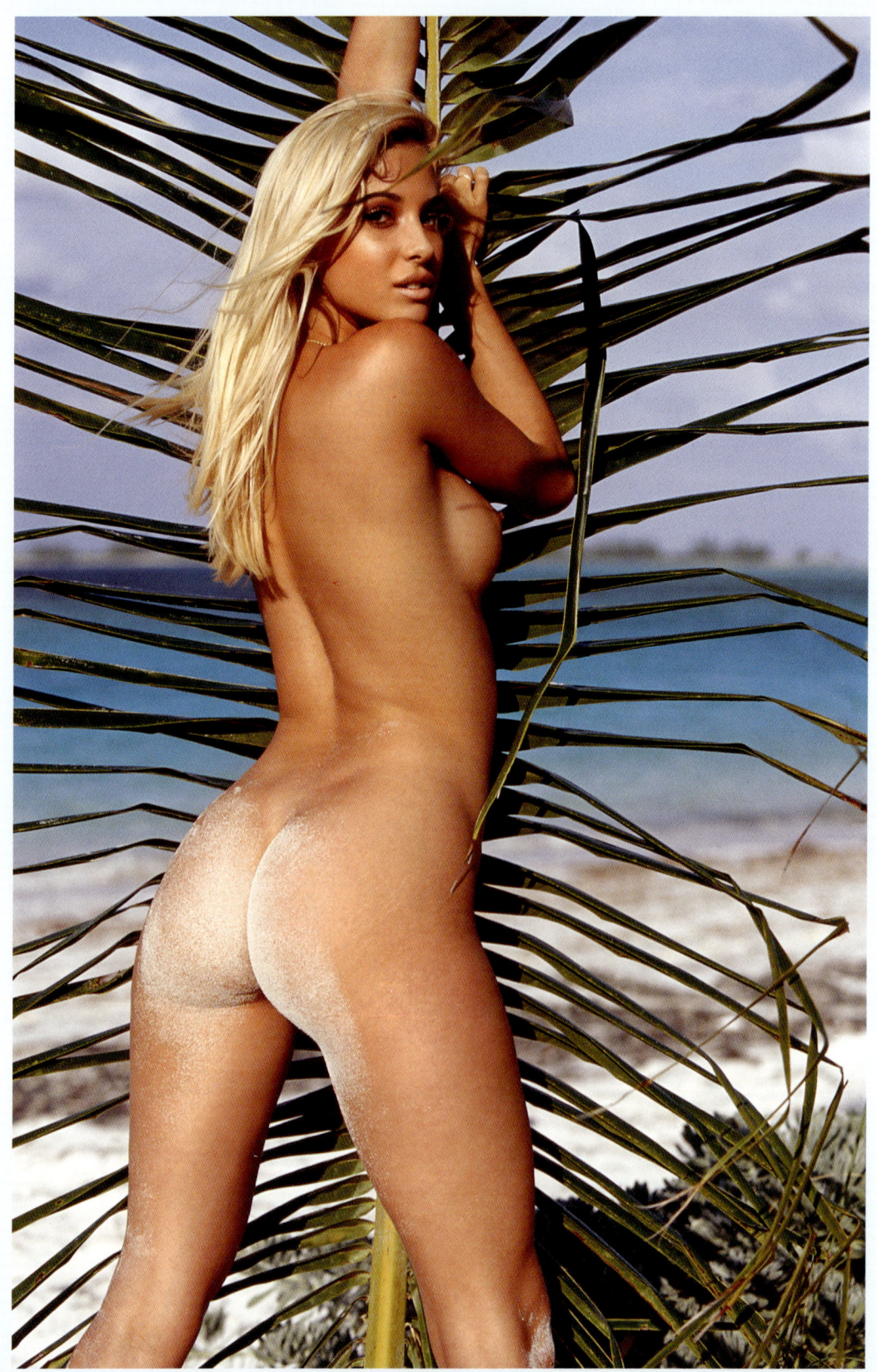

JANA

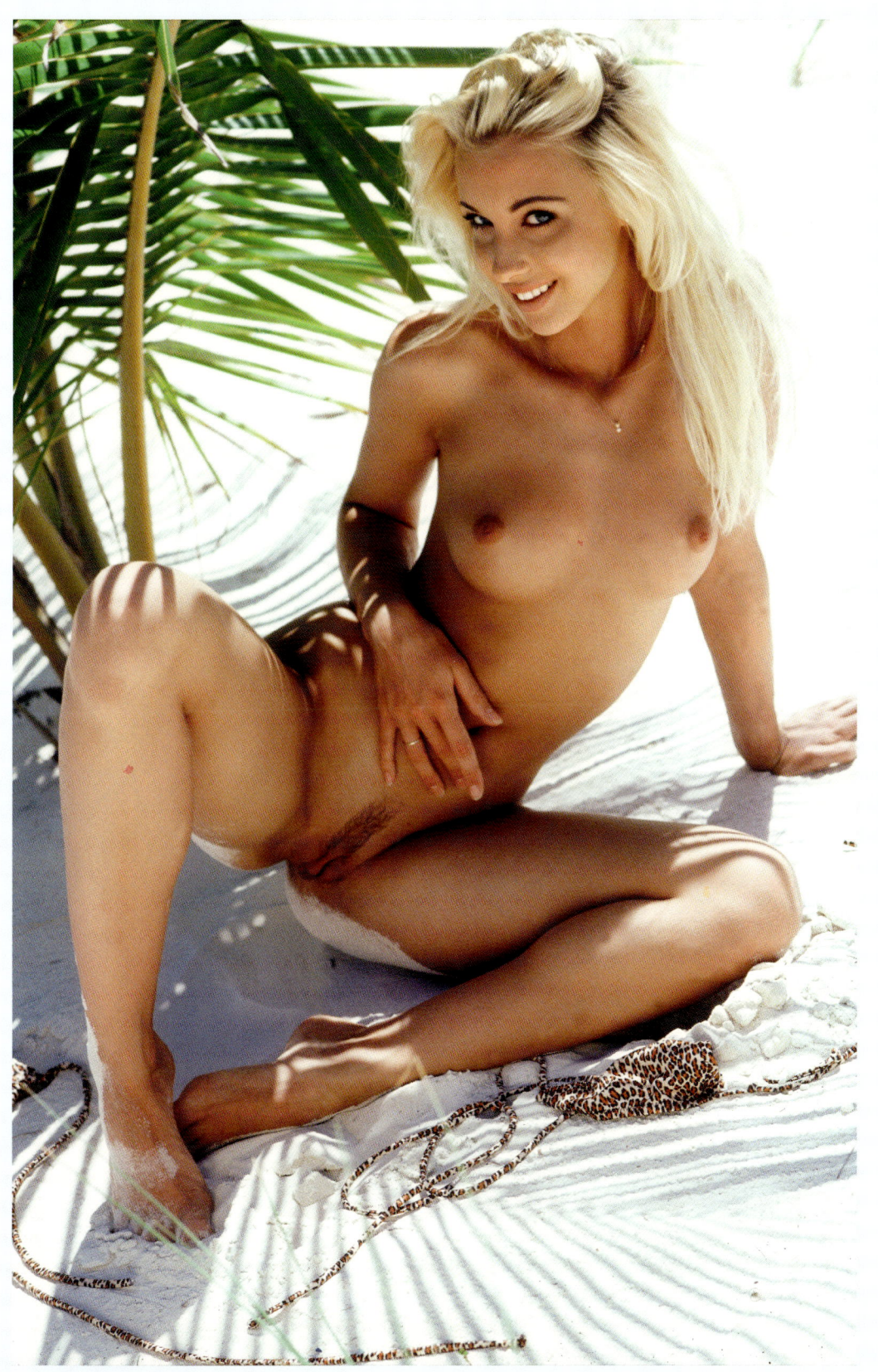

JANA

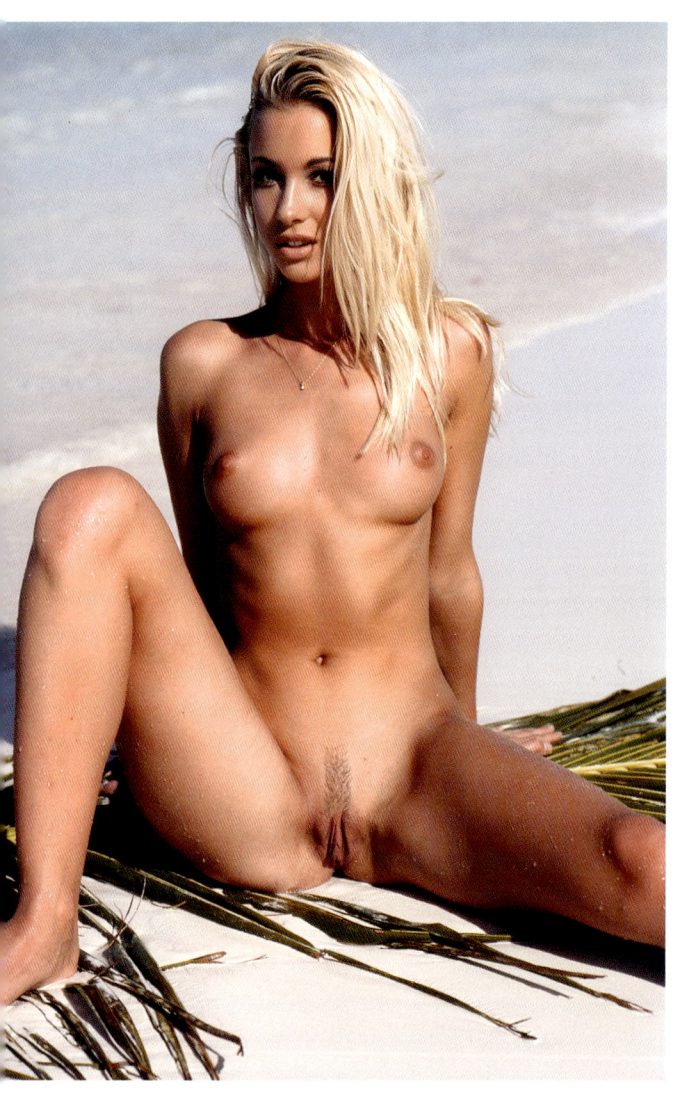
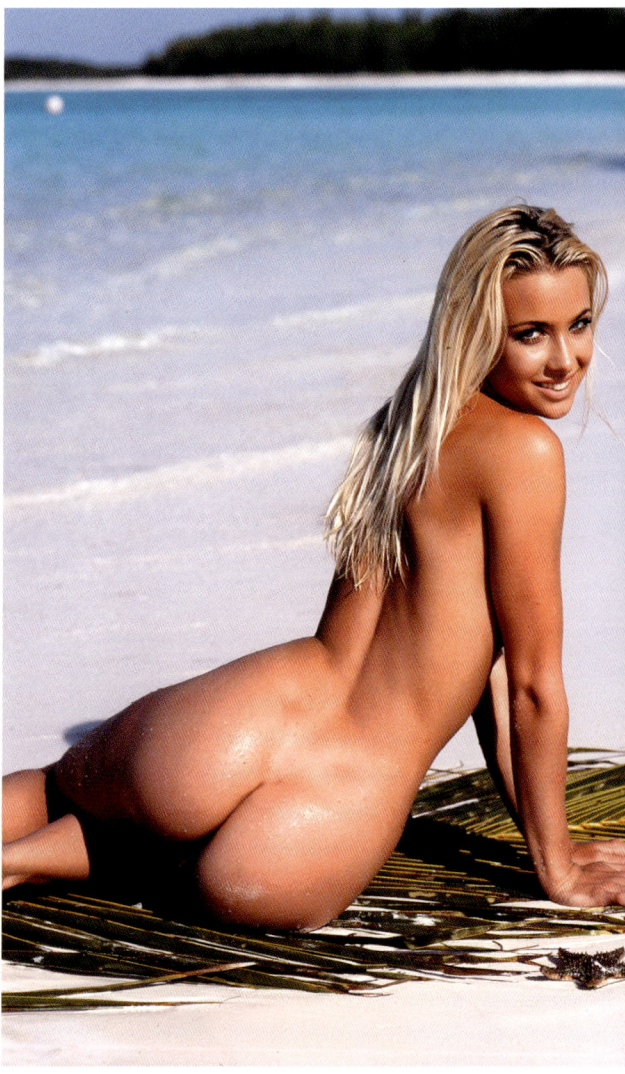

JANA

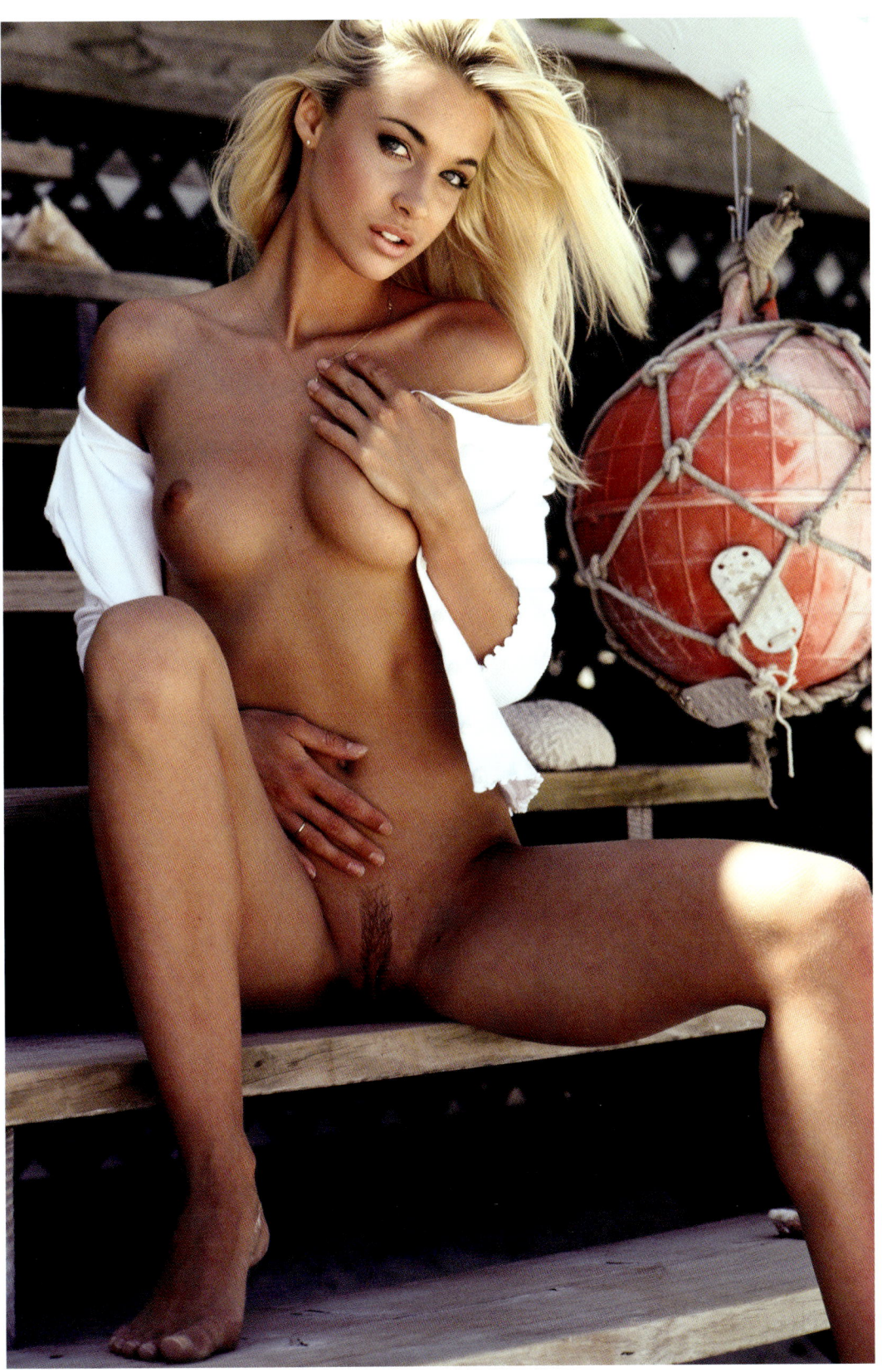

JANA

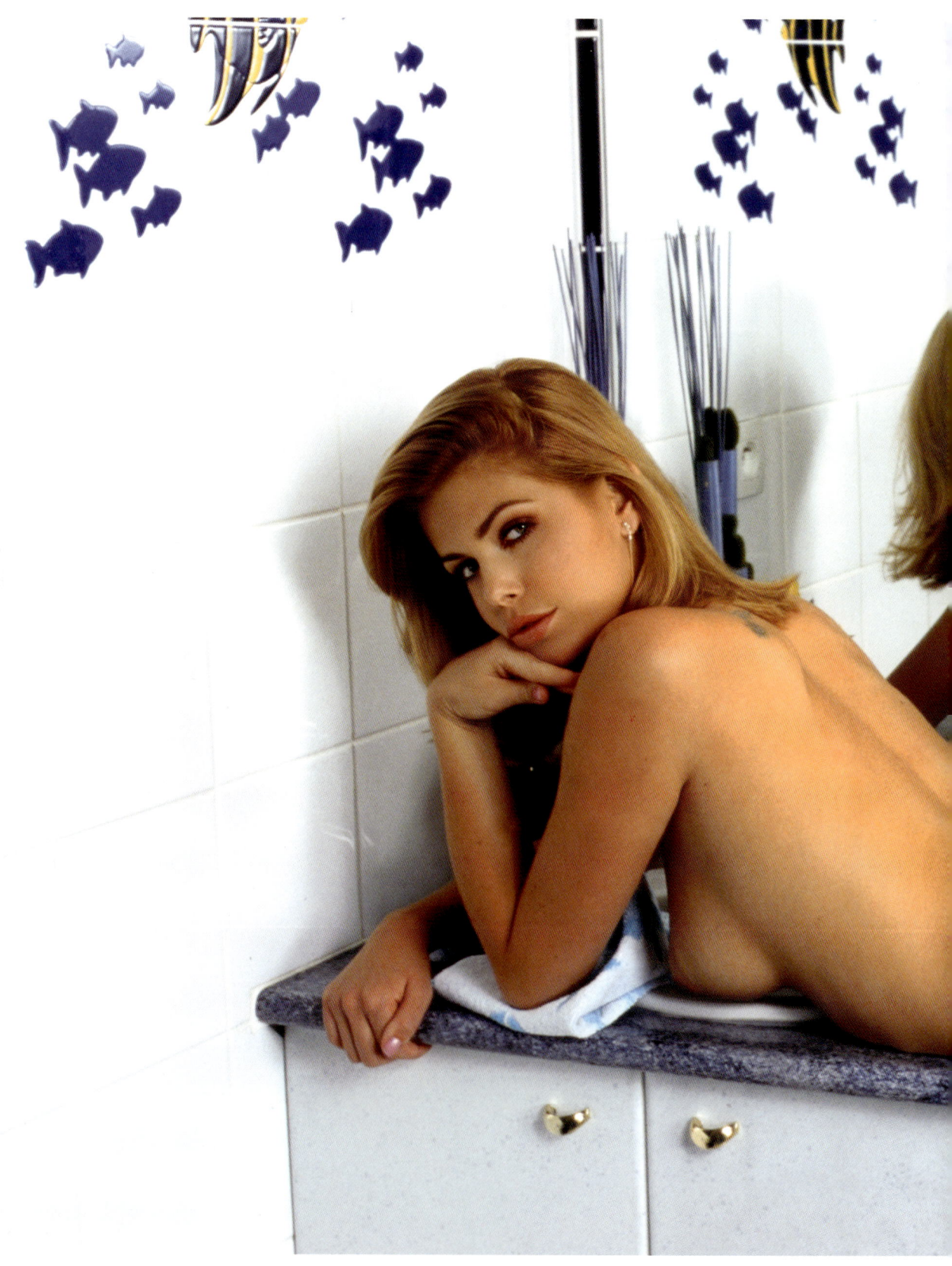

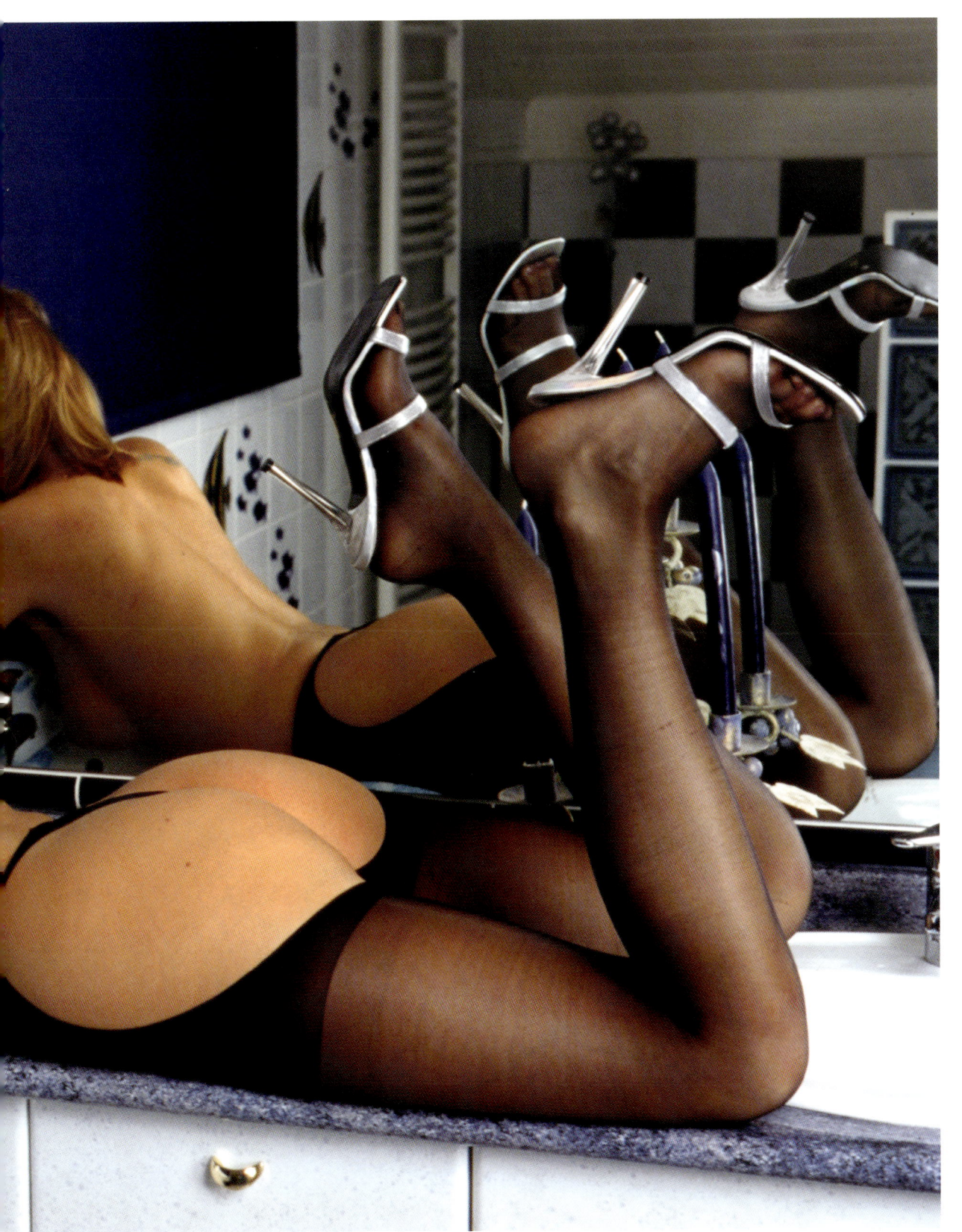

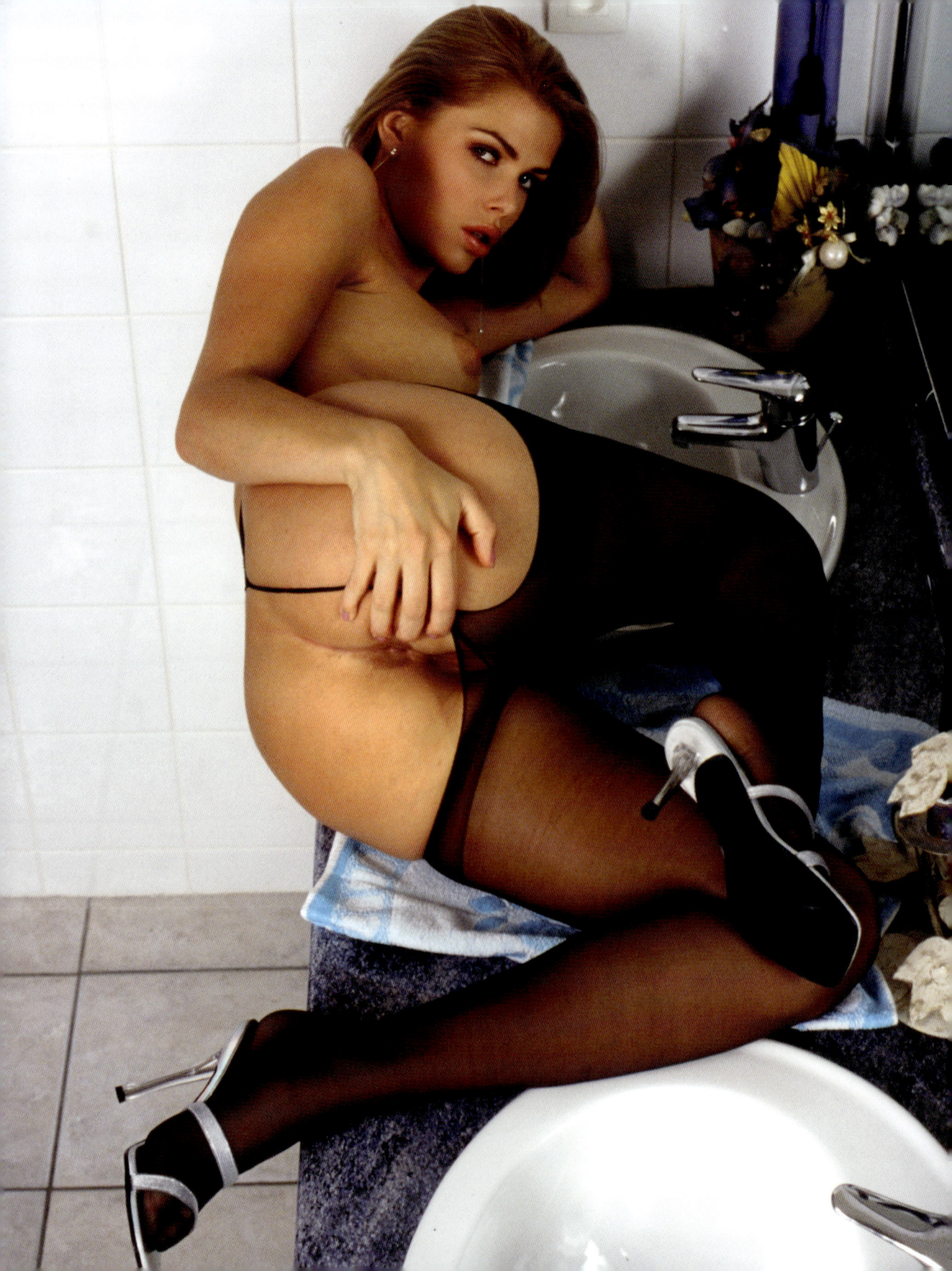

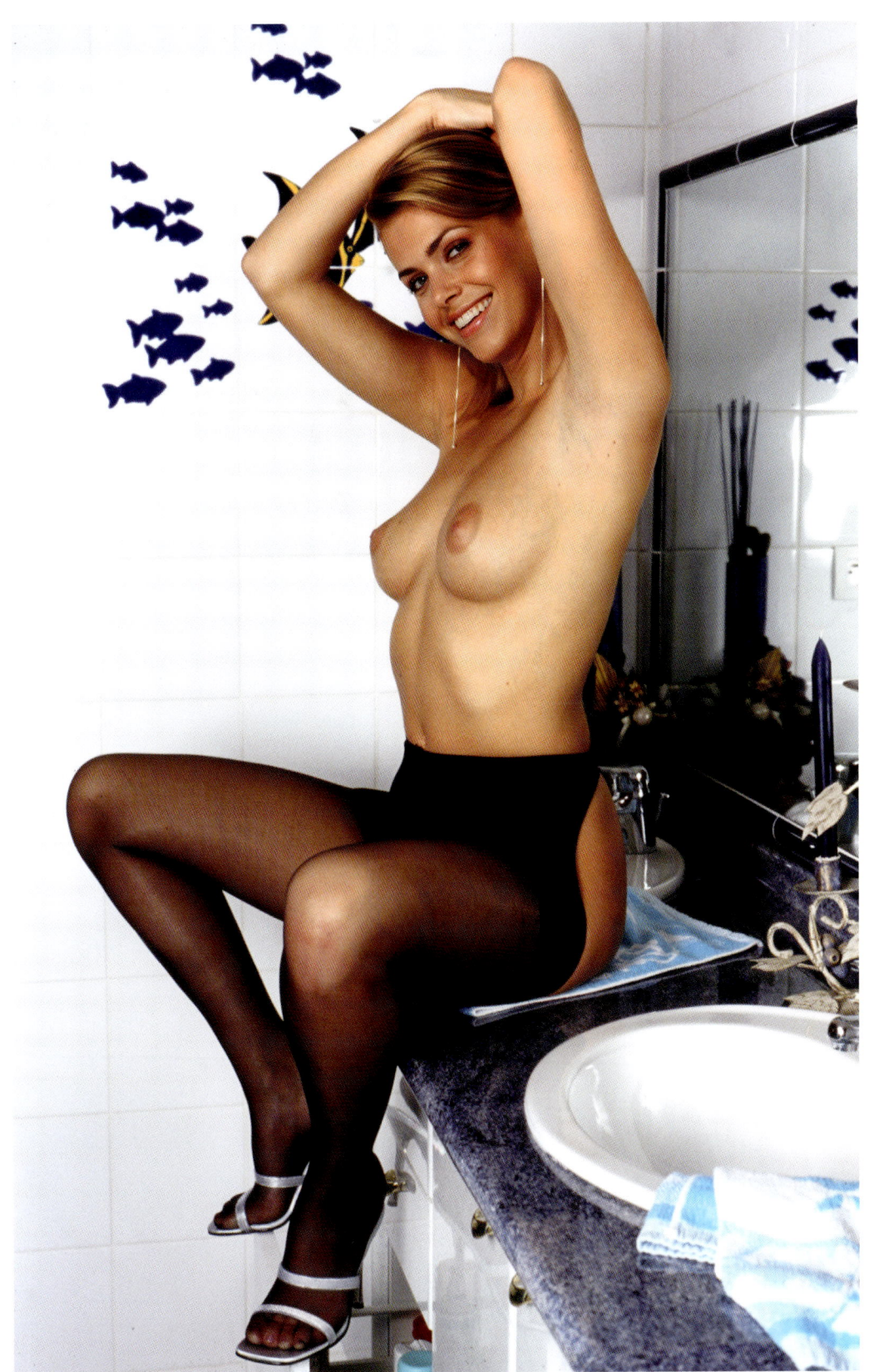

KATALINE K

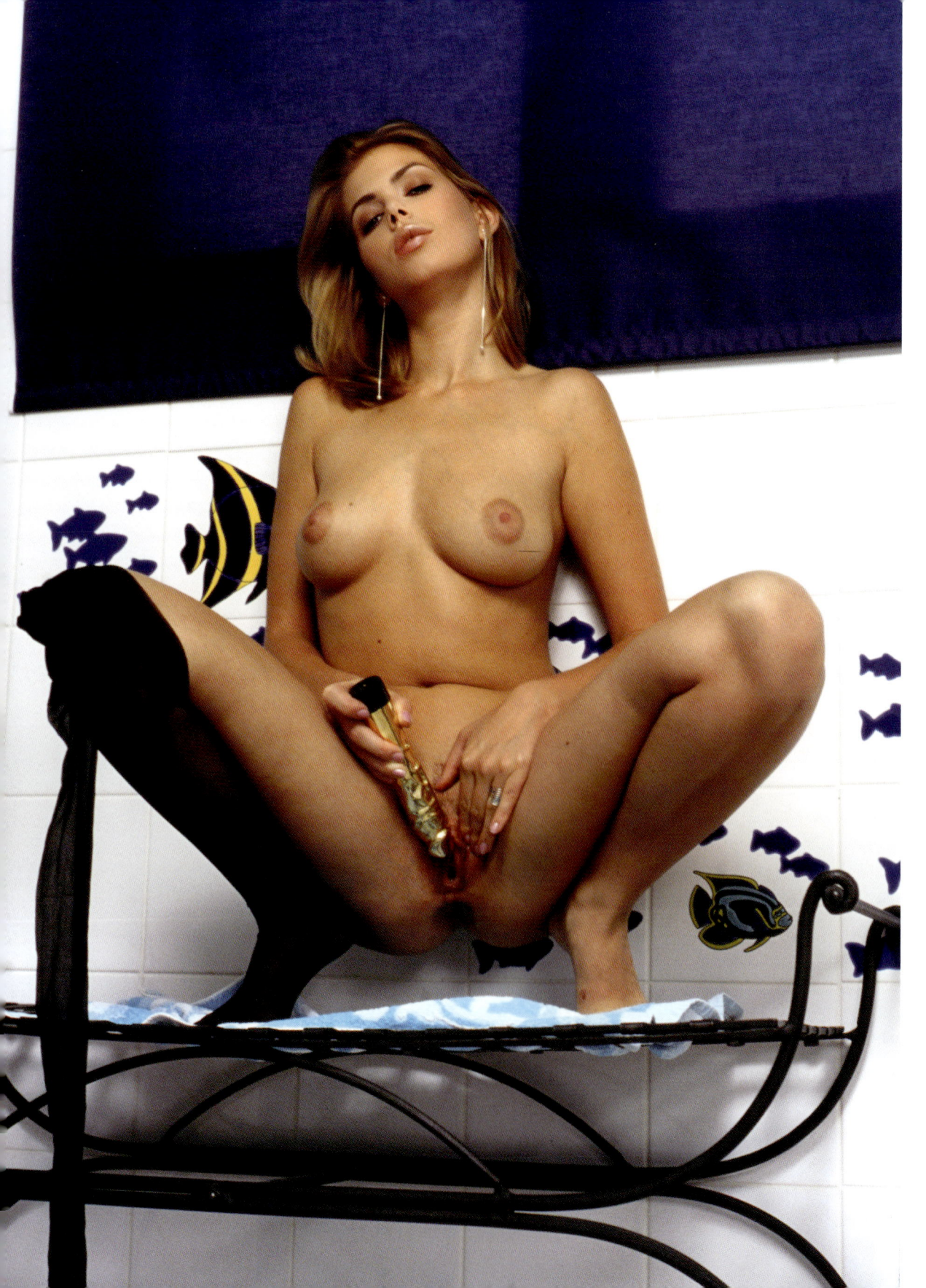

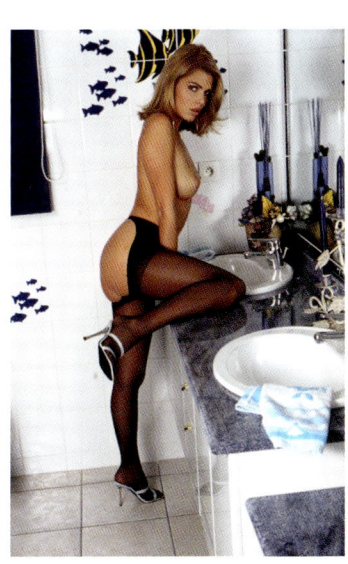
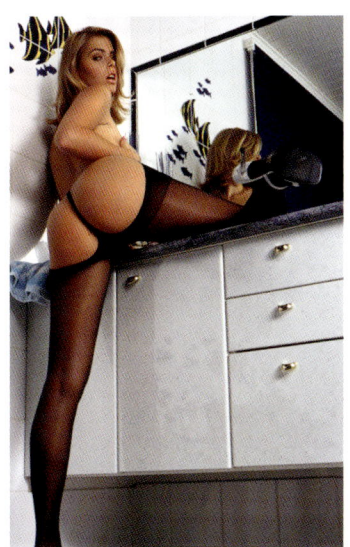
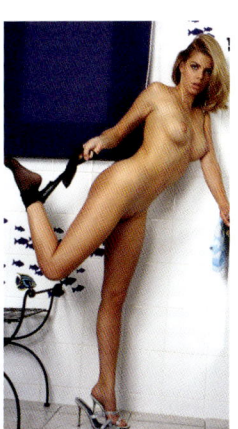
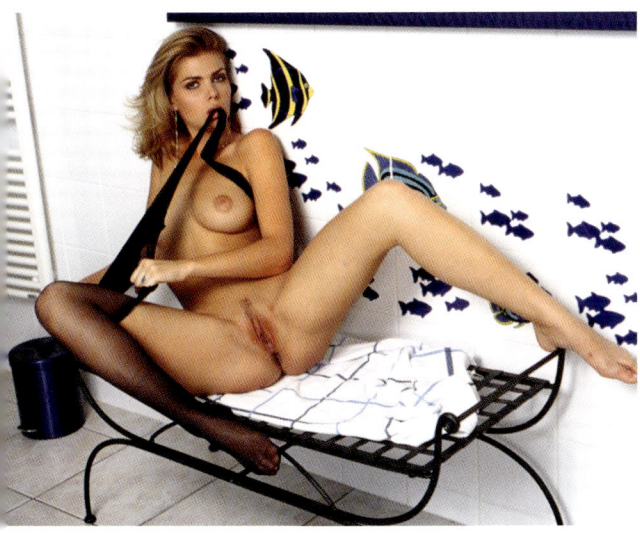
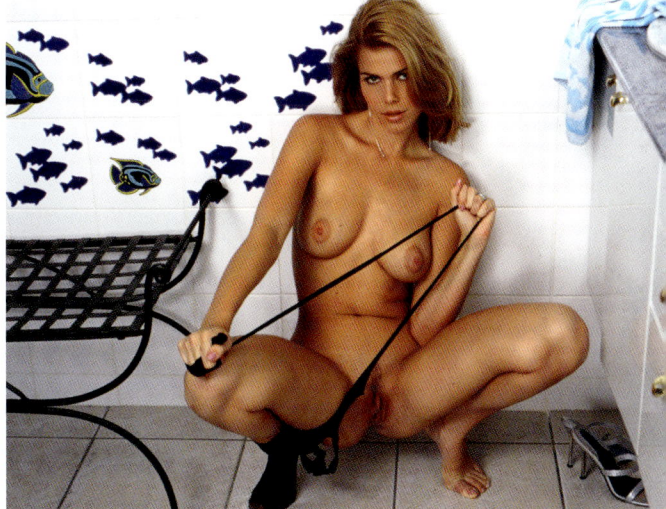

KATALINE K

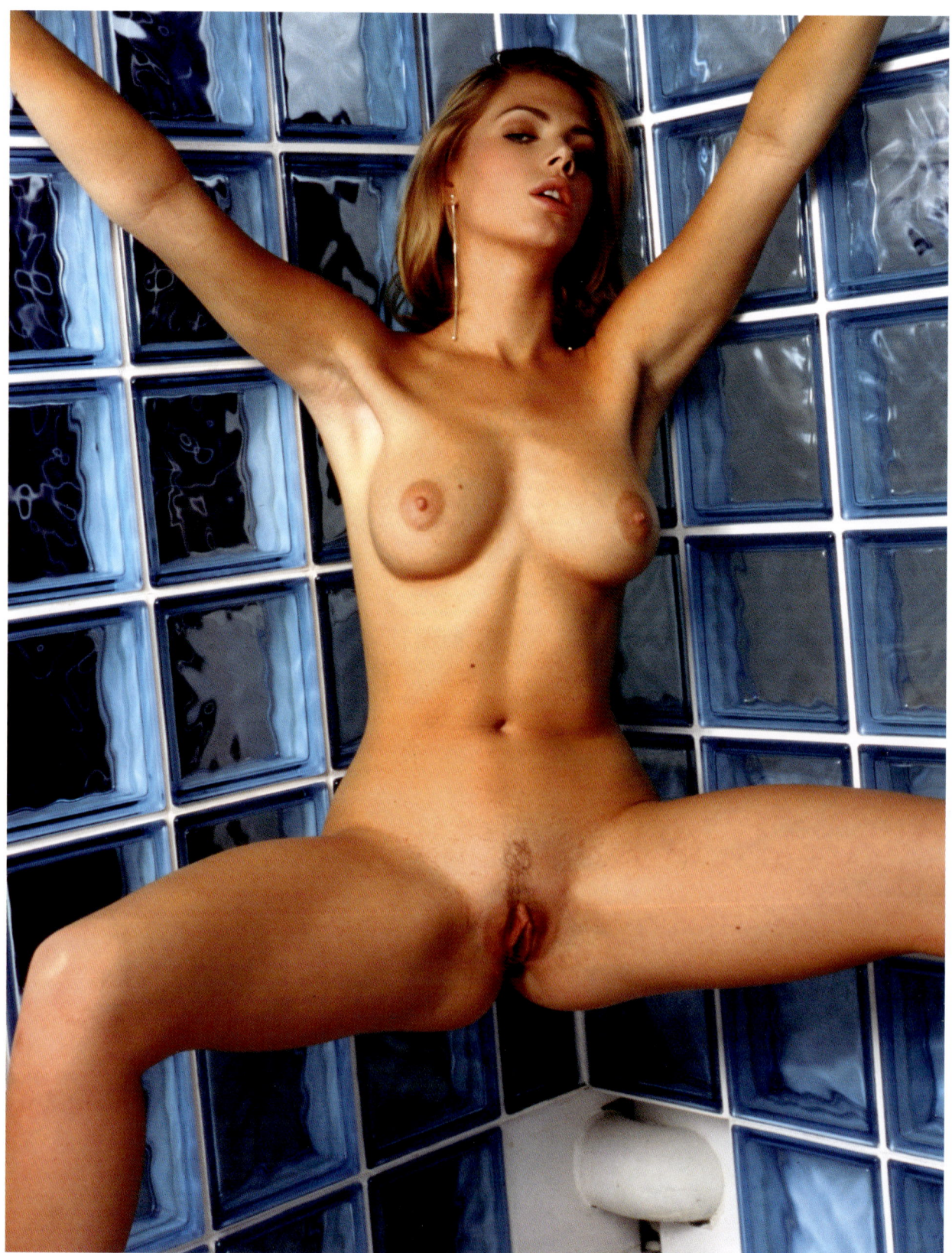

KATALINE K

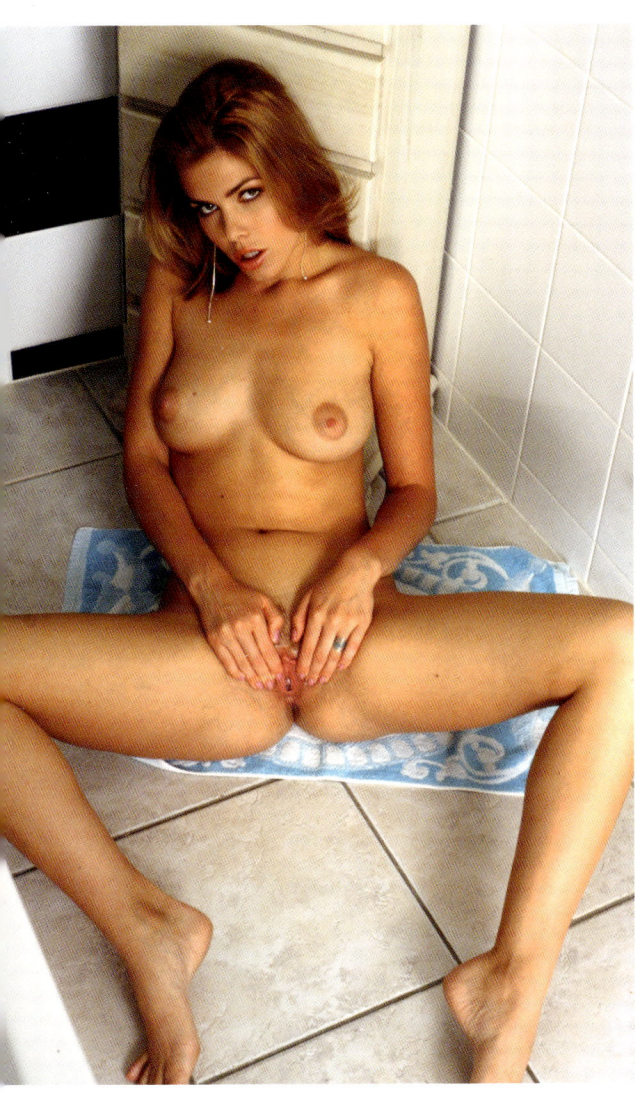
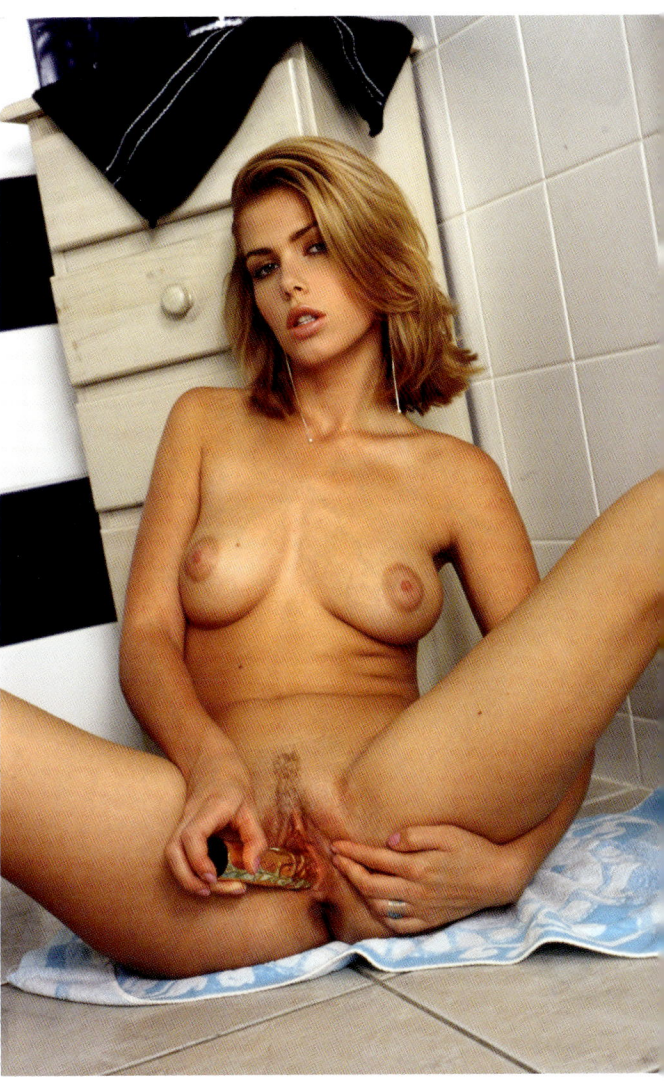

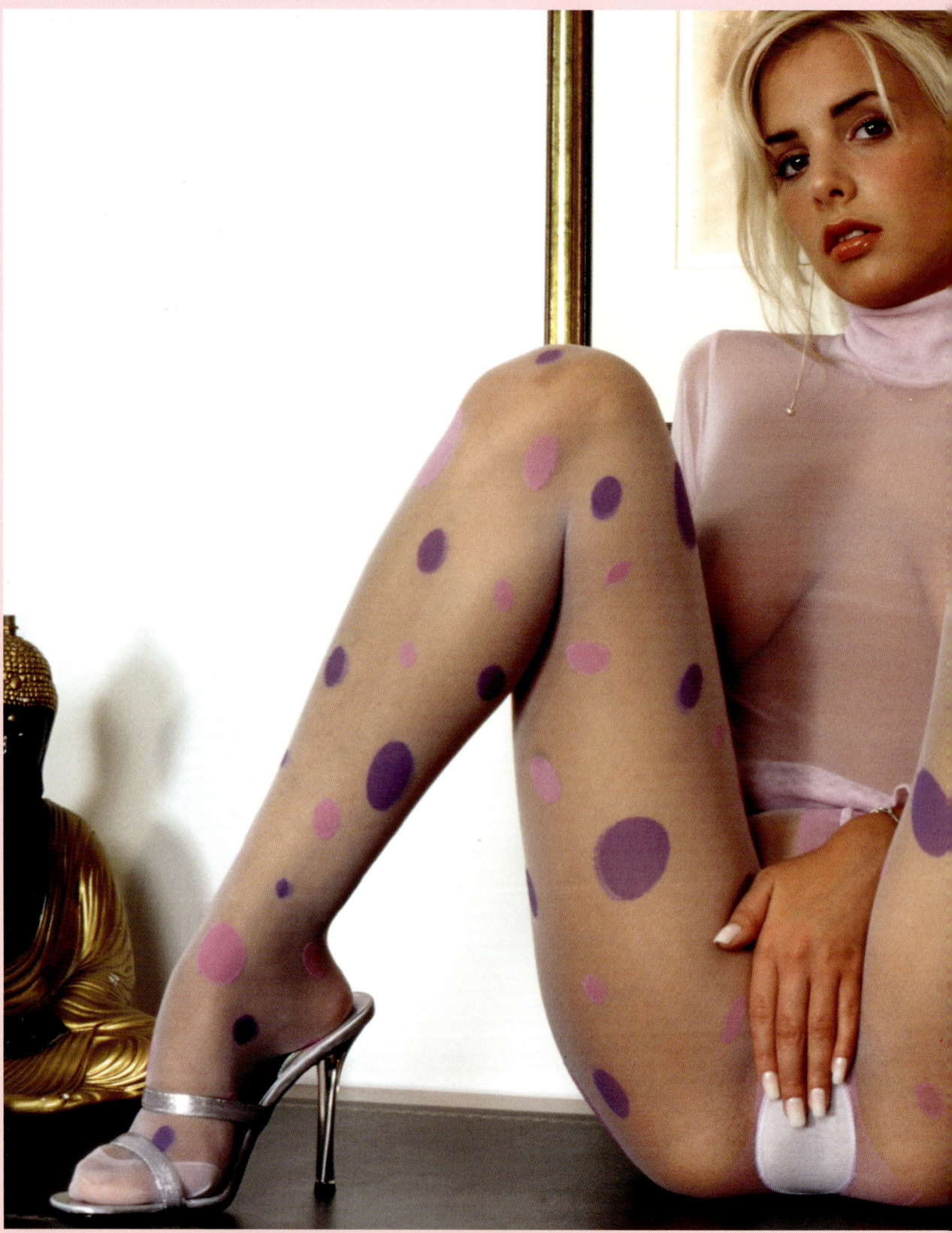

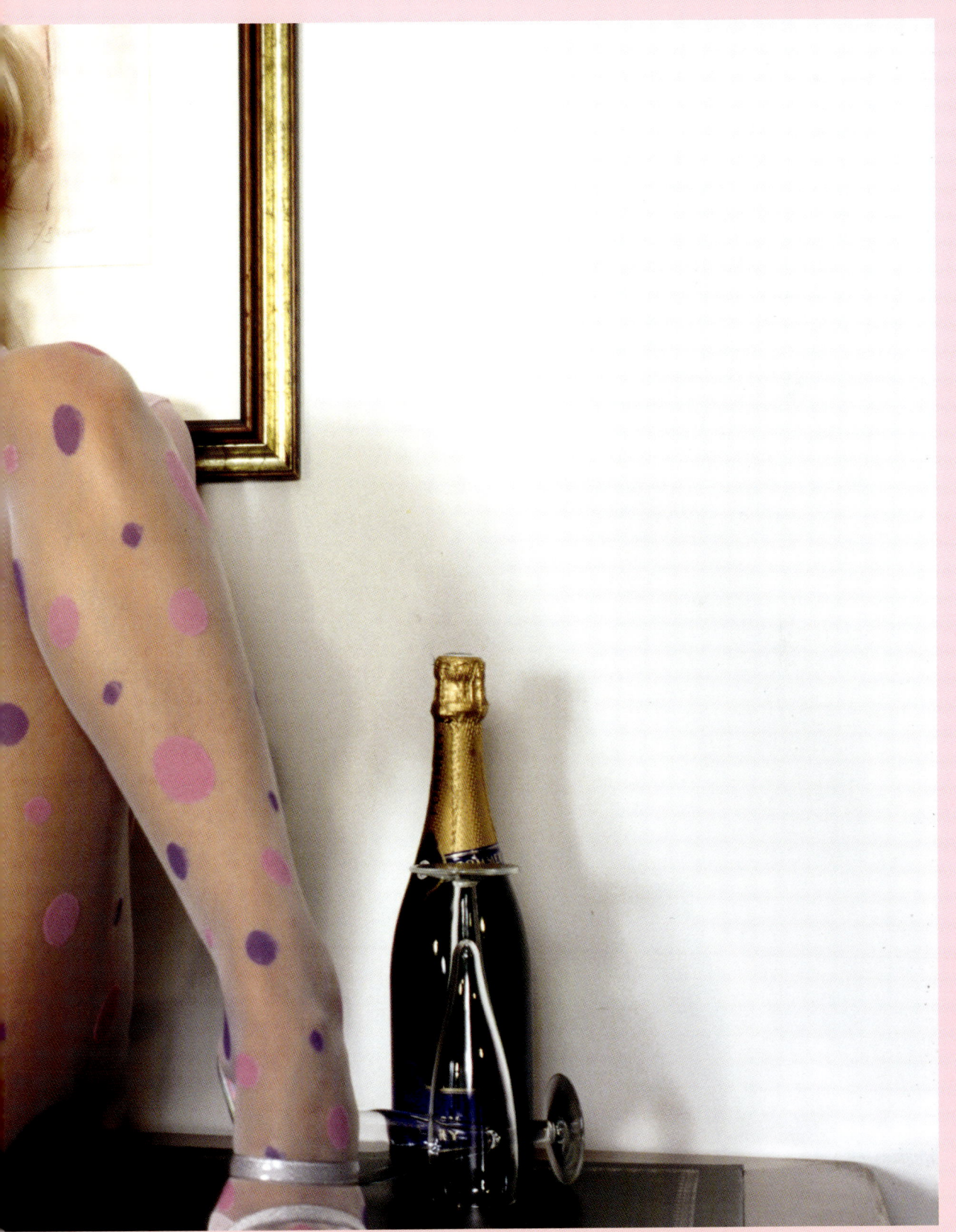

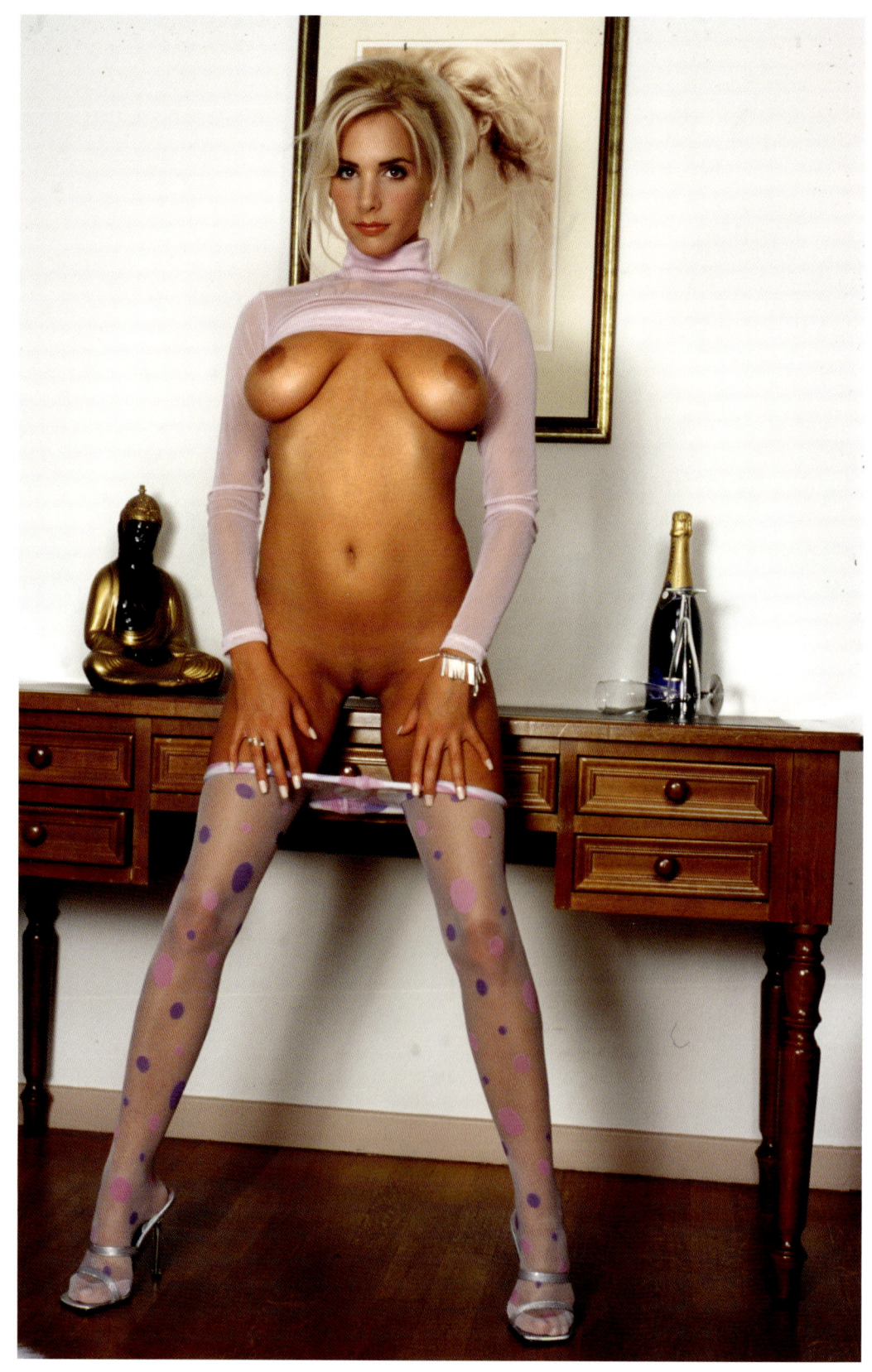

KATALINE V

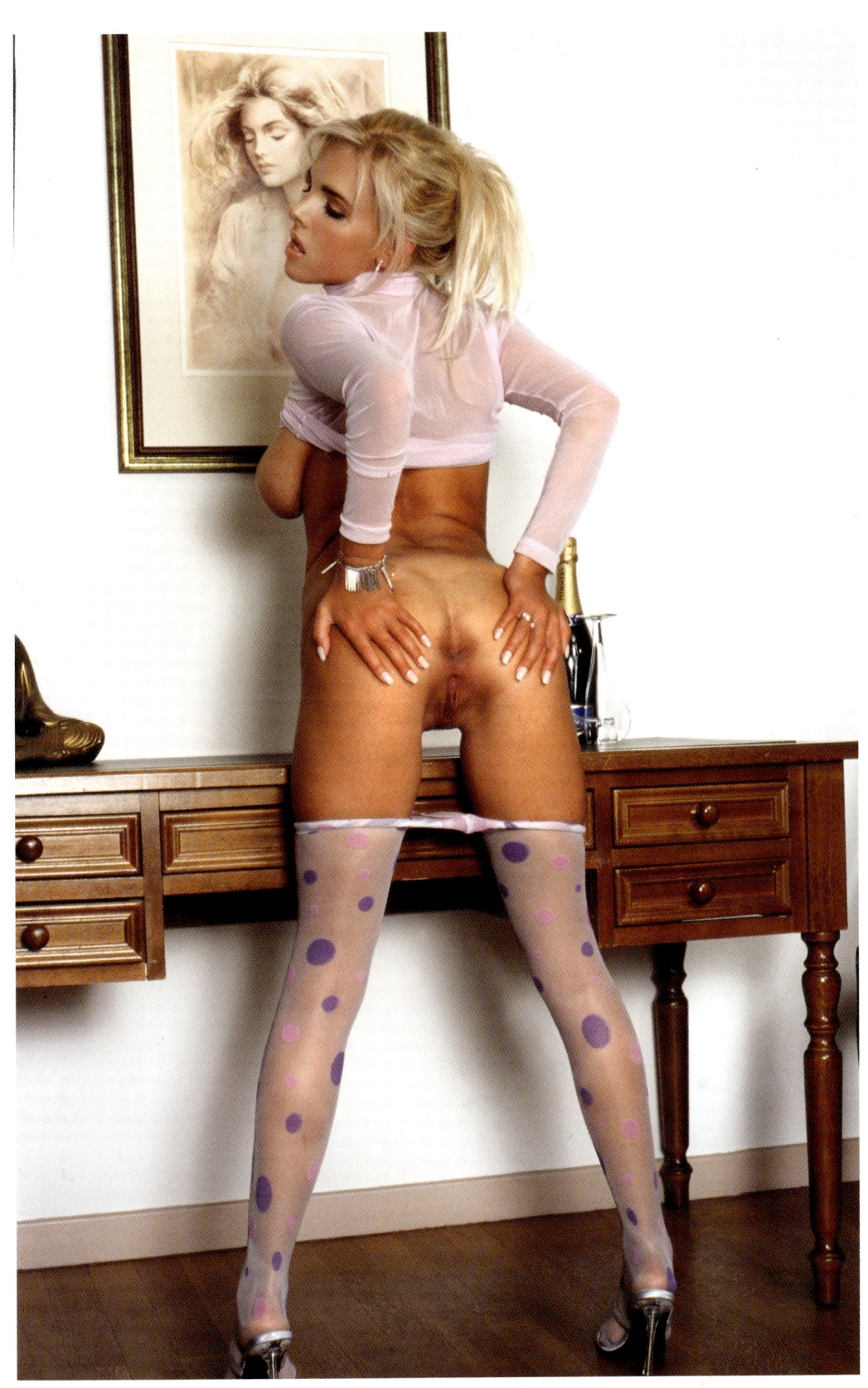

KATALINE V

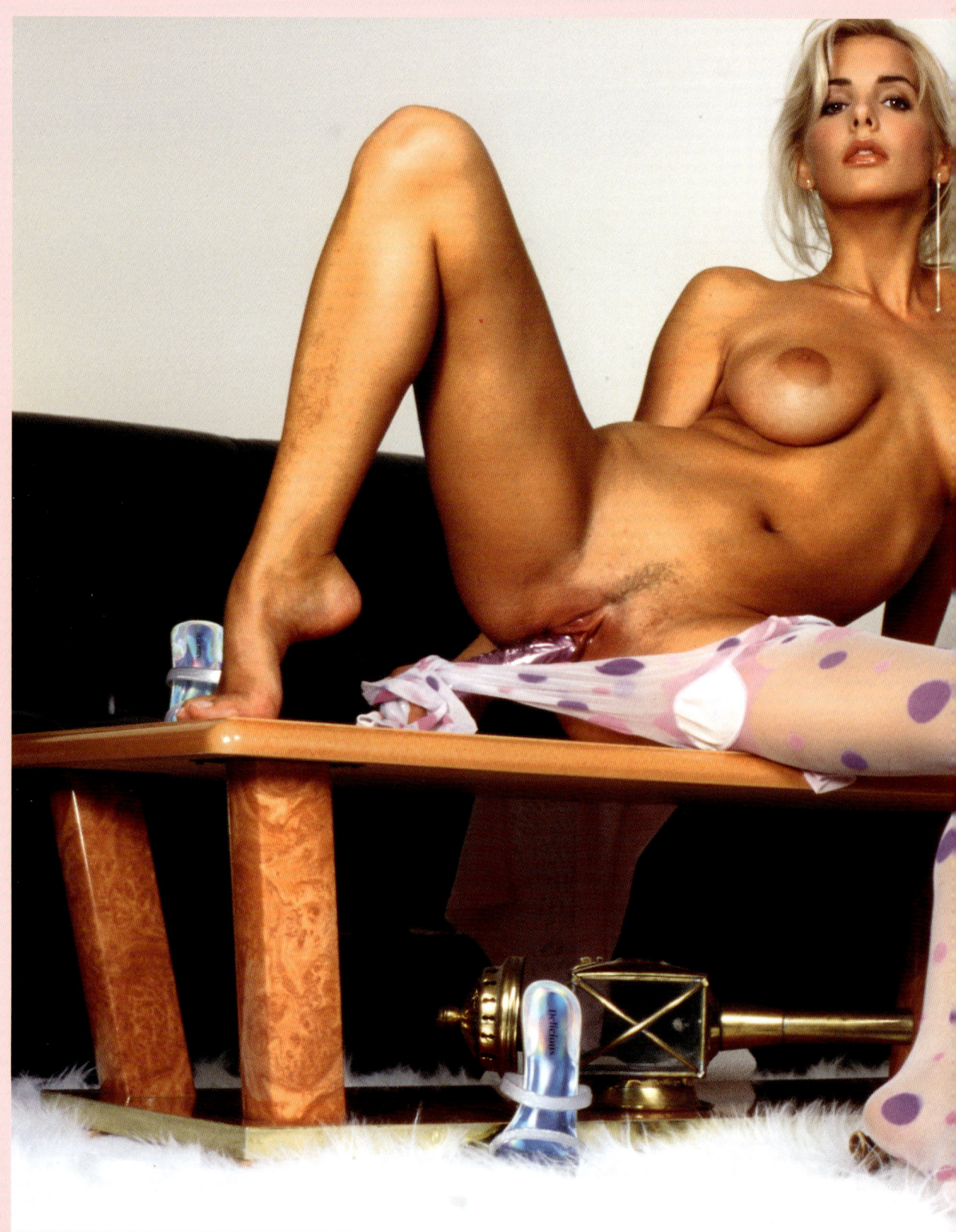

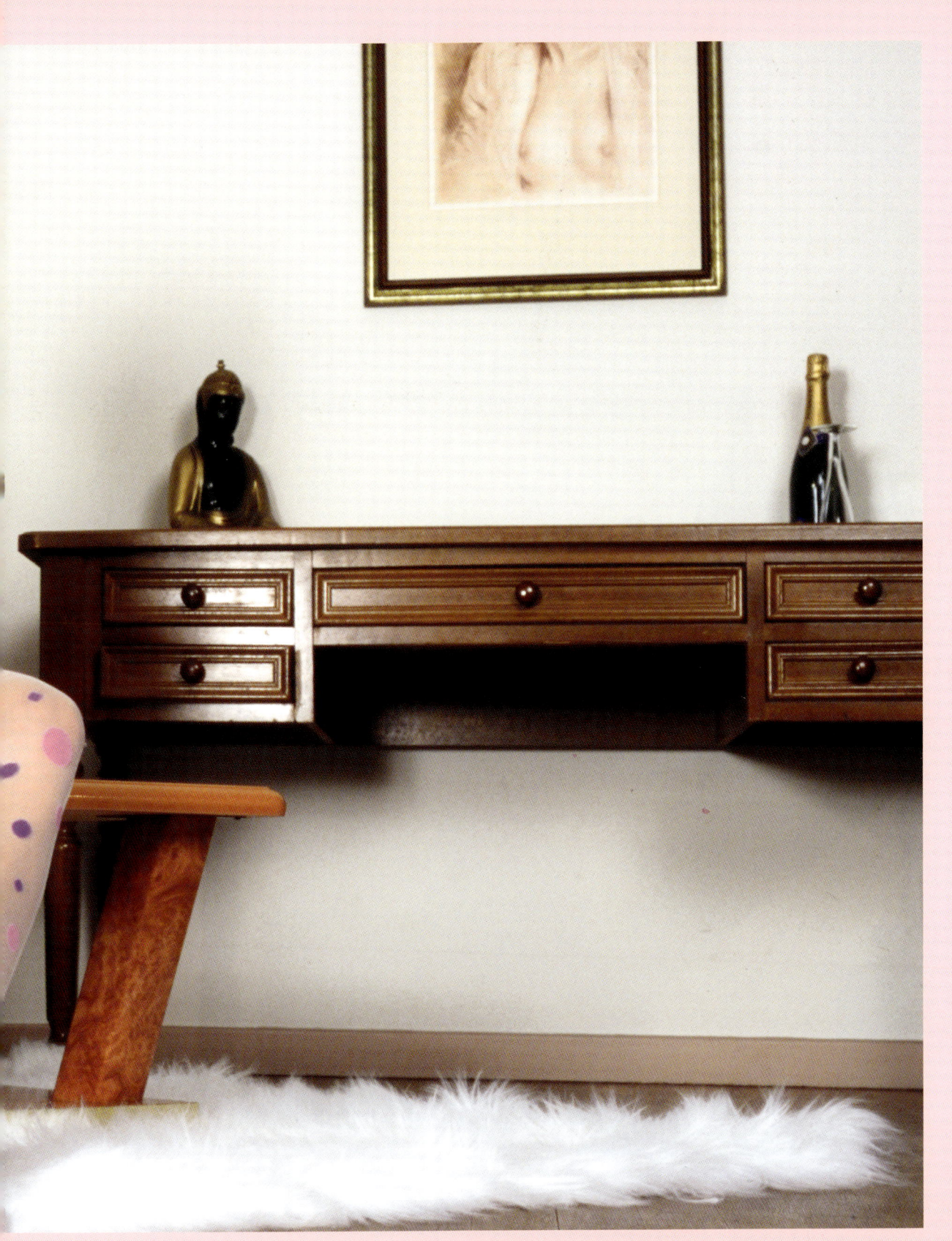

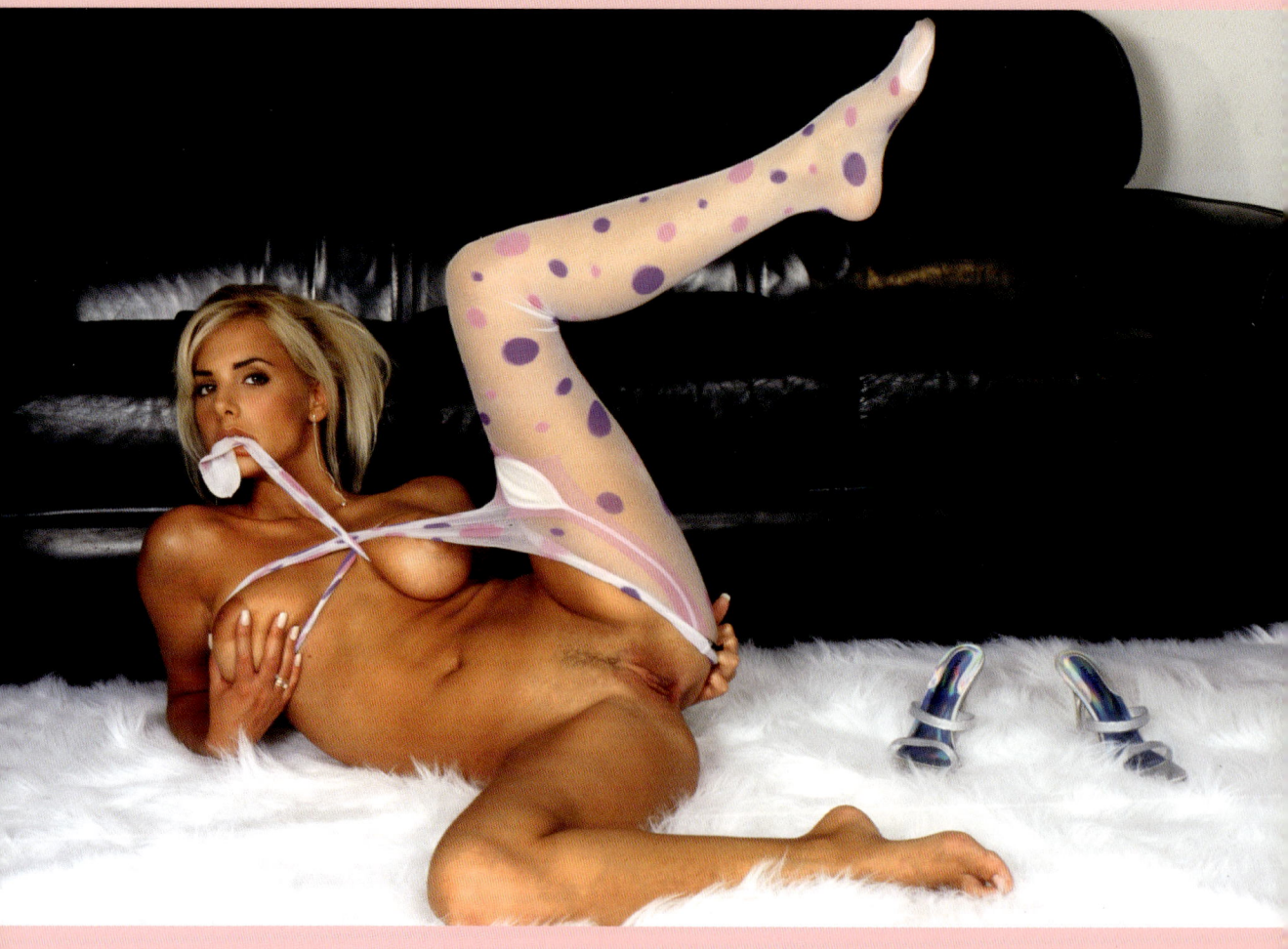

KATALINE V

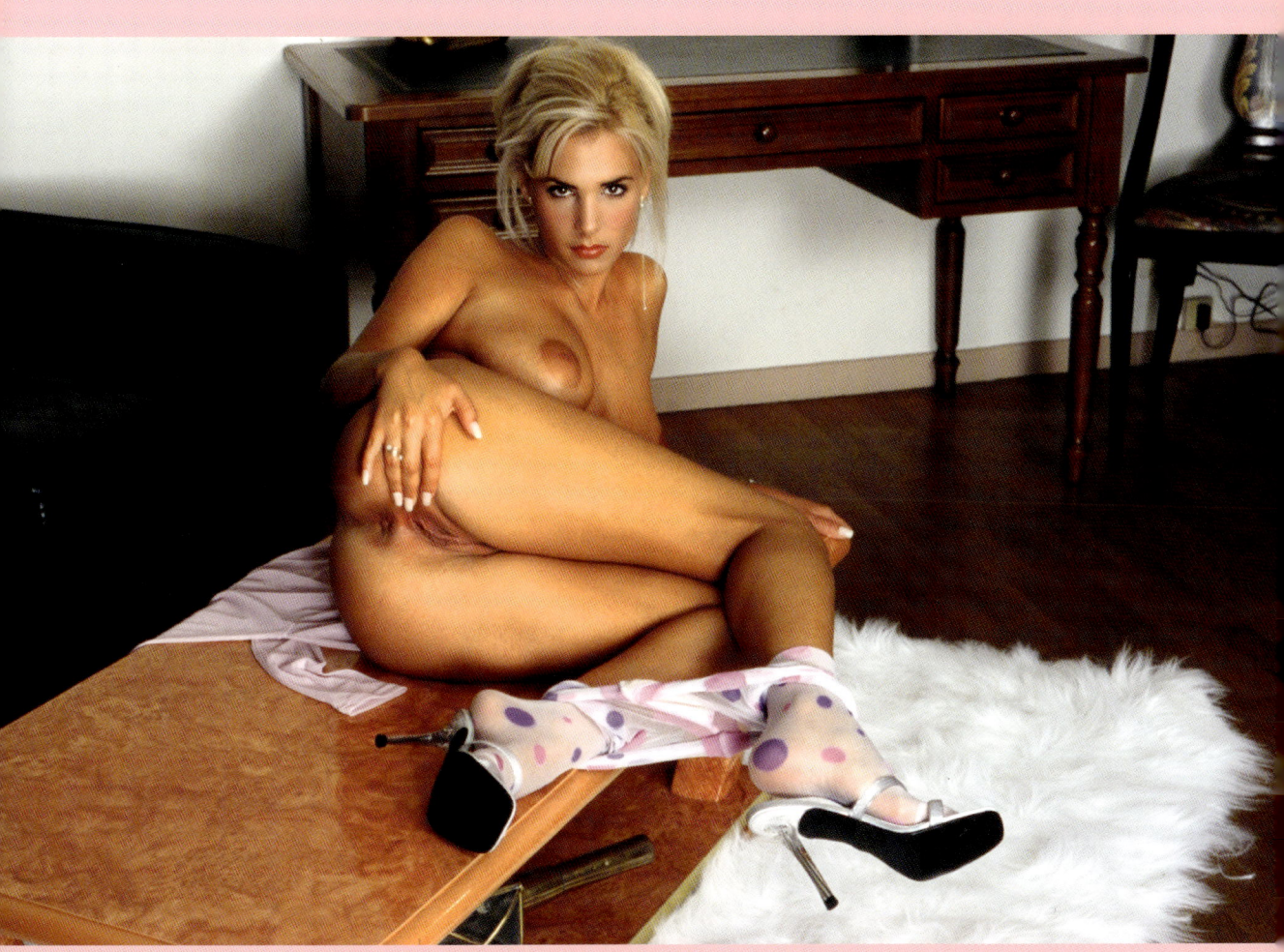

KATALINE V

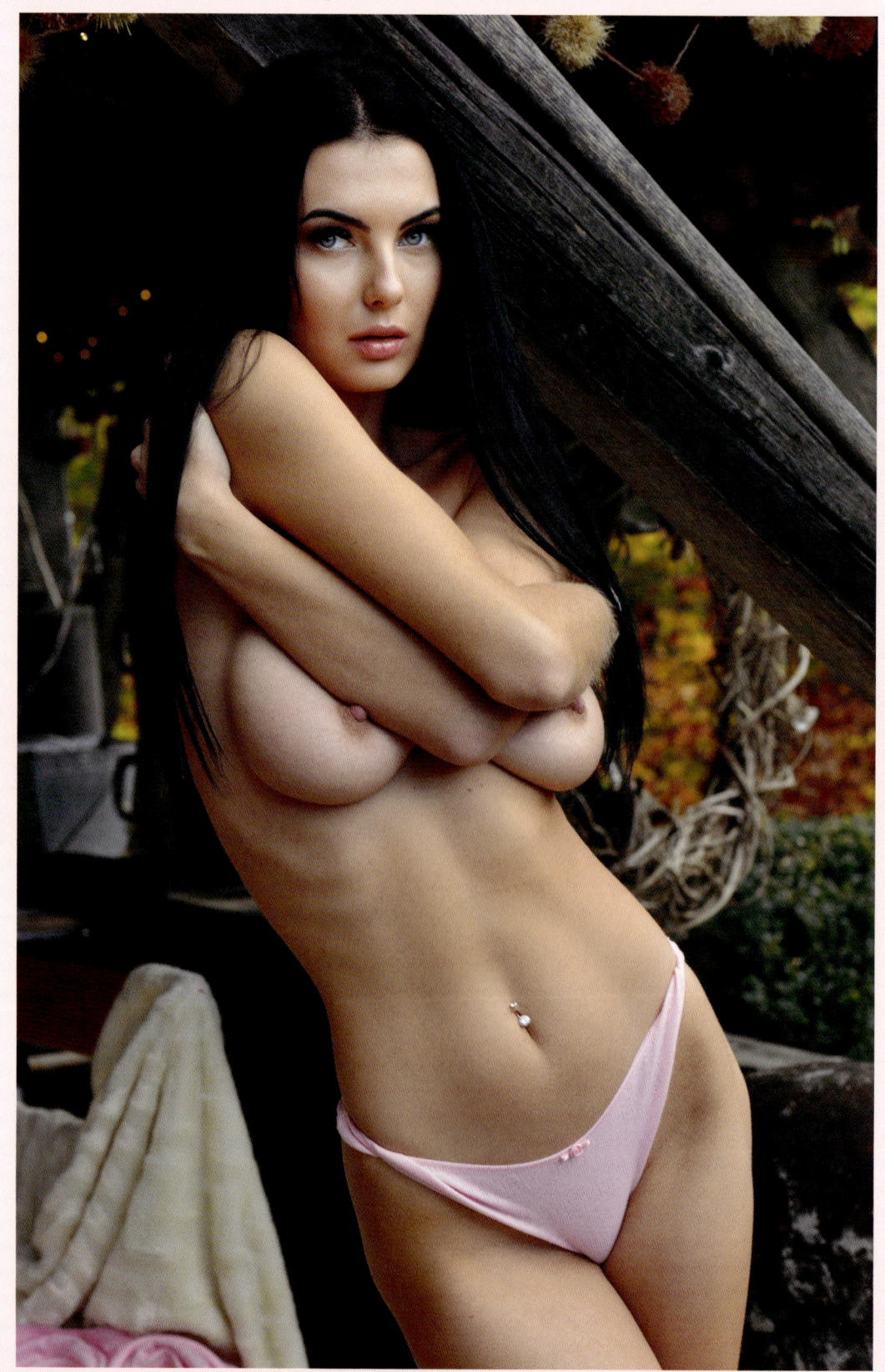

KITTY

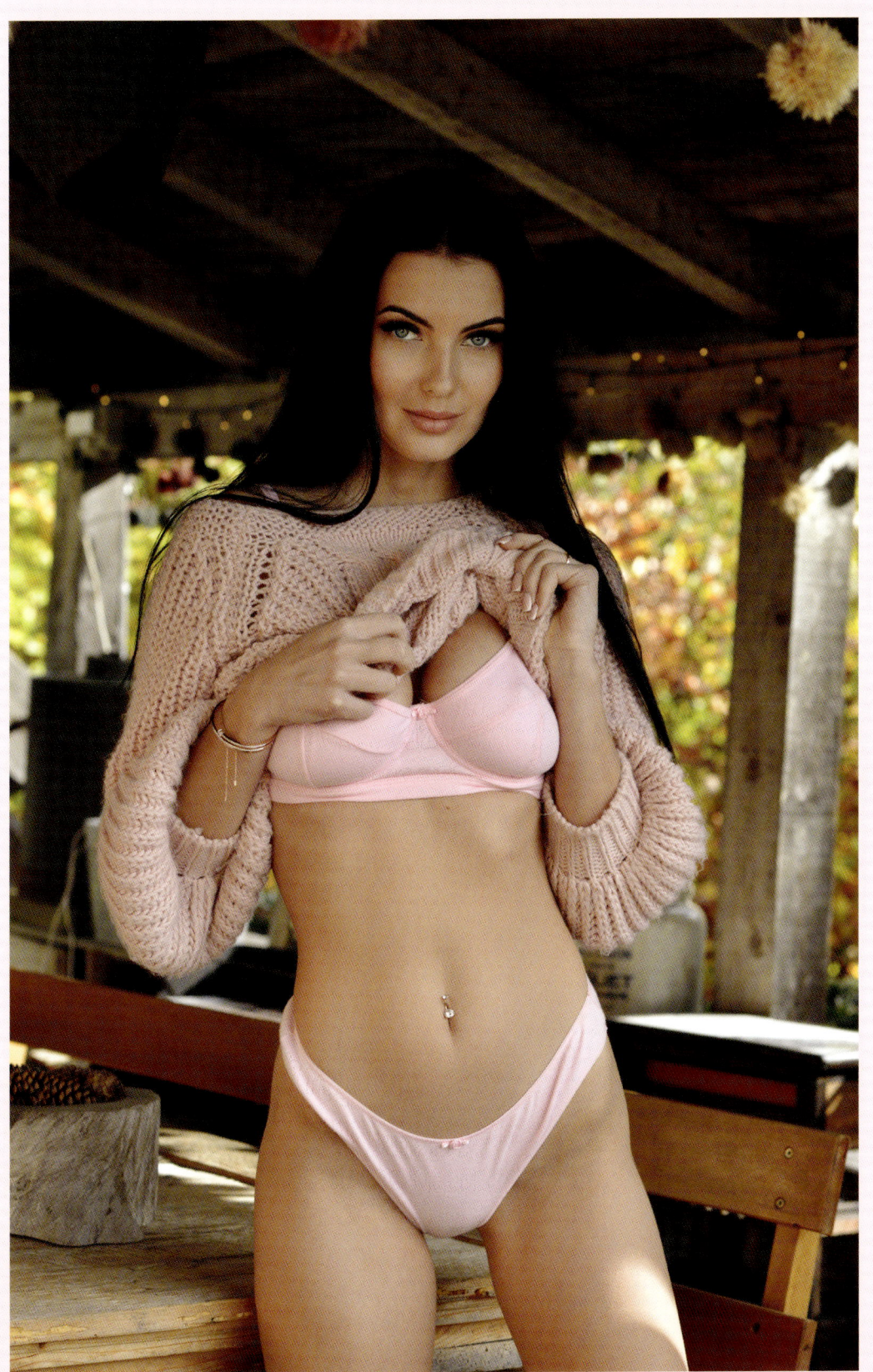

KITTY

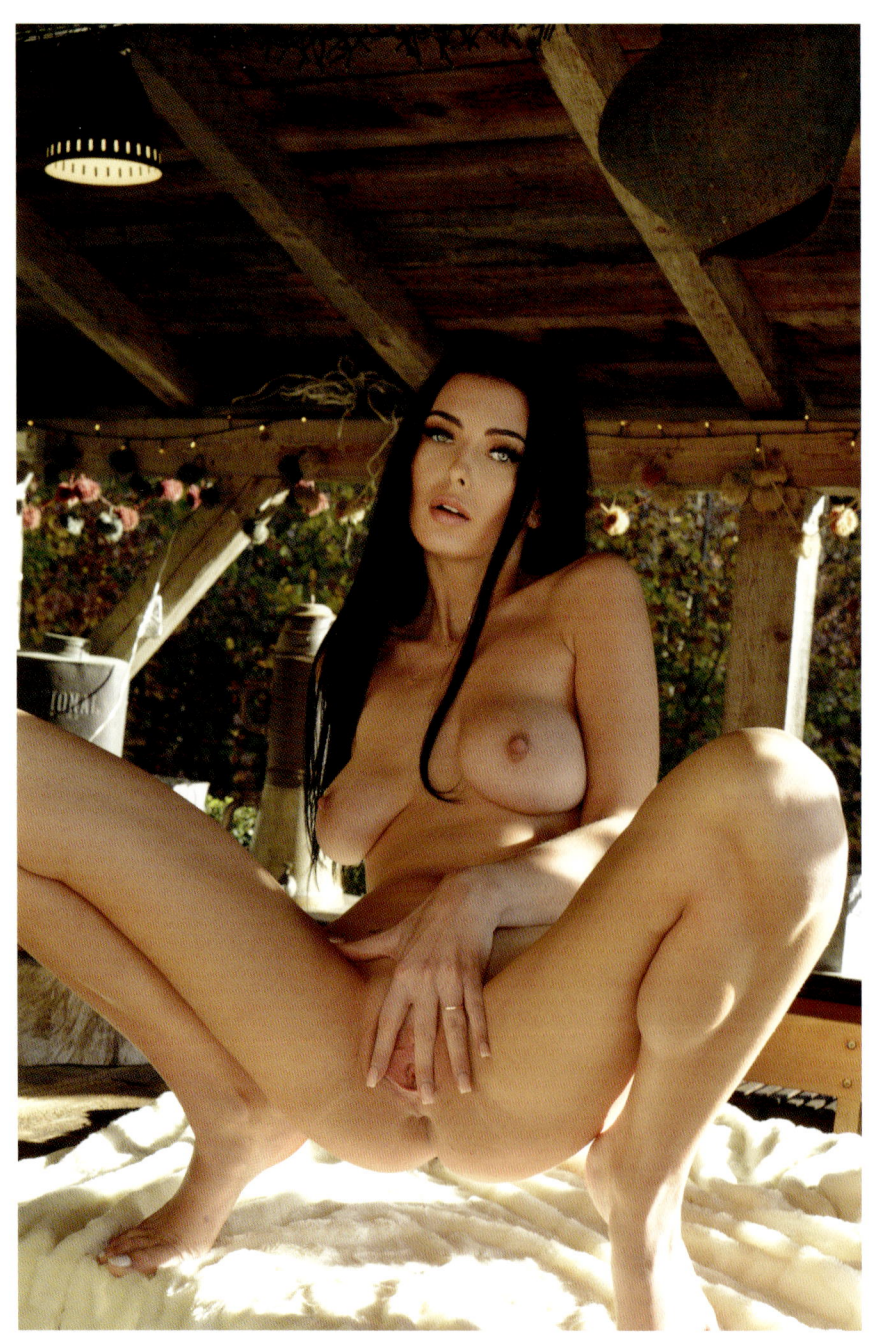

KITTY

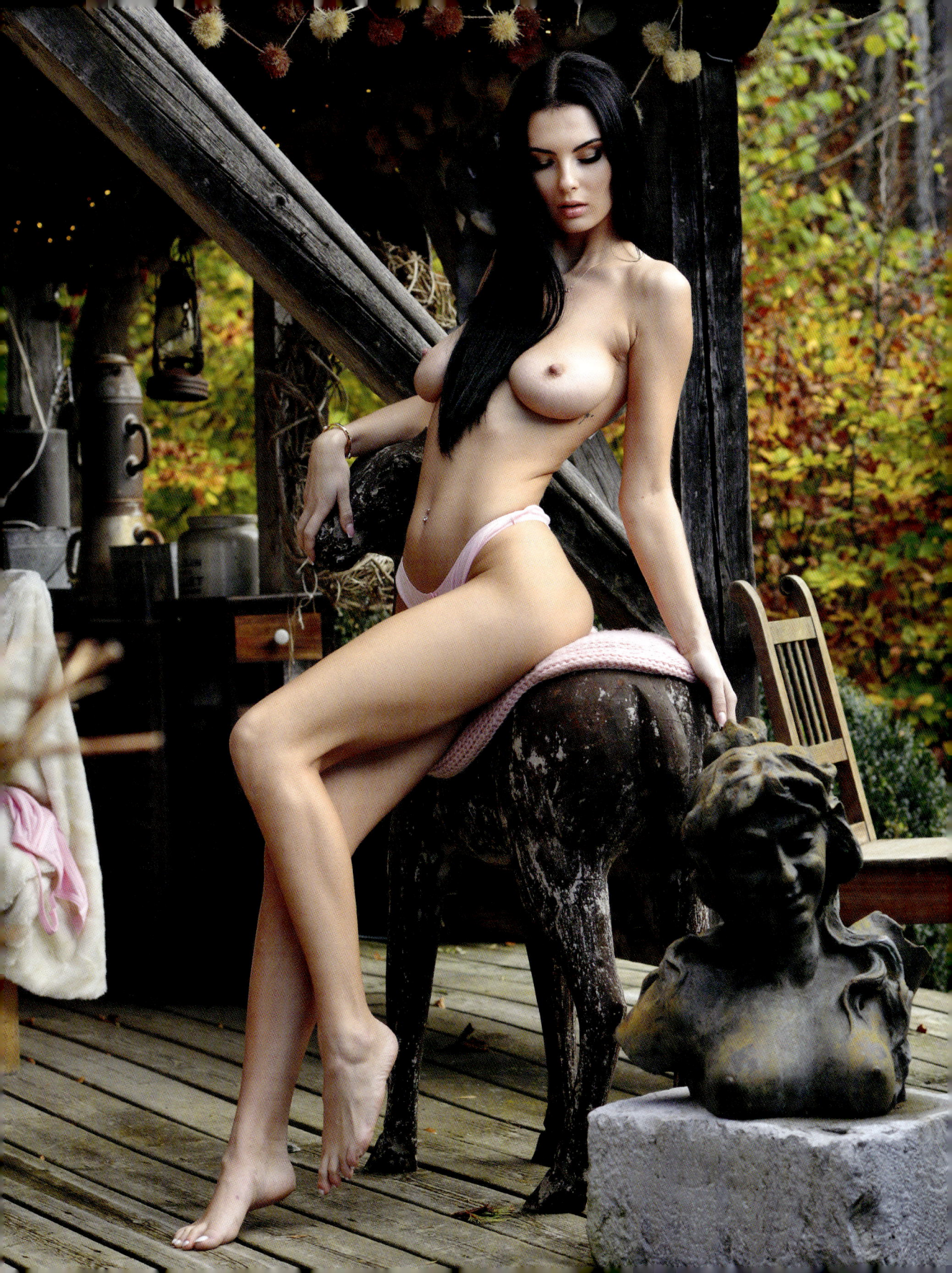

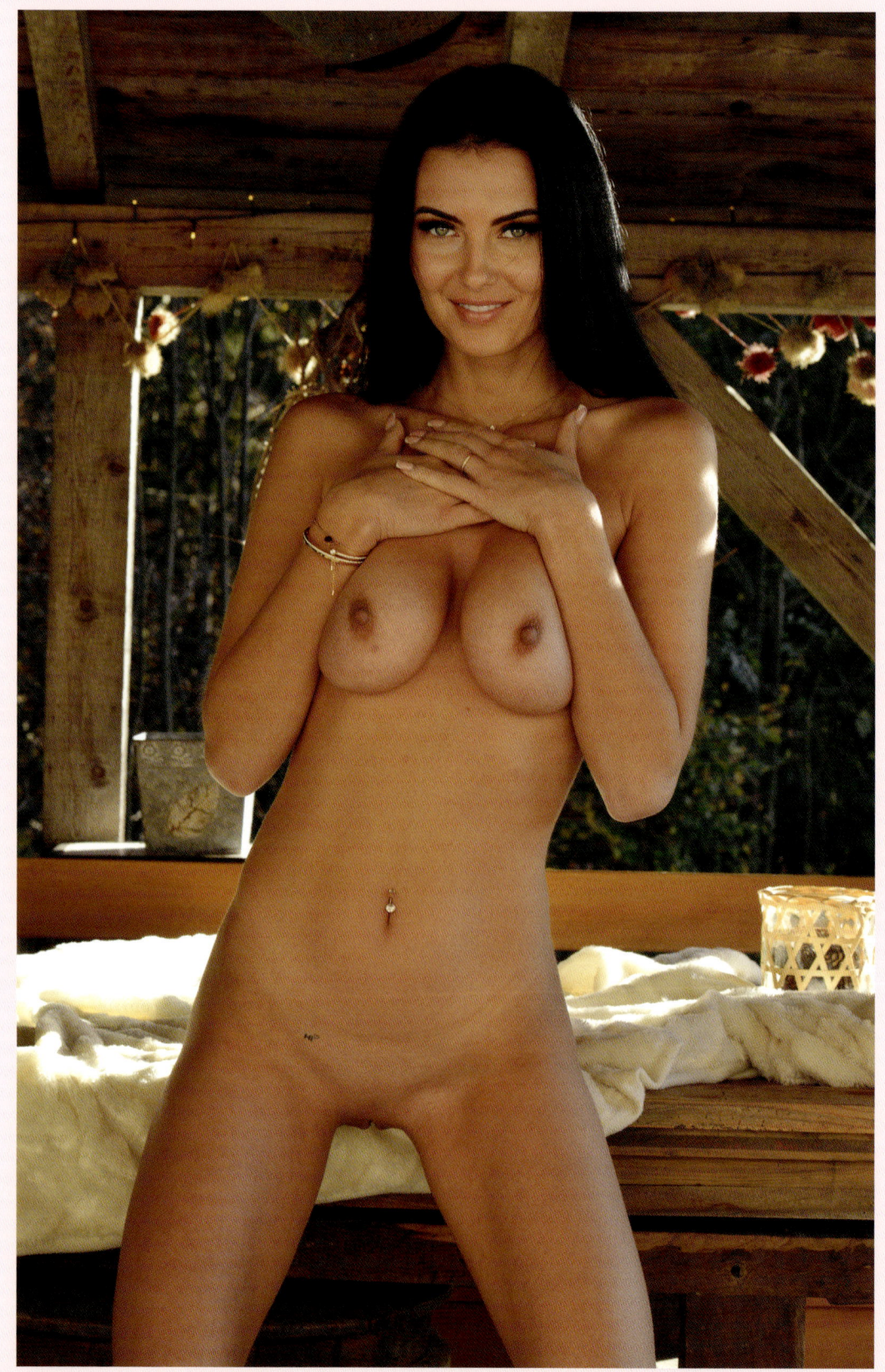

KITTY

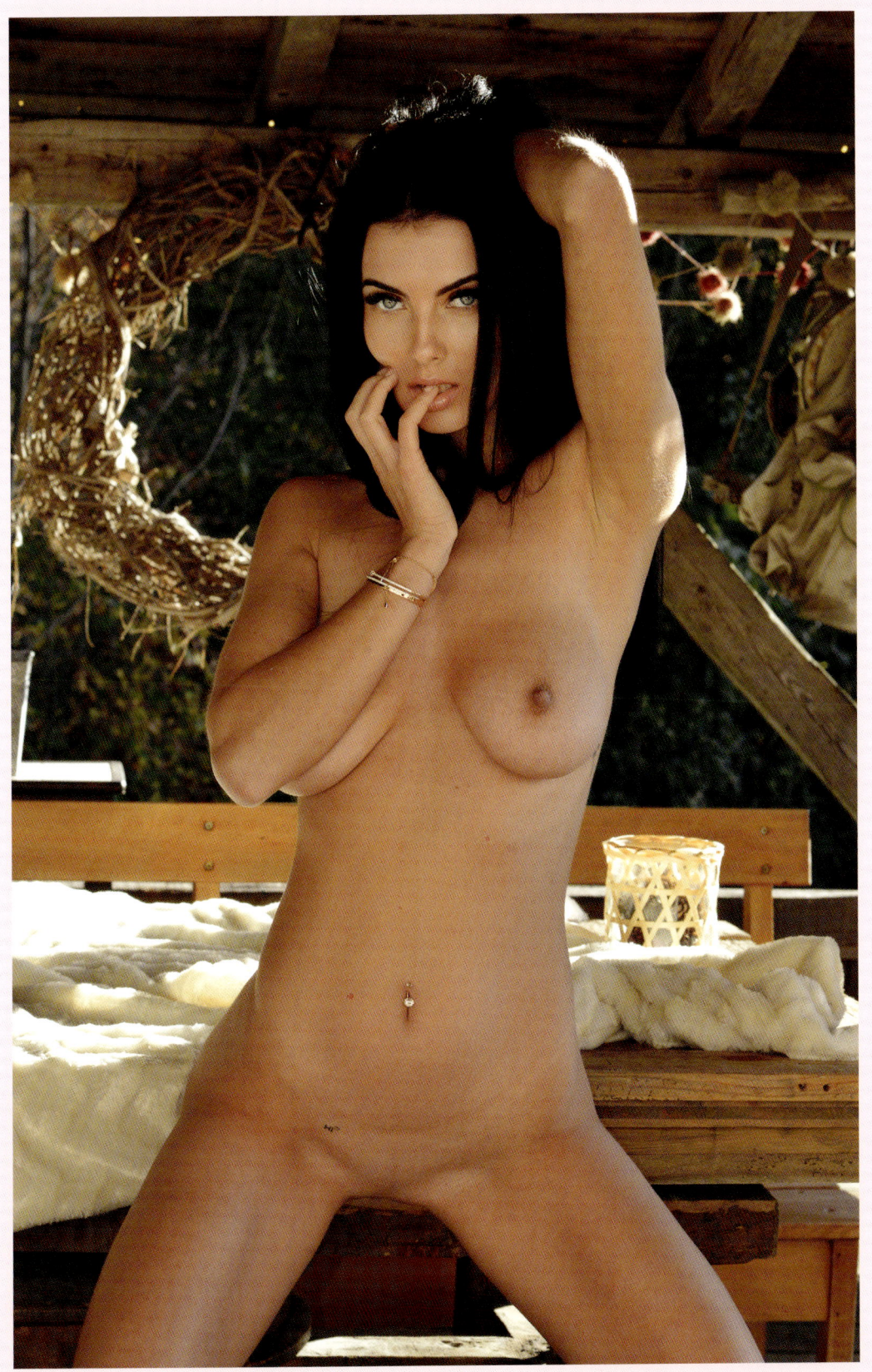

KITTY

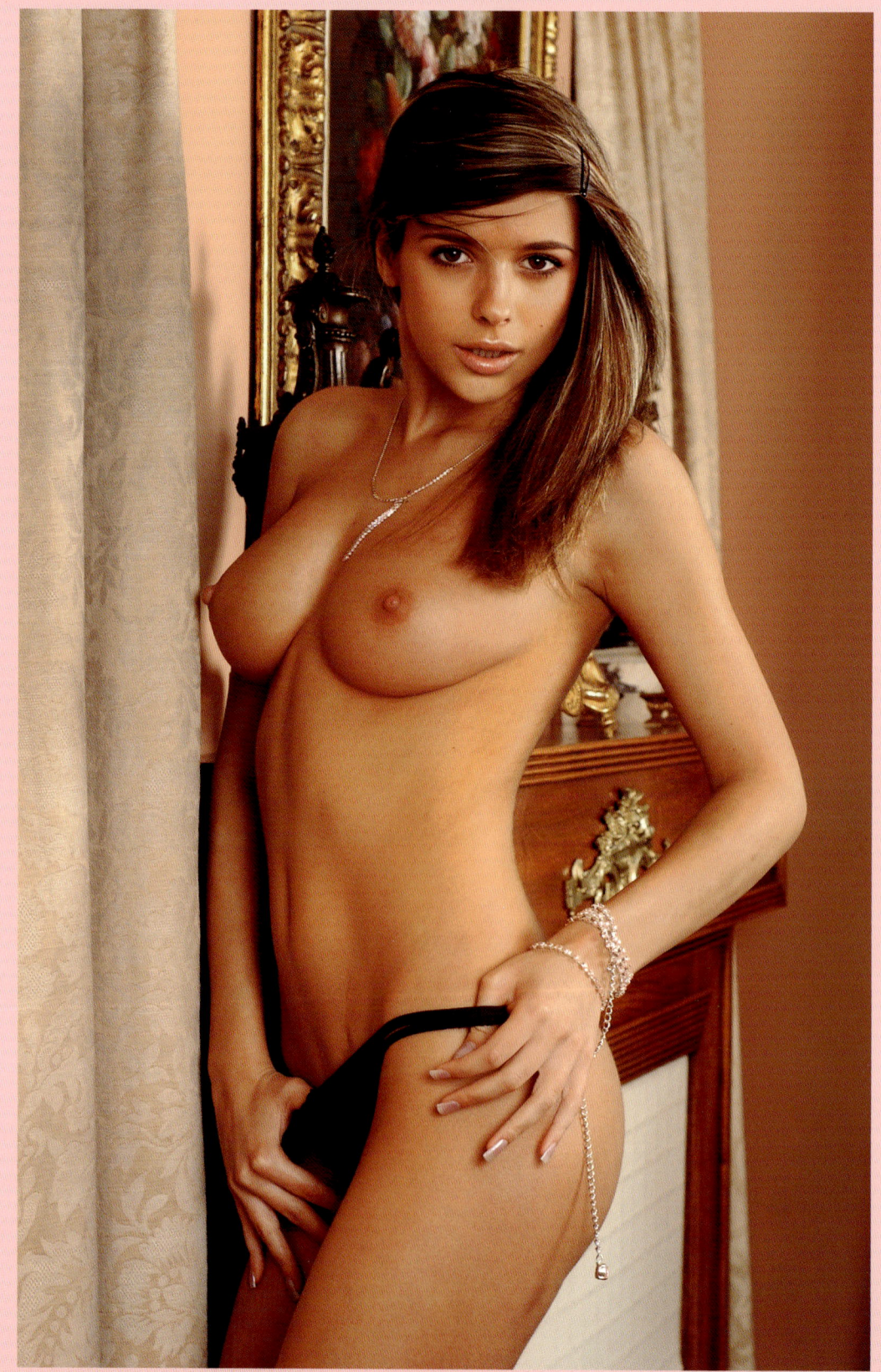

KLAUDIA

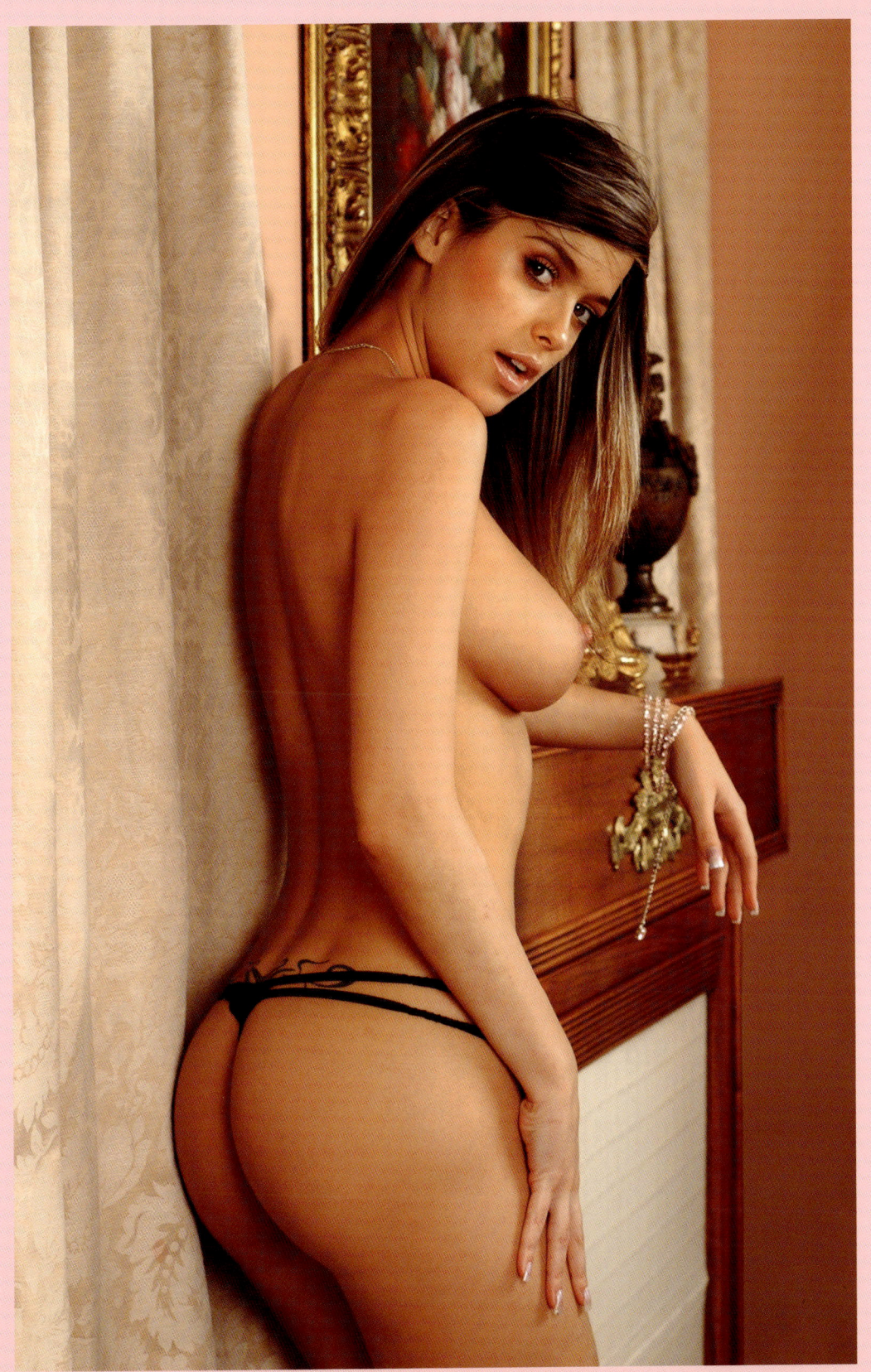

KLAUDIA

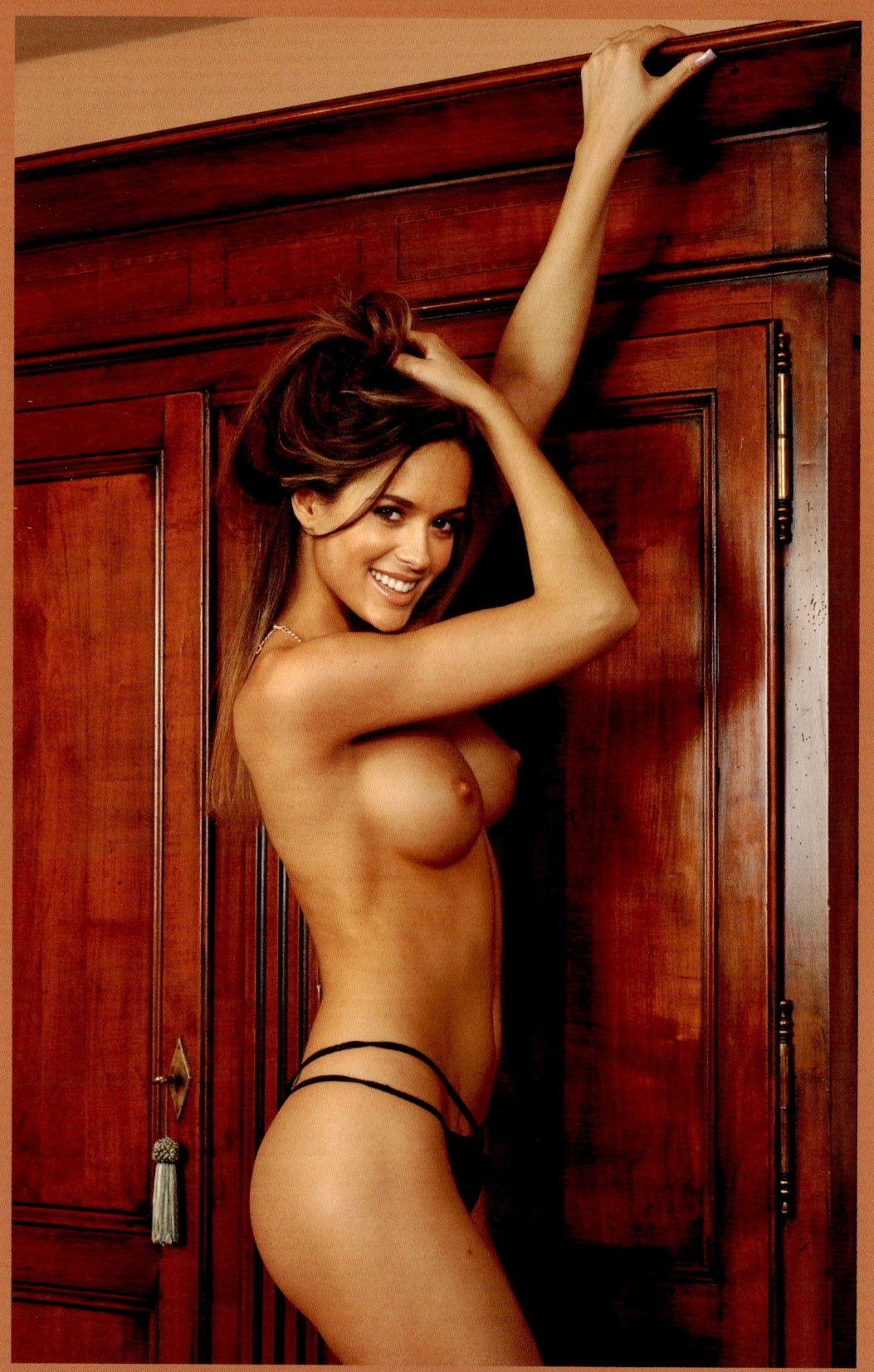

KLAUDIA

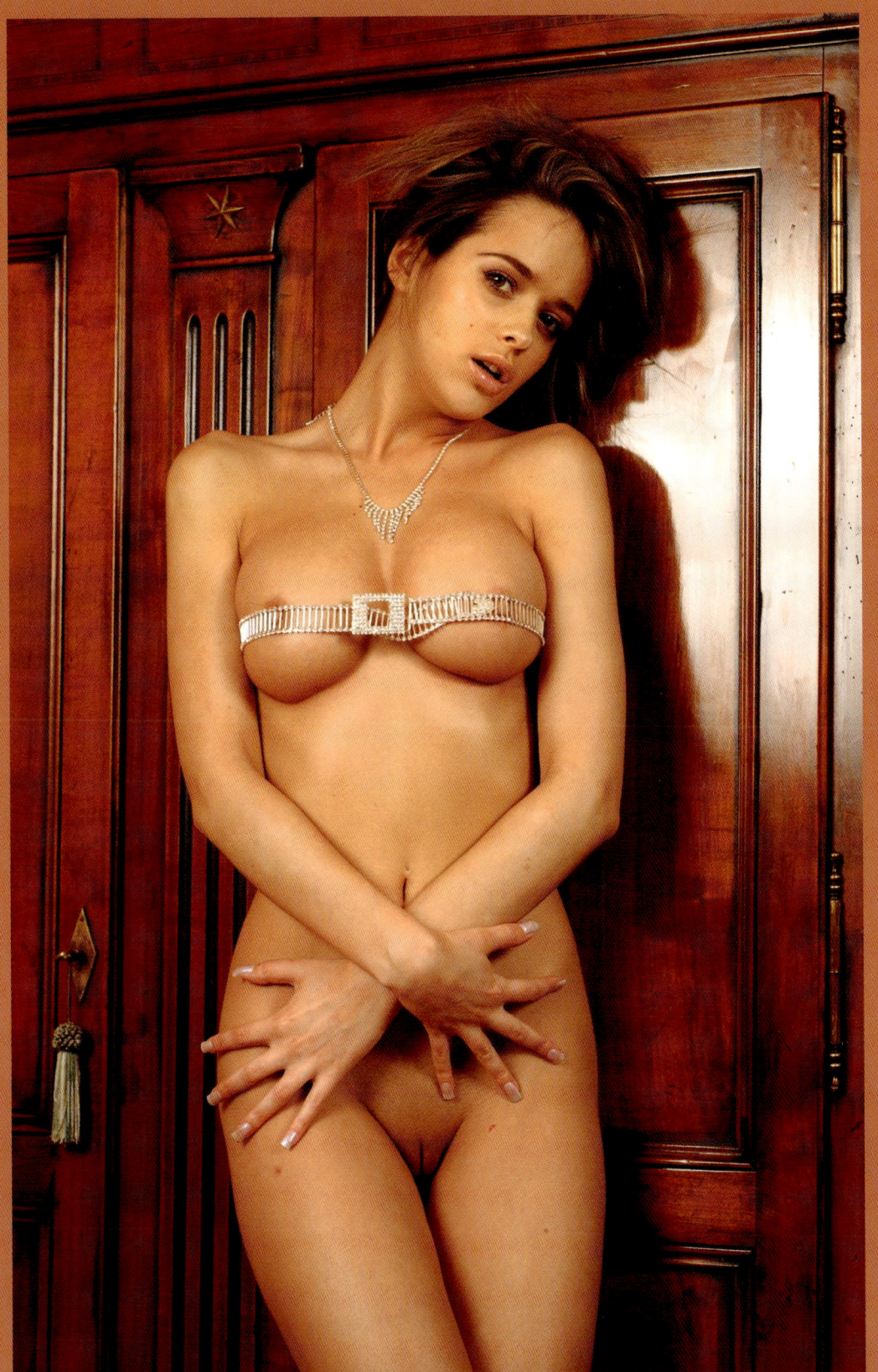

KLAUDIA

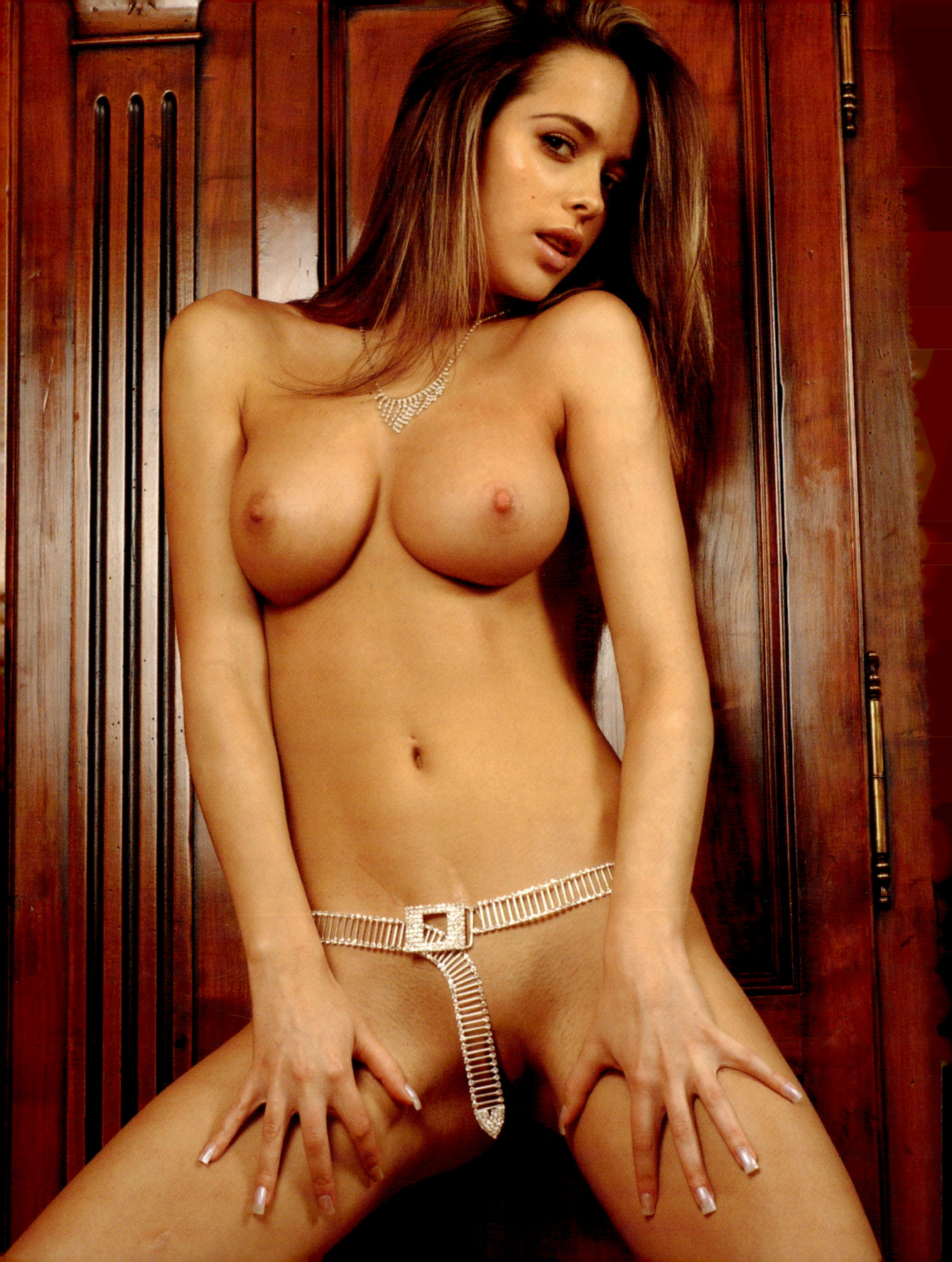

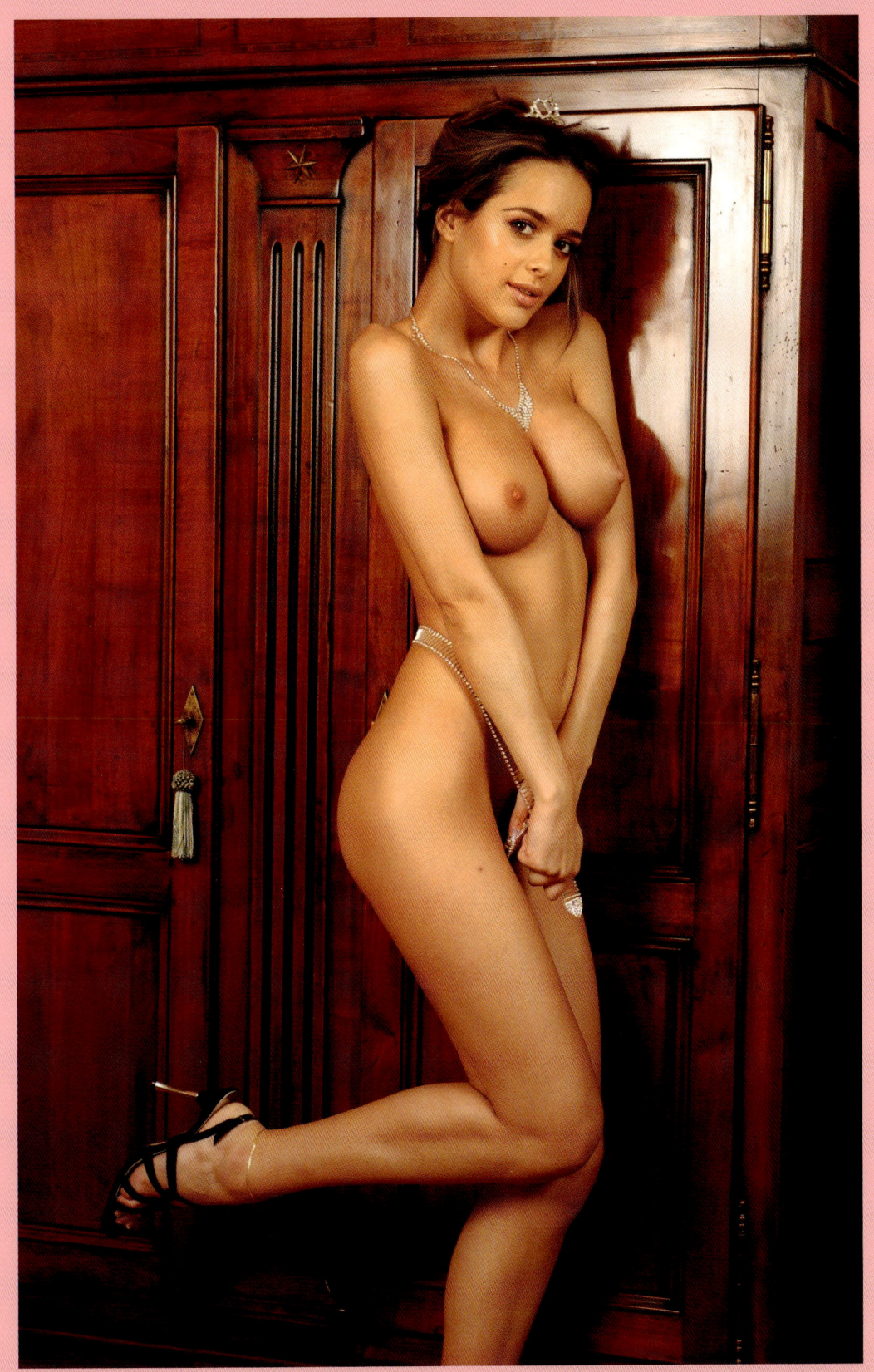

KLAUDIA

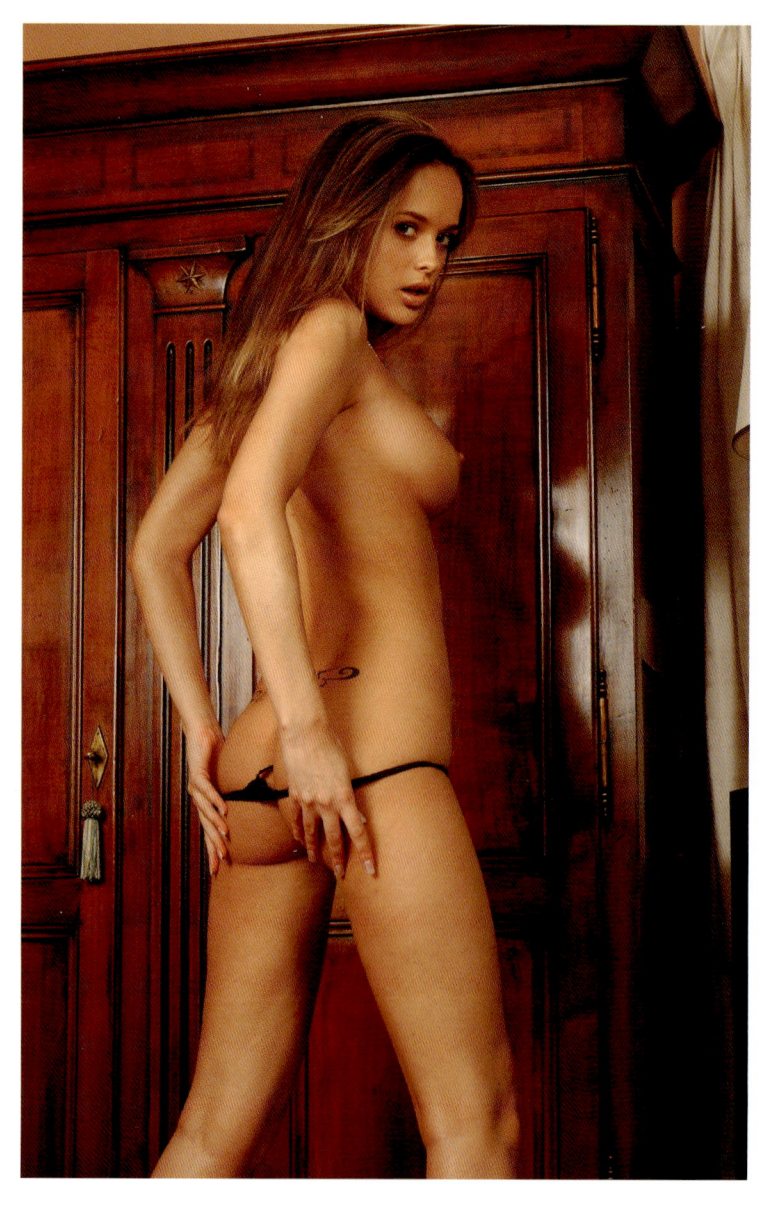

KLAUDIA

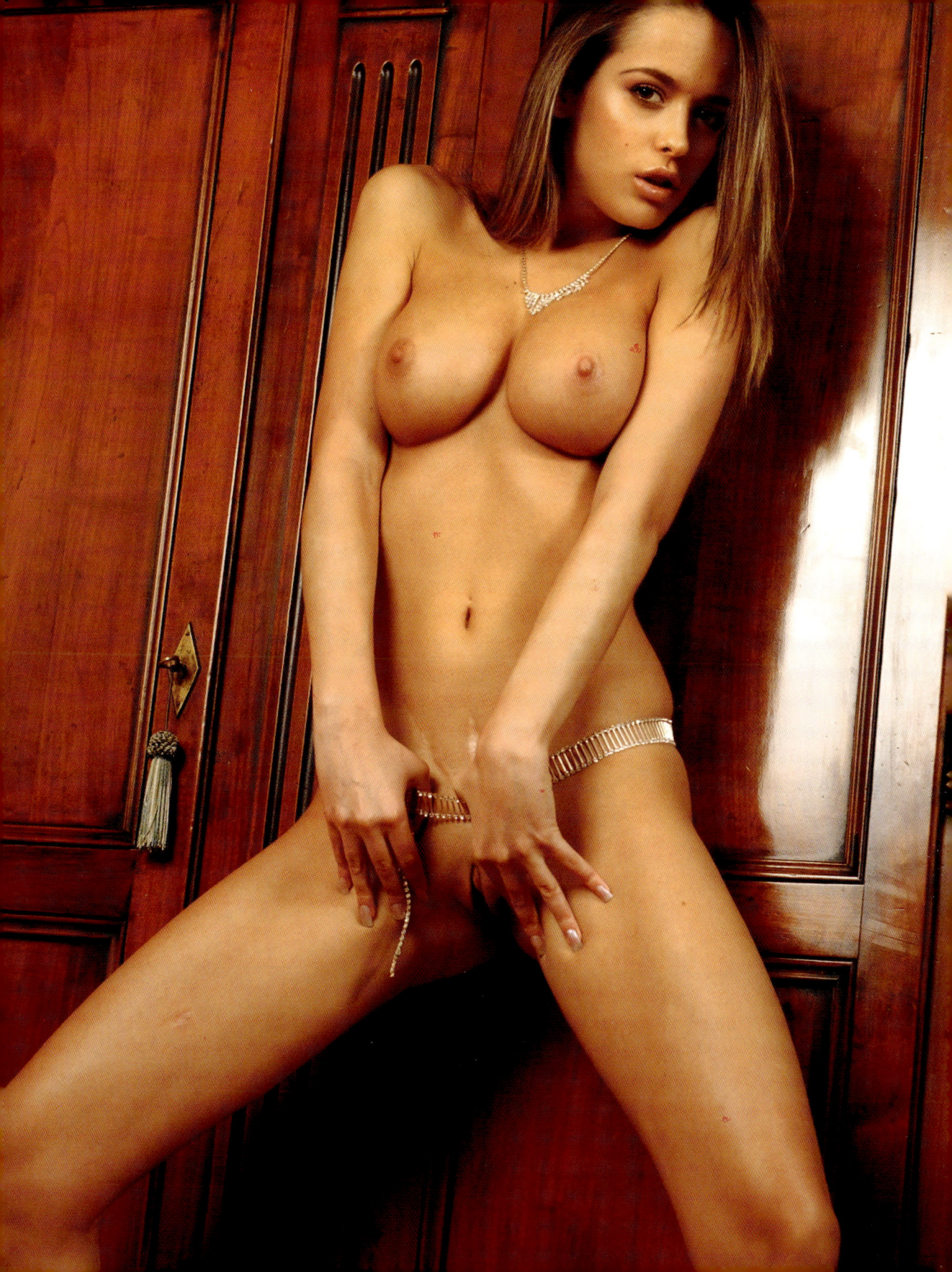

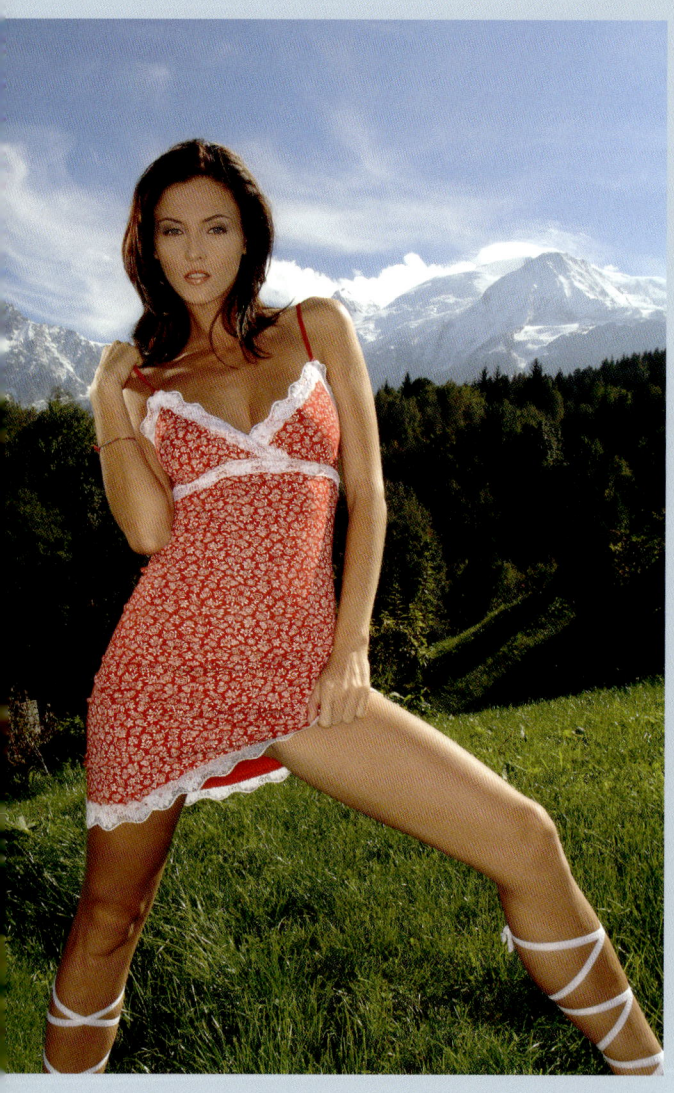 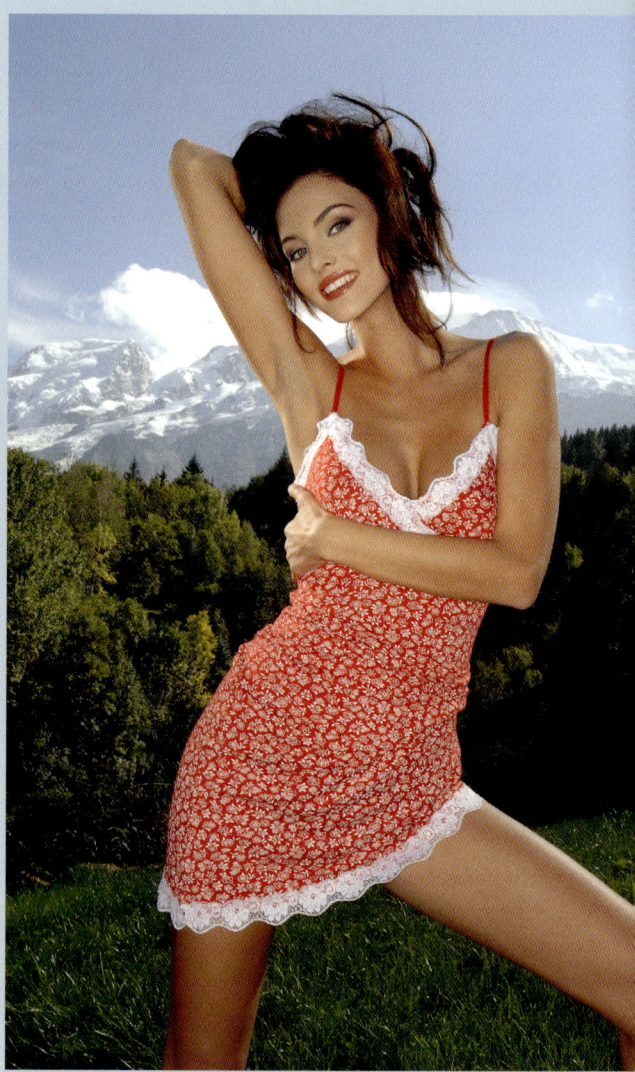

LINDA

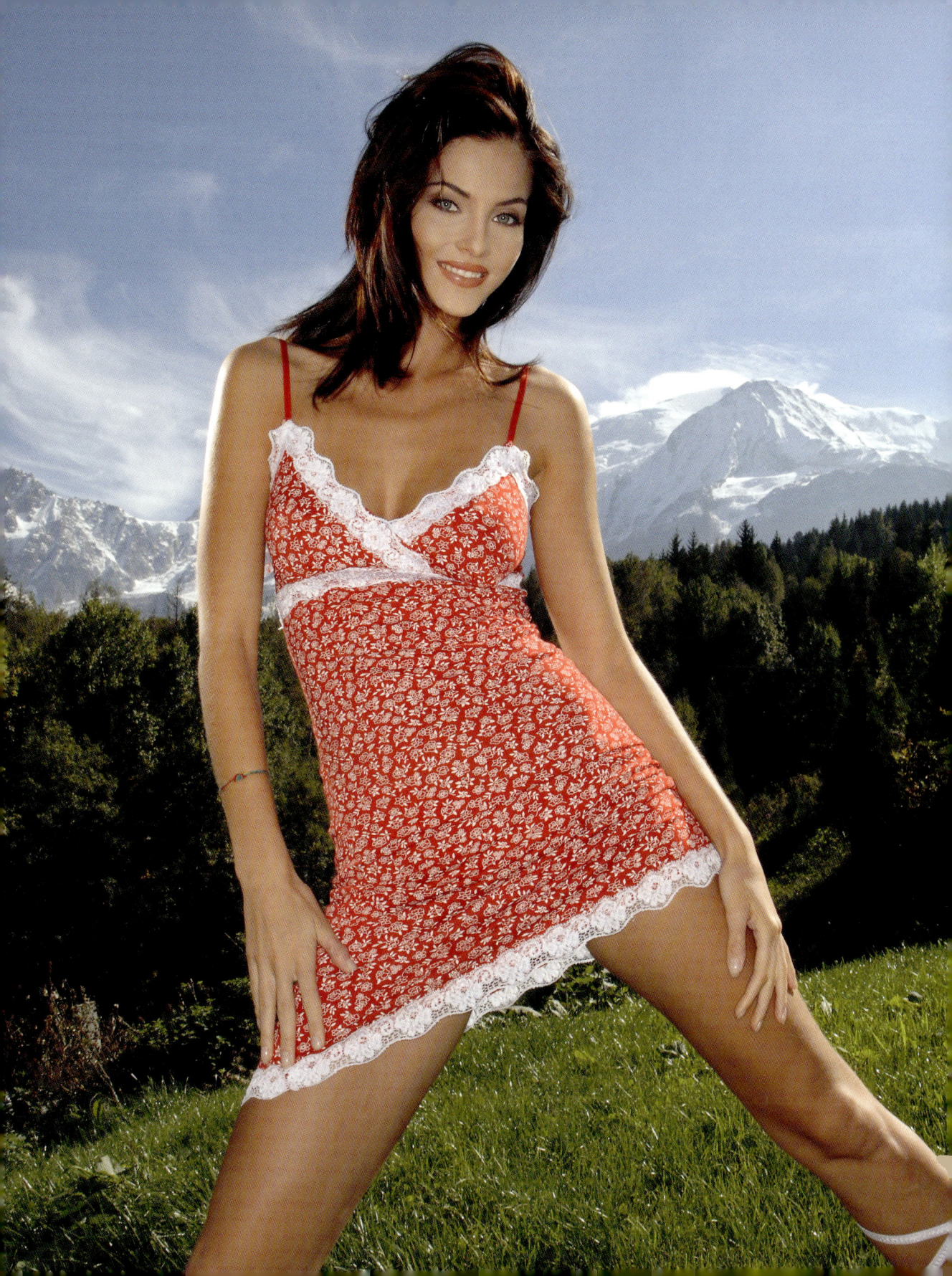

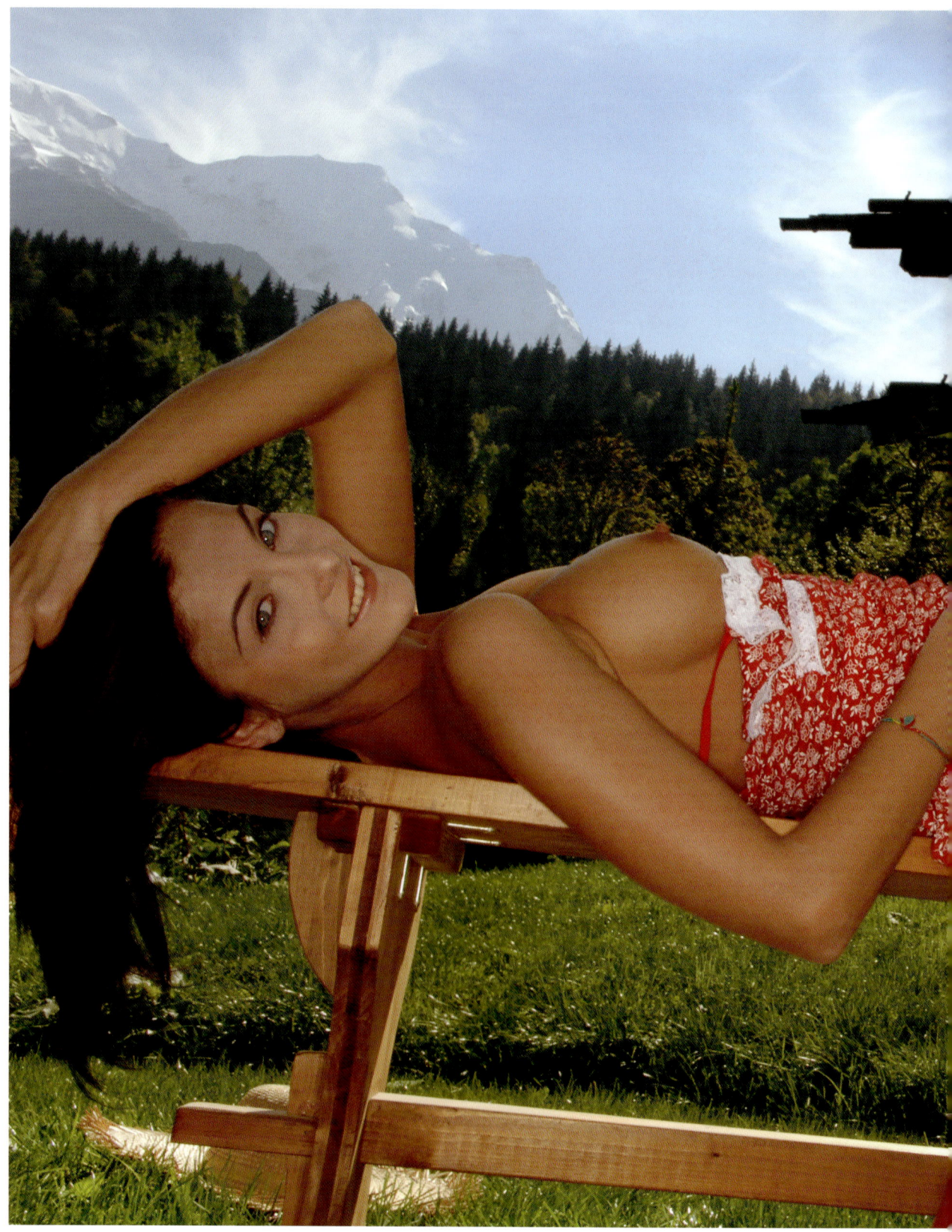

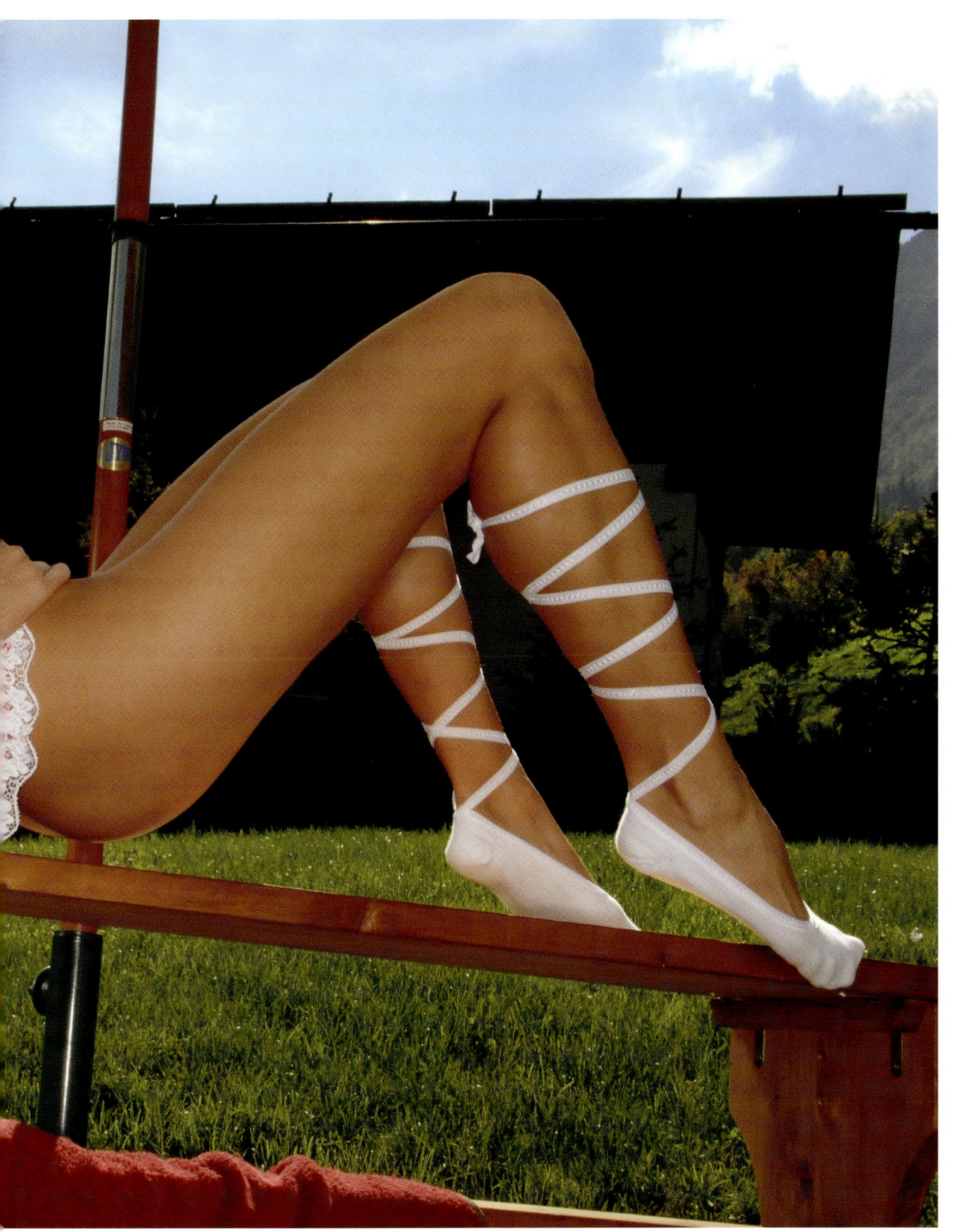

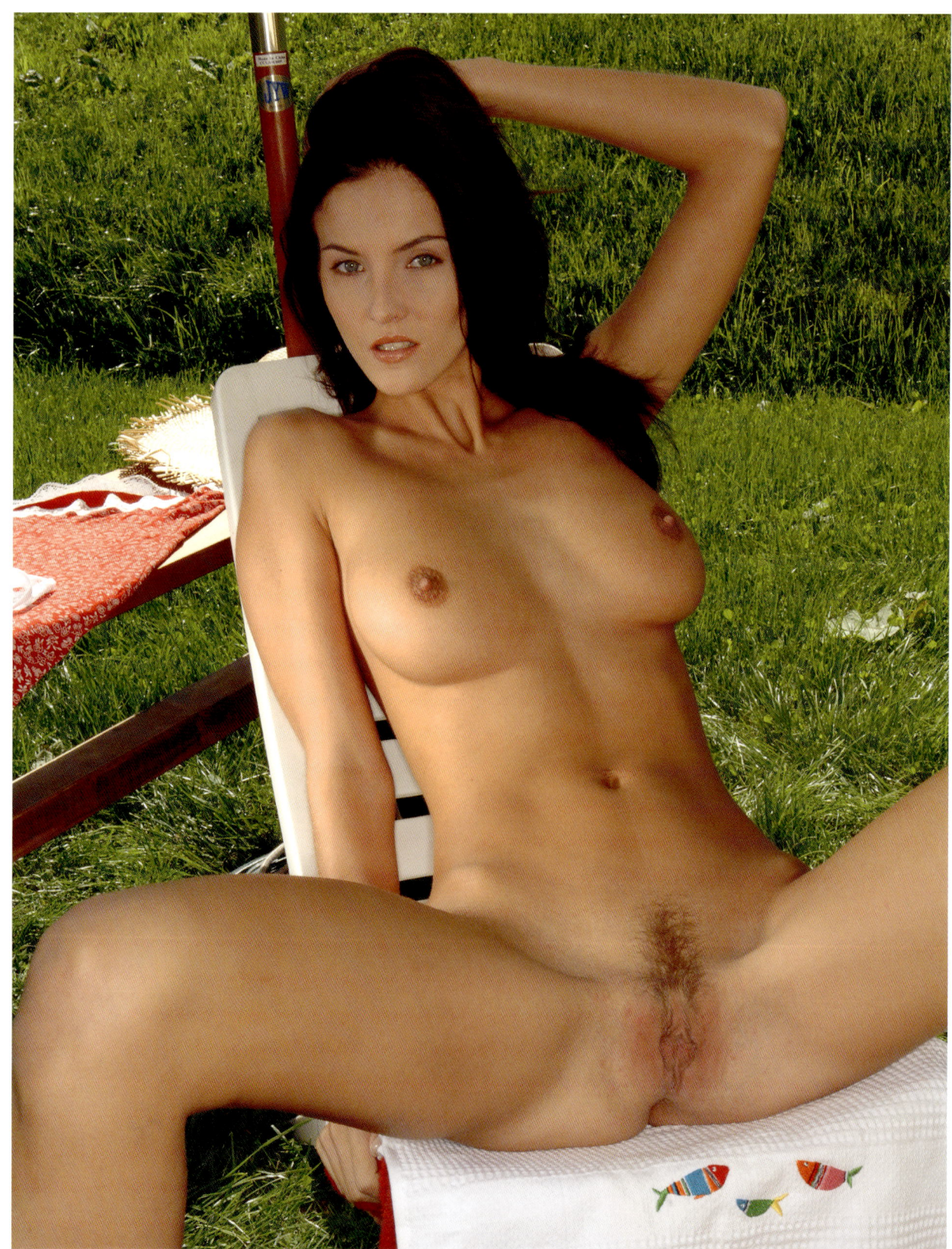

LINDA

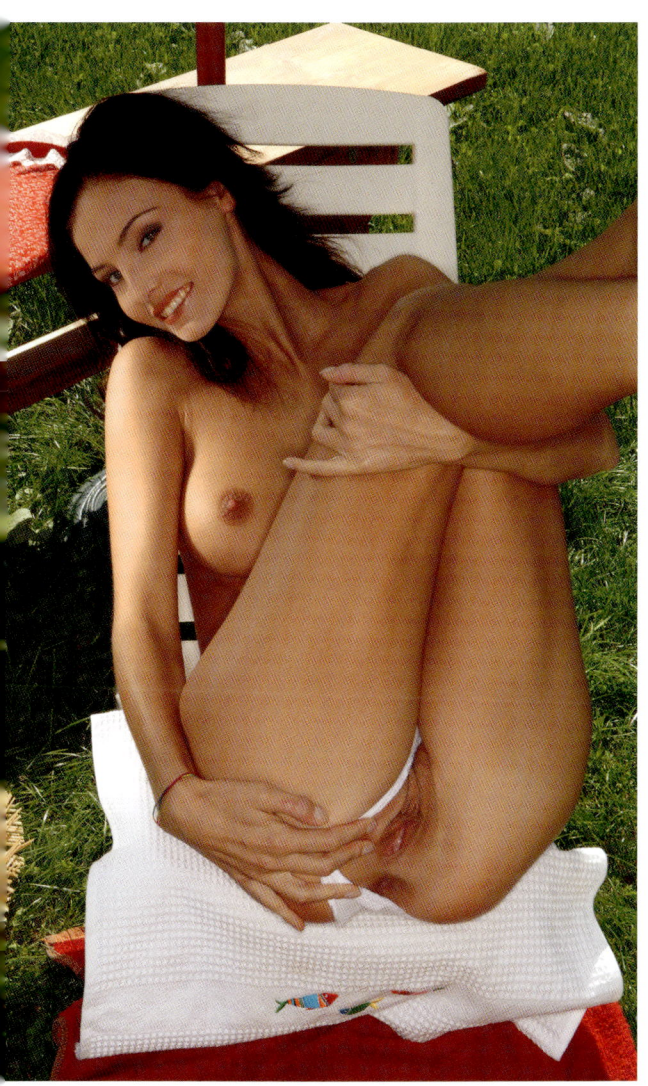
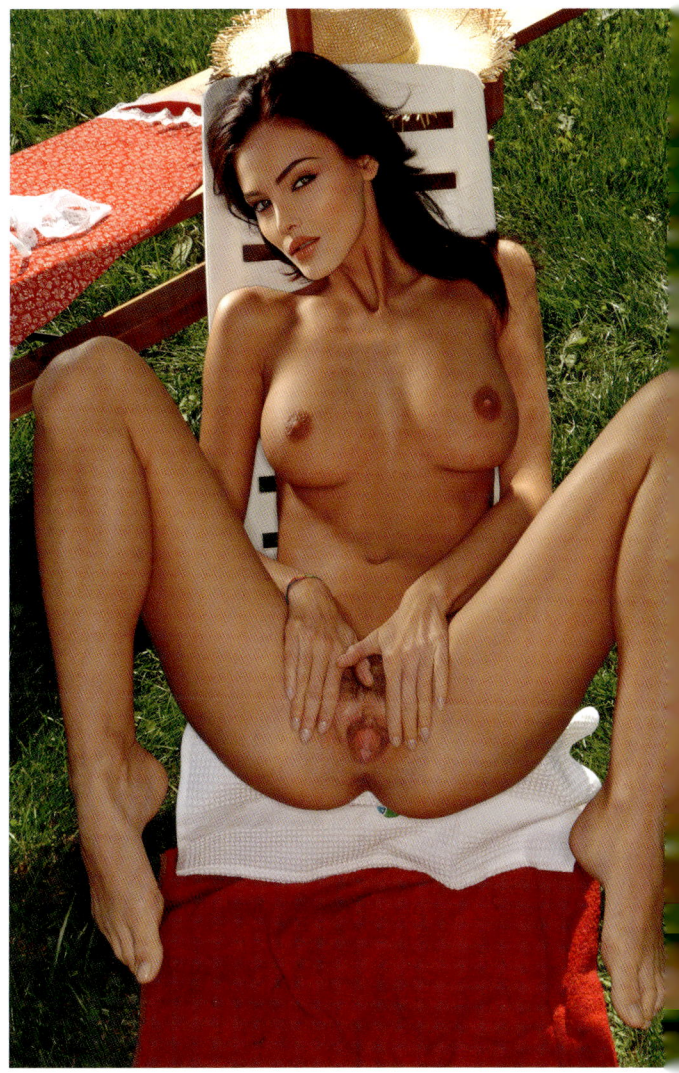

LINDA

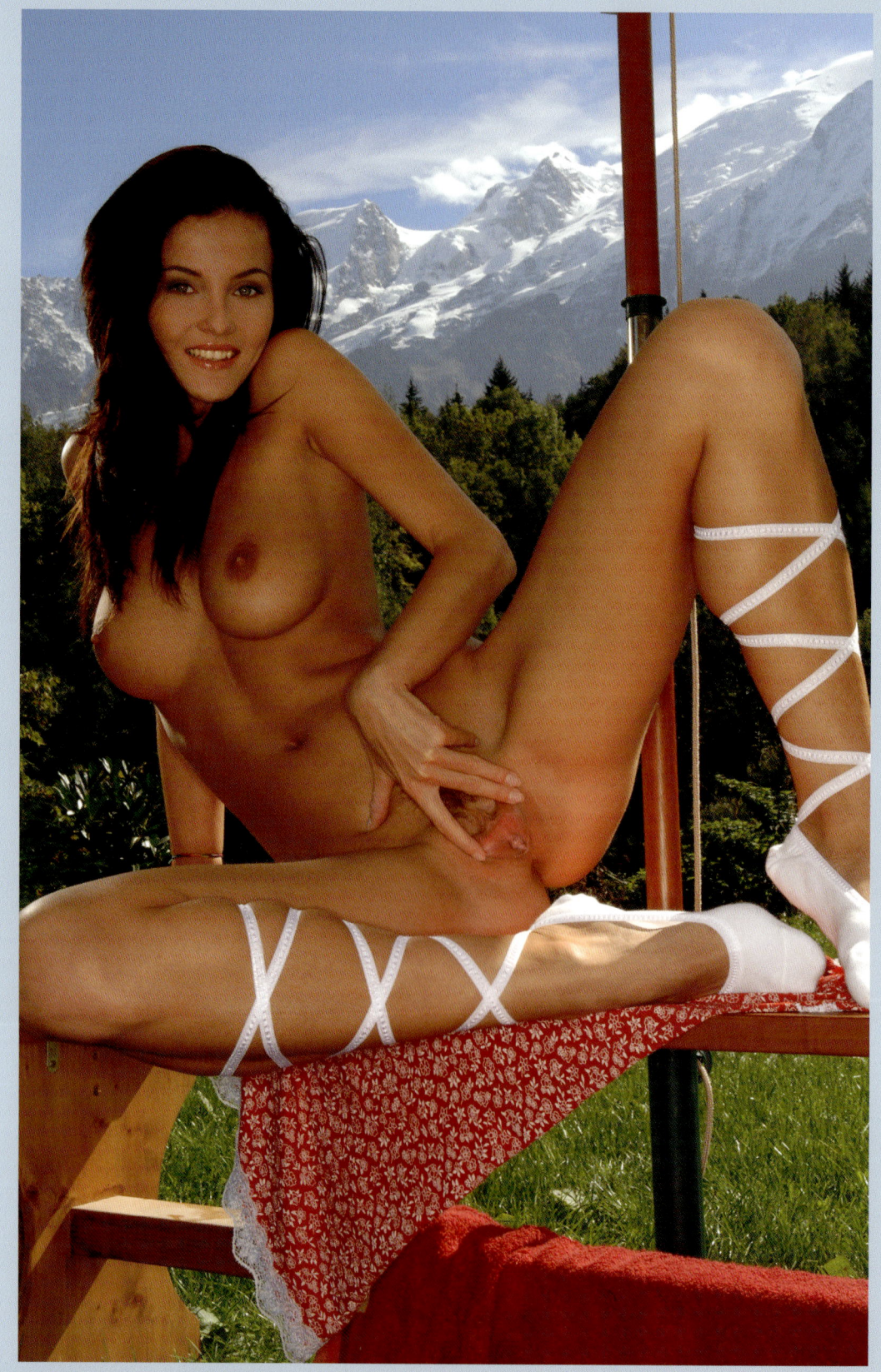

LINDA

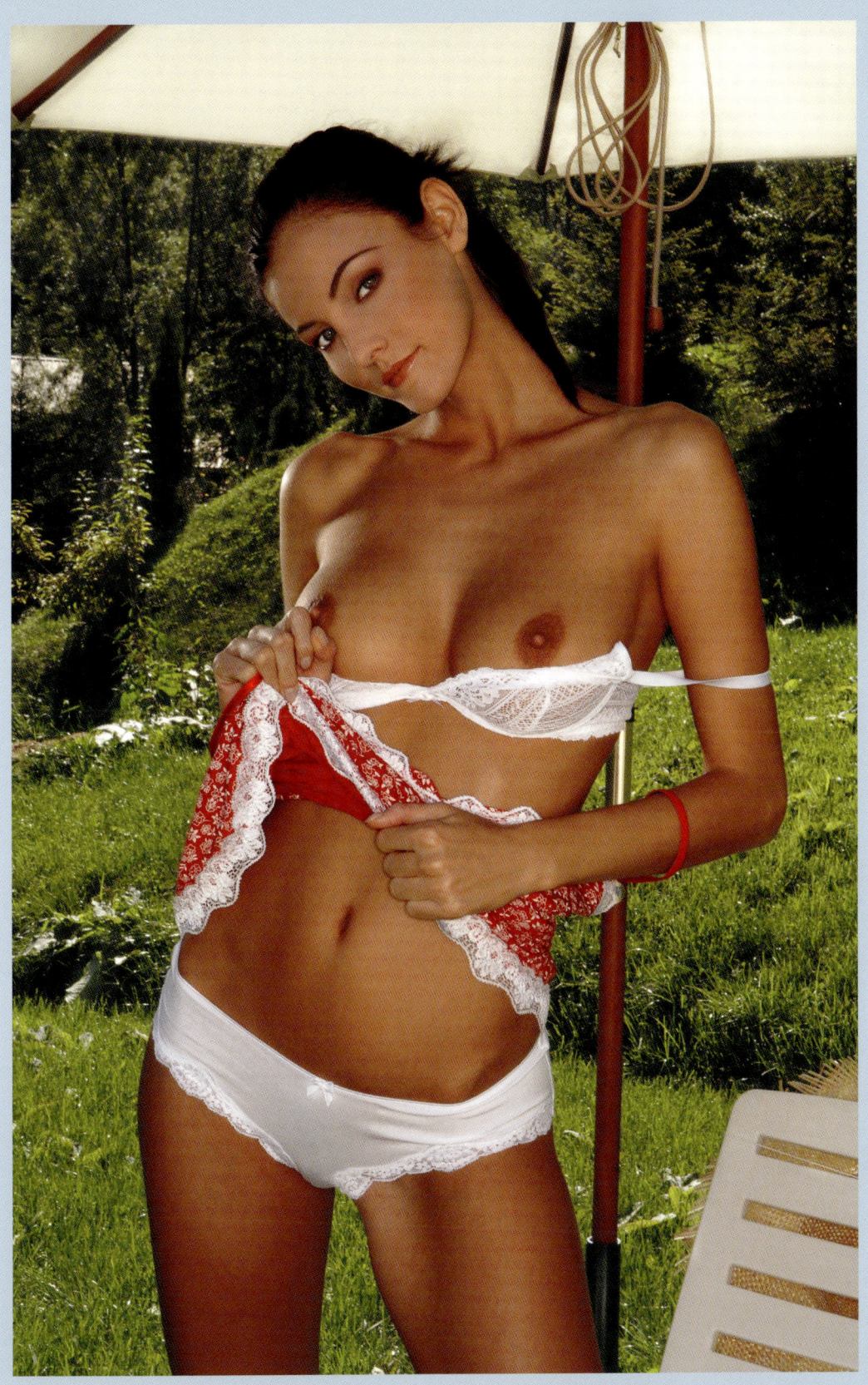

LINDA

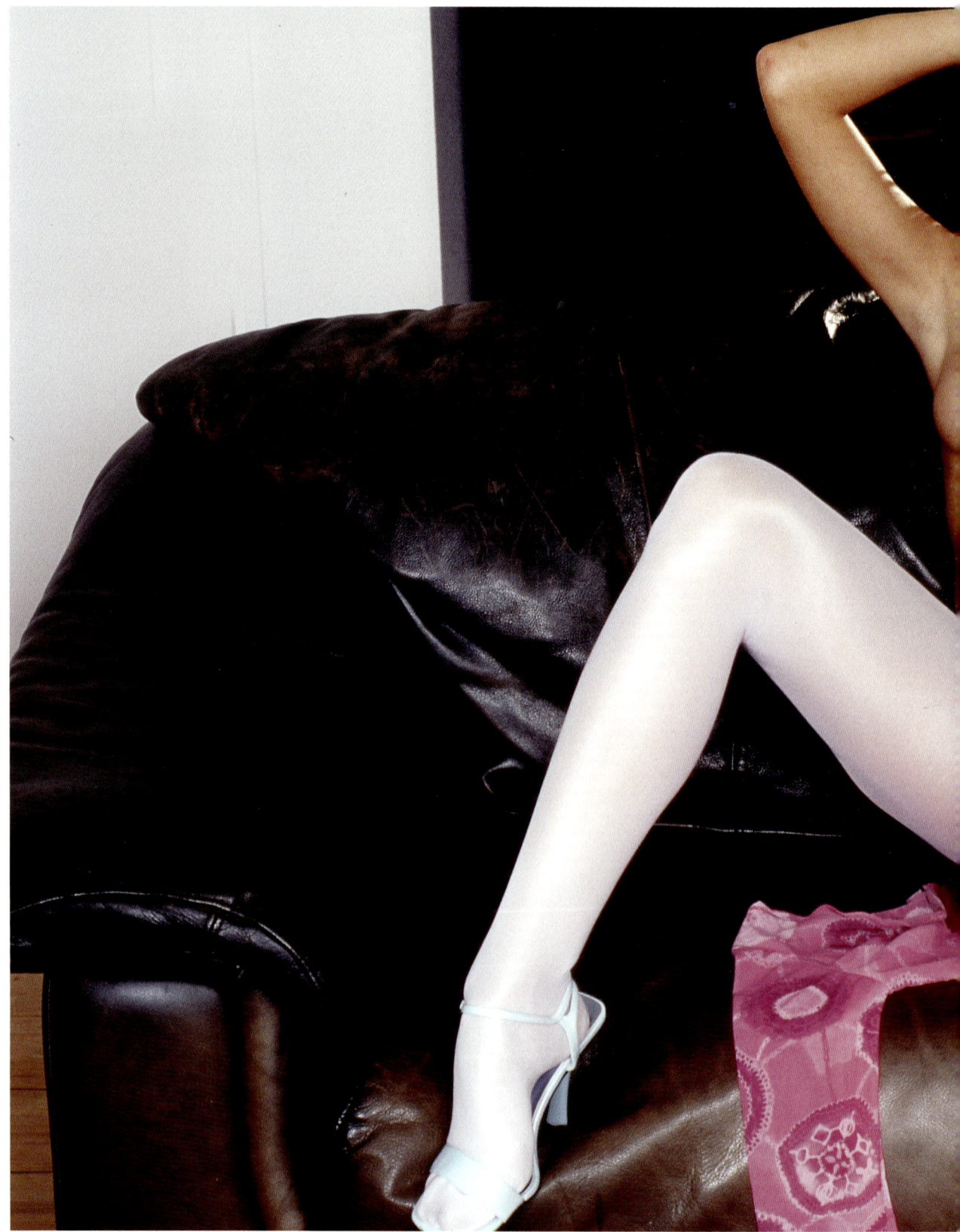

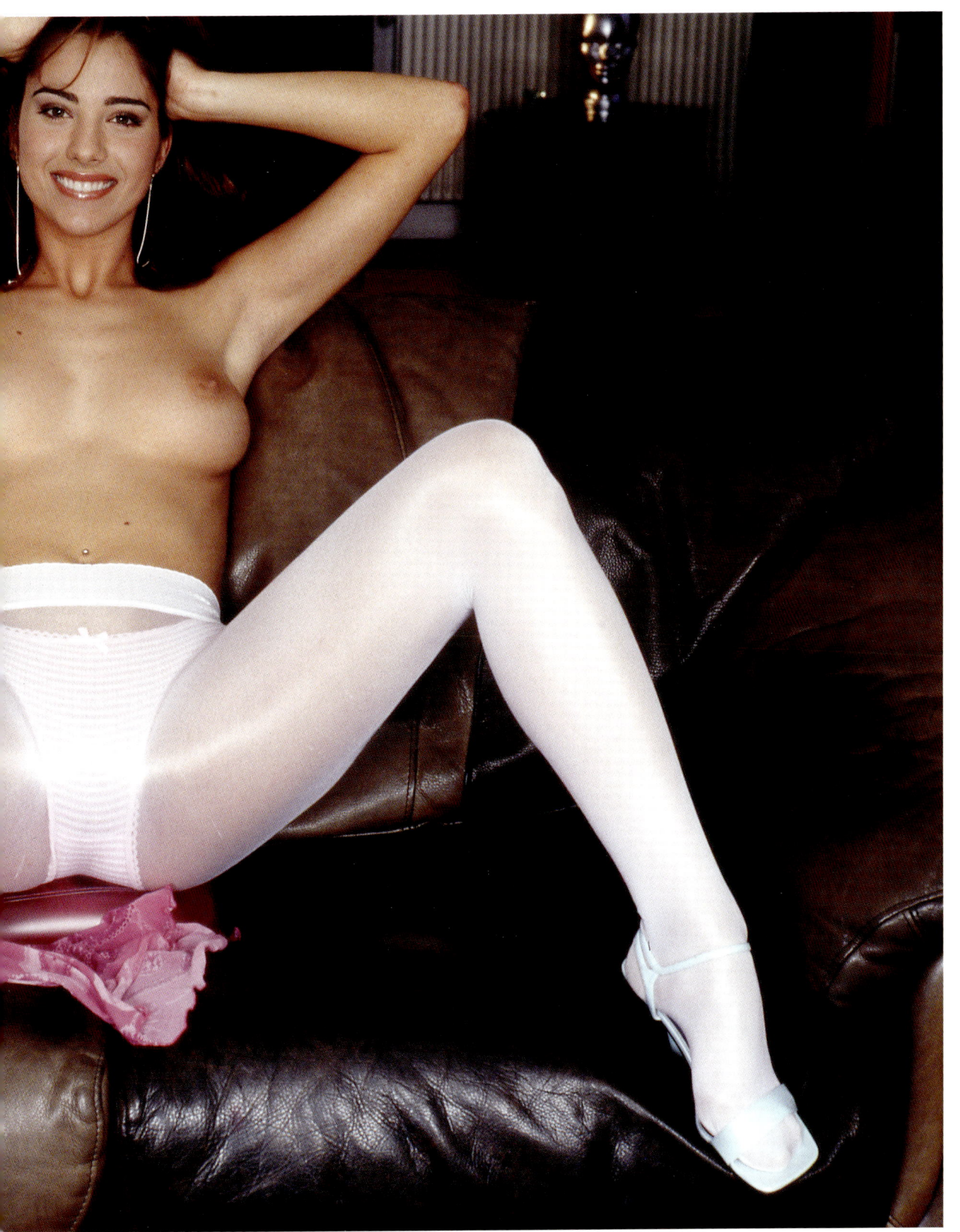

MARIA

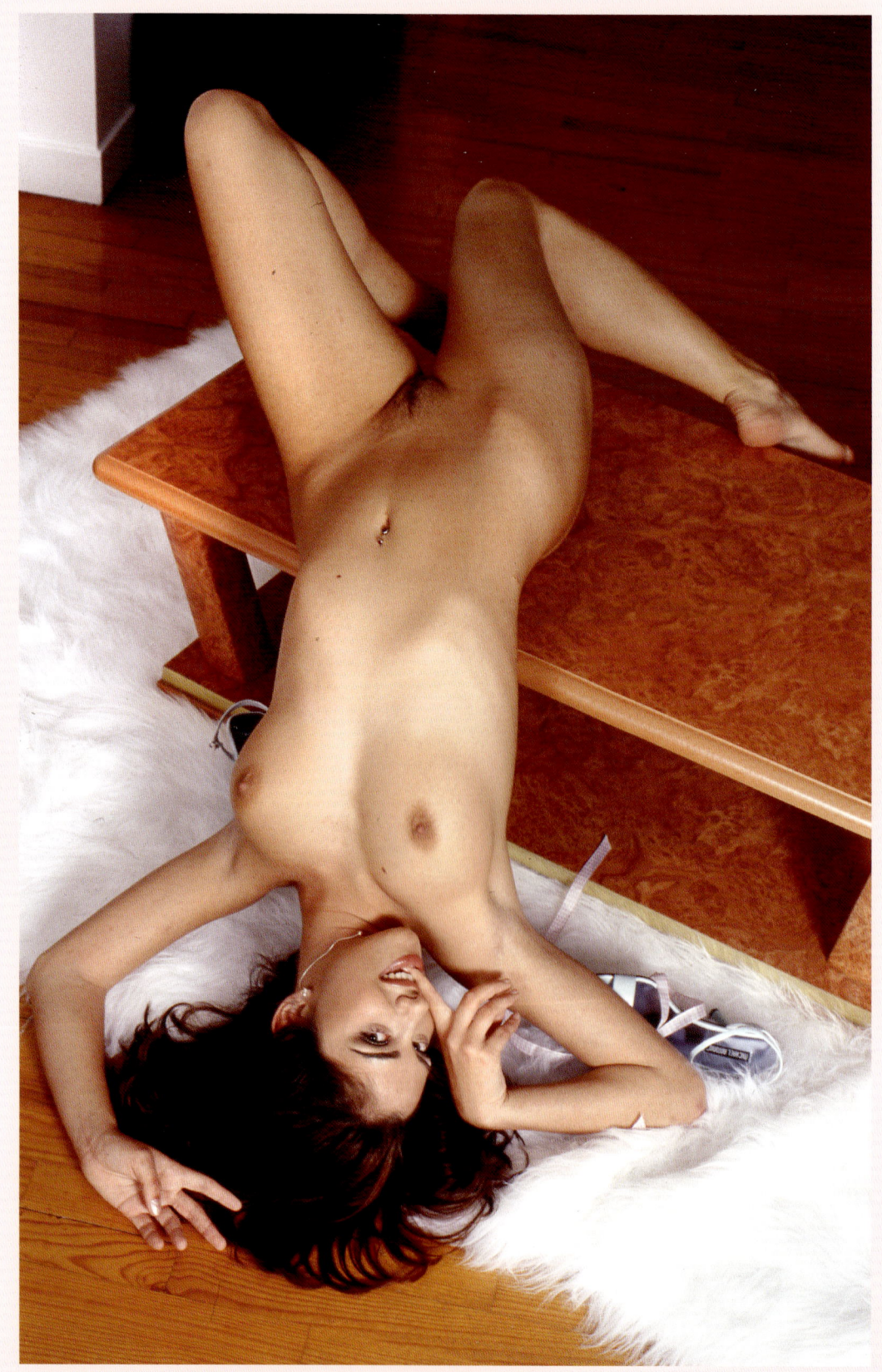

MARIA

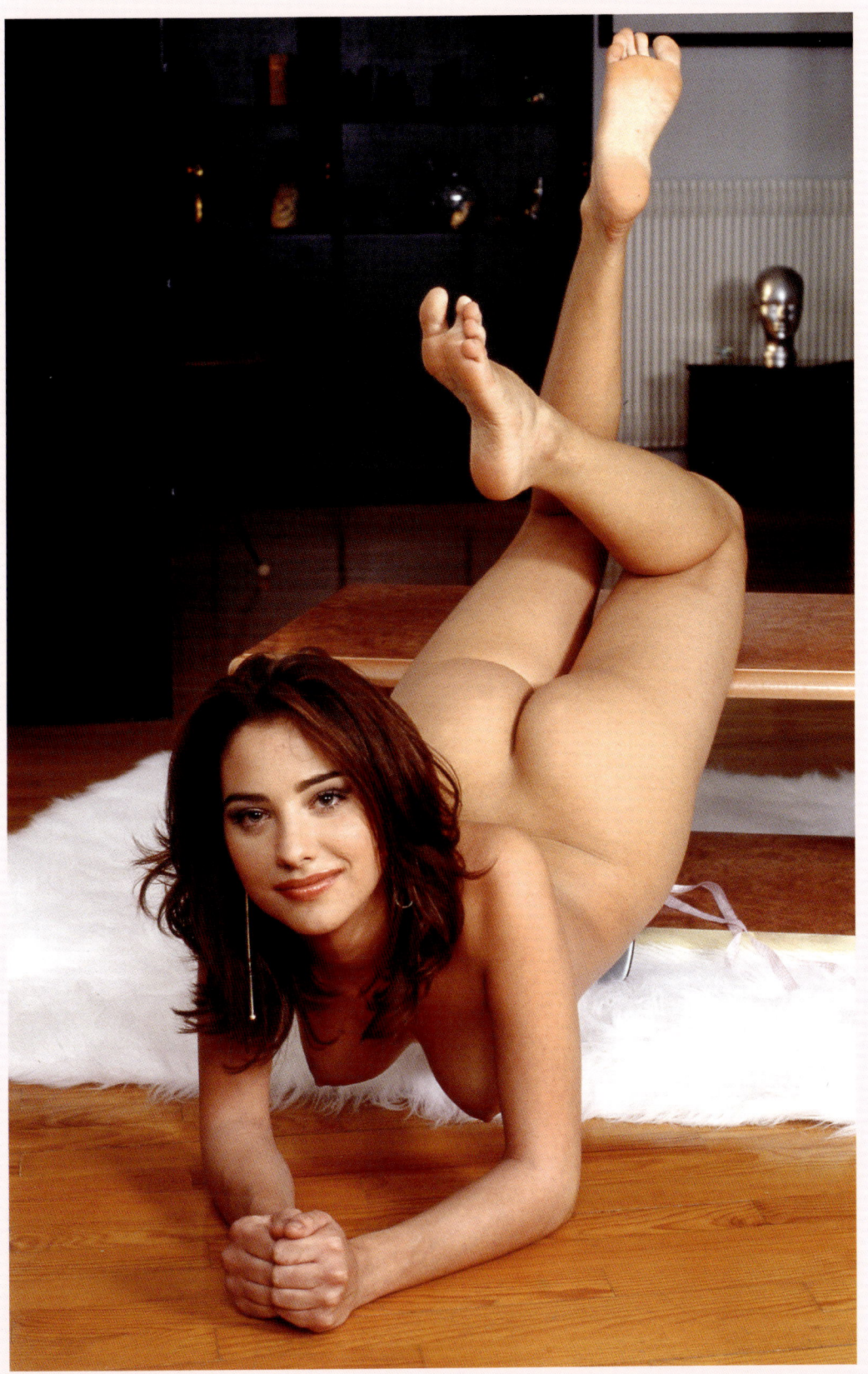

MARIA

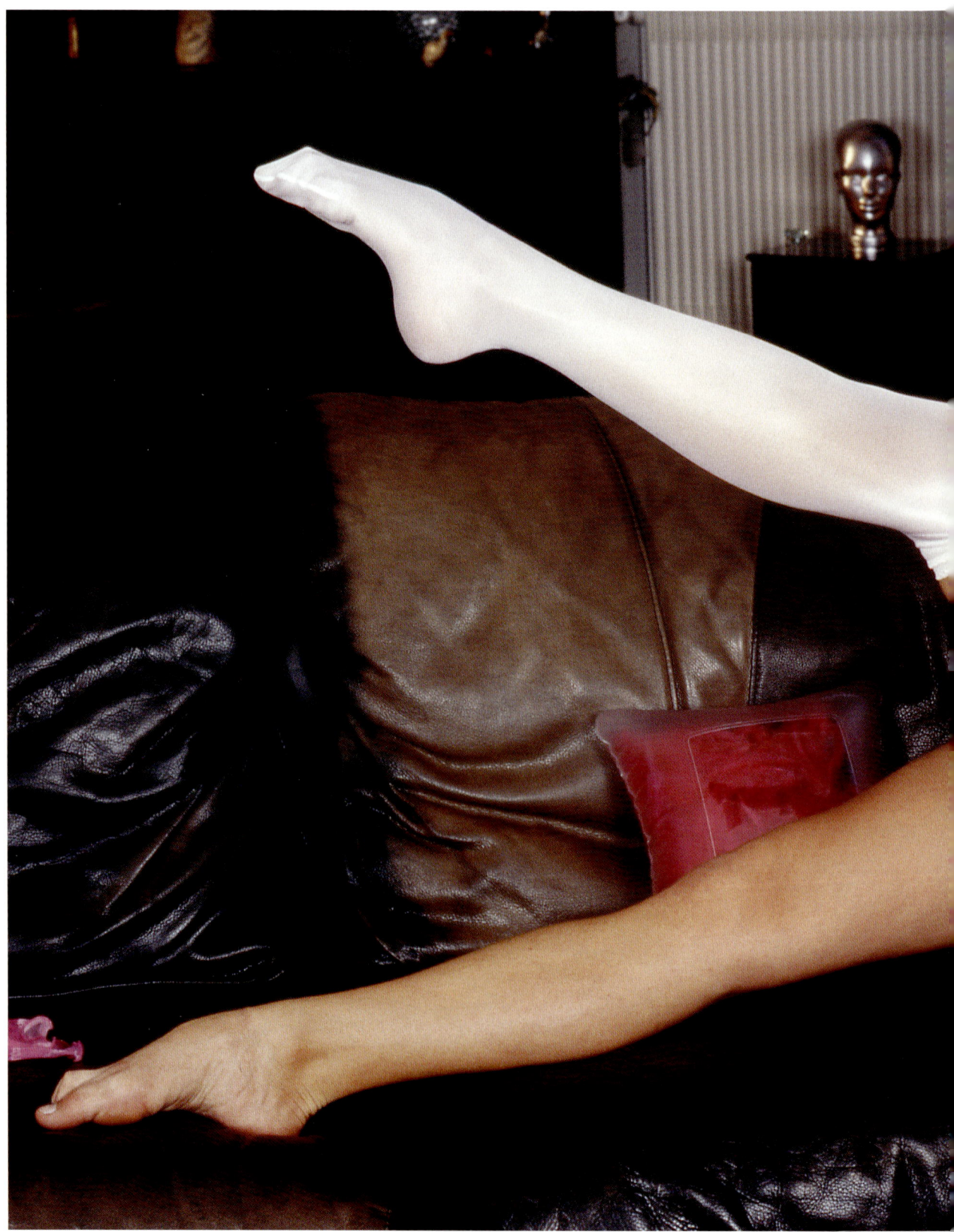

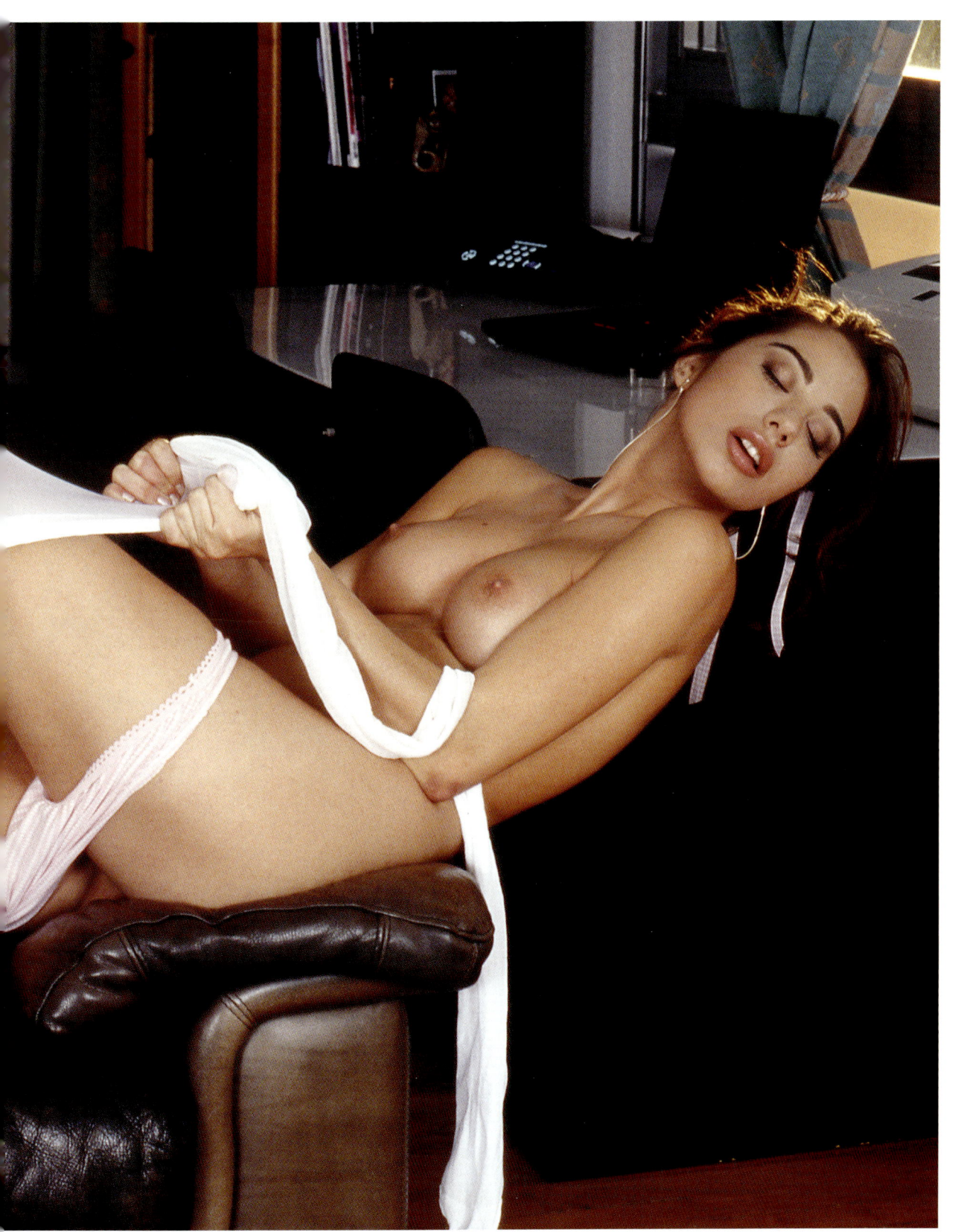

MARIA

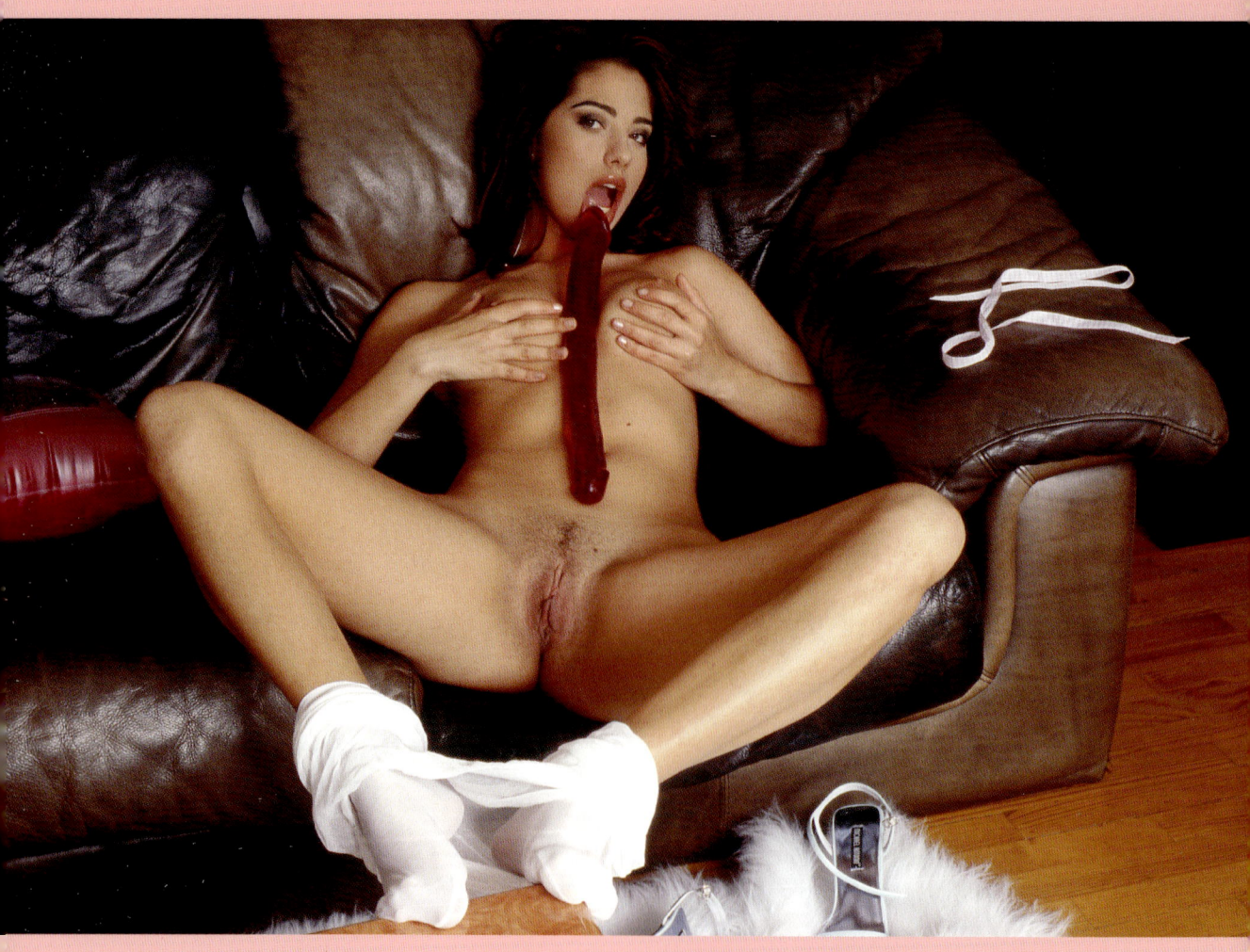

MARIA

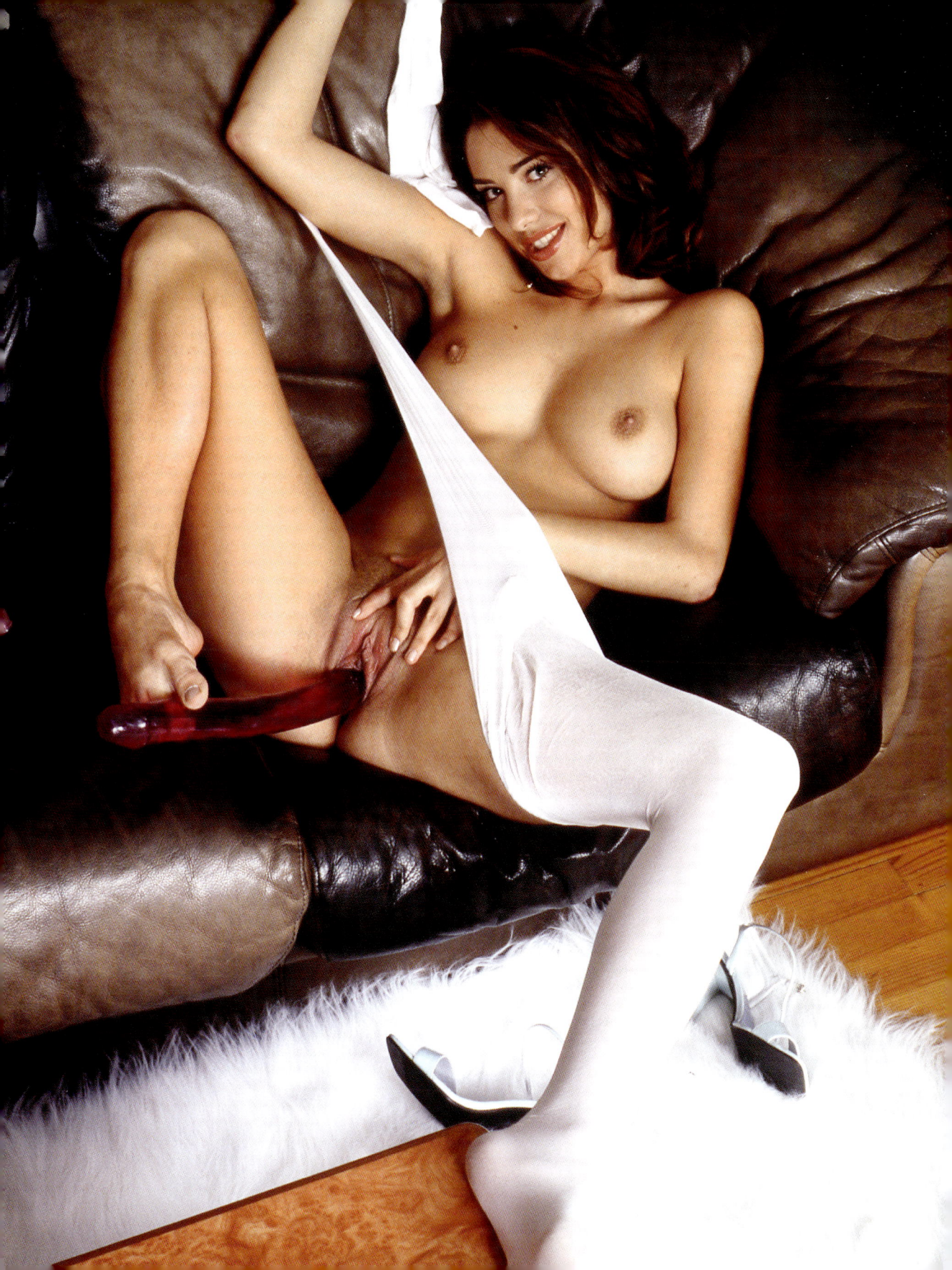

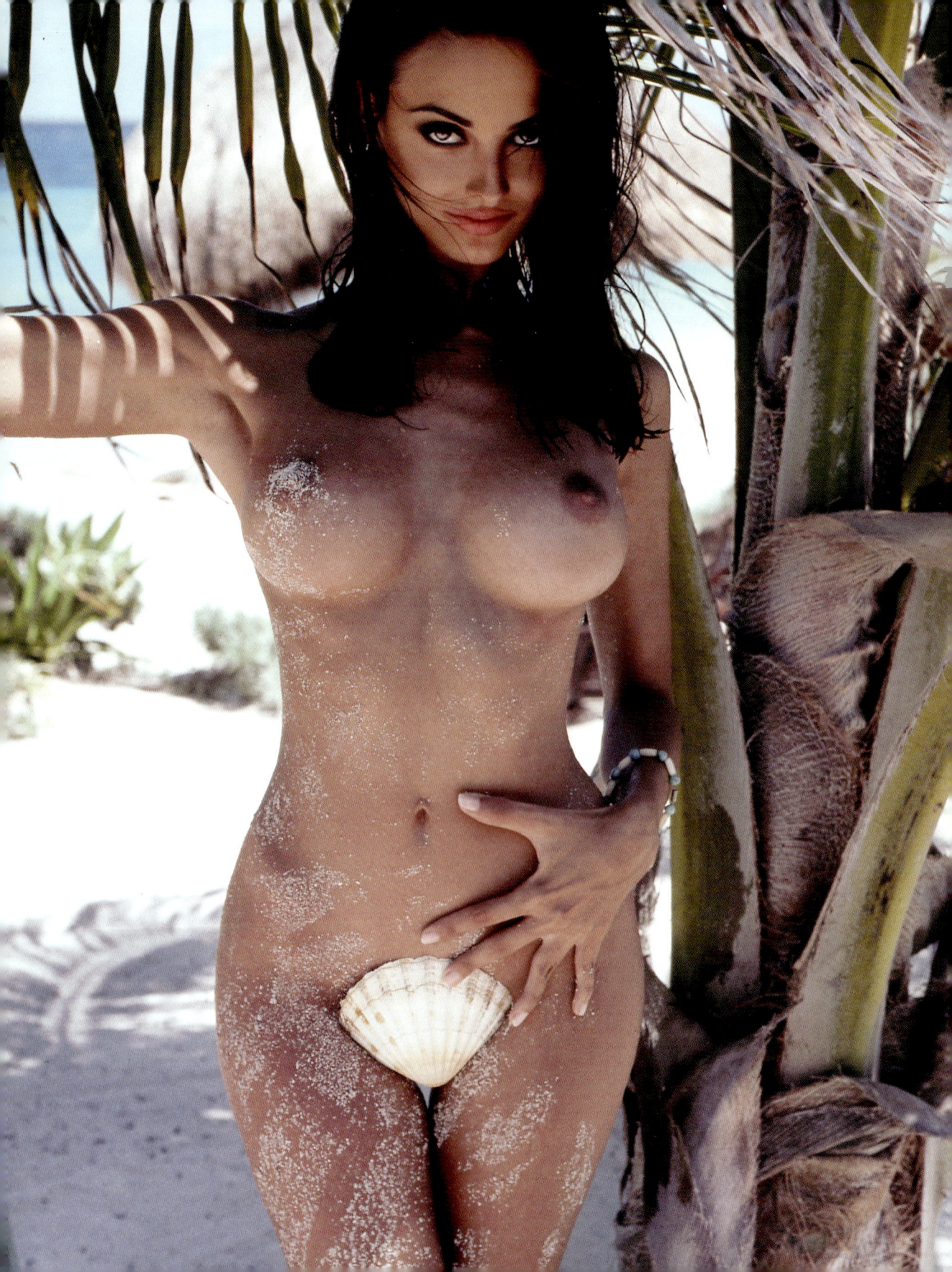

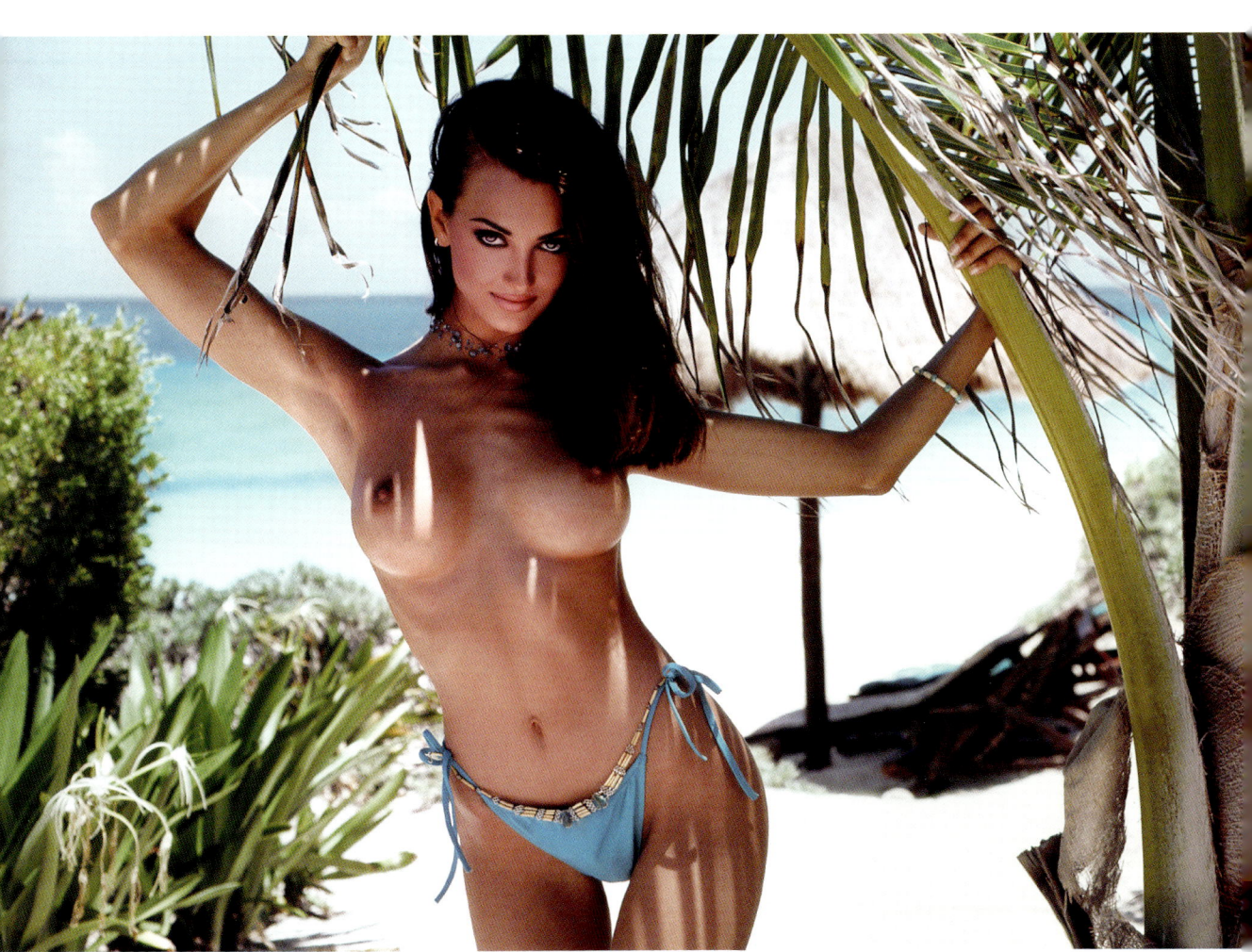

SANJA

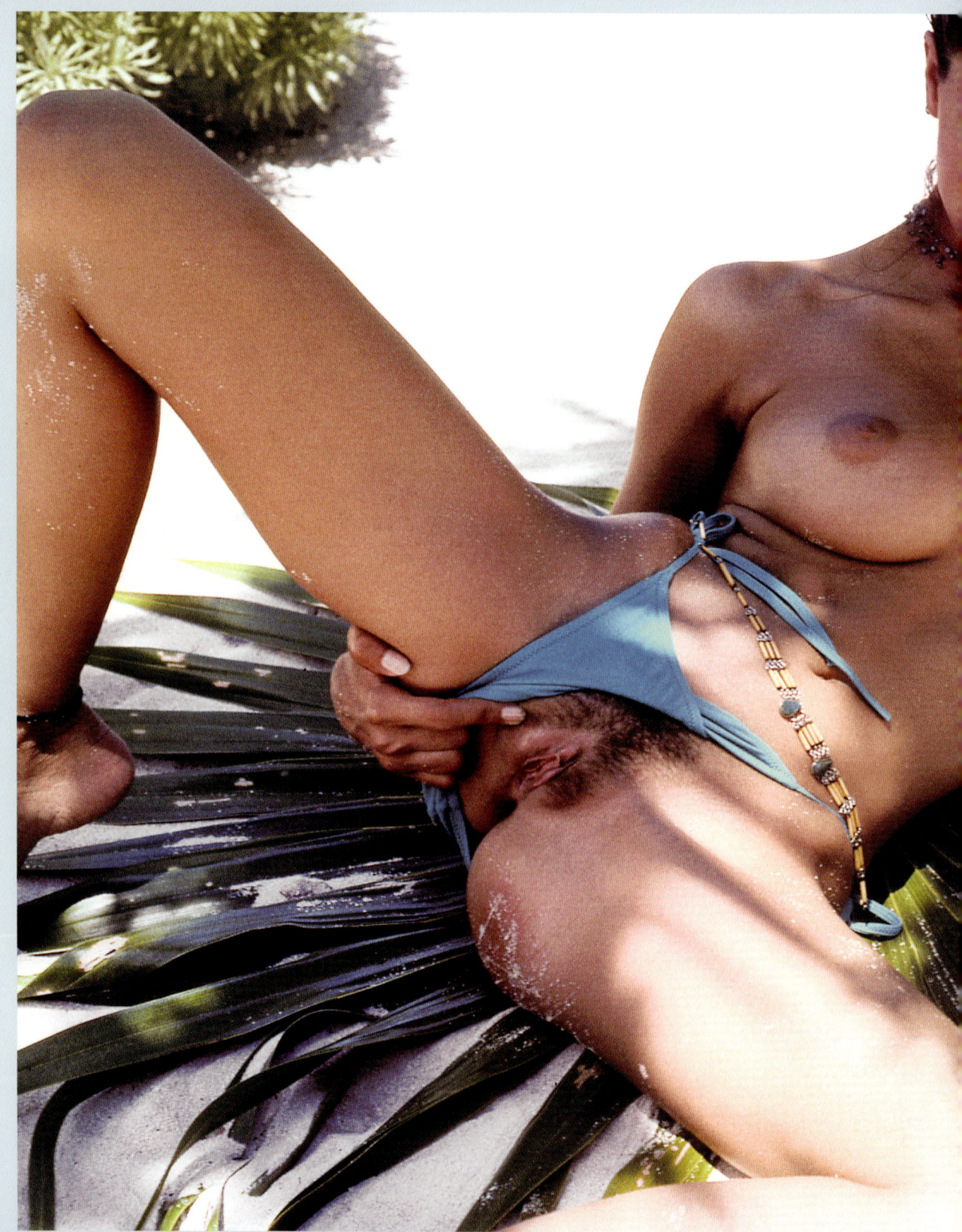

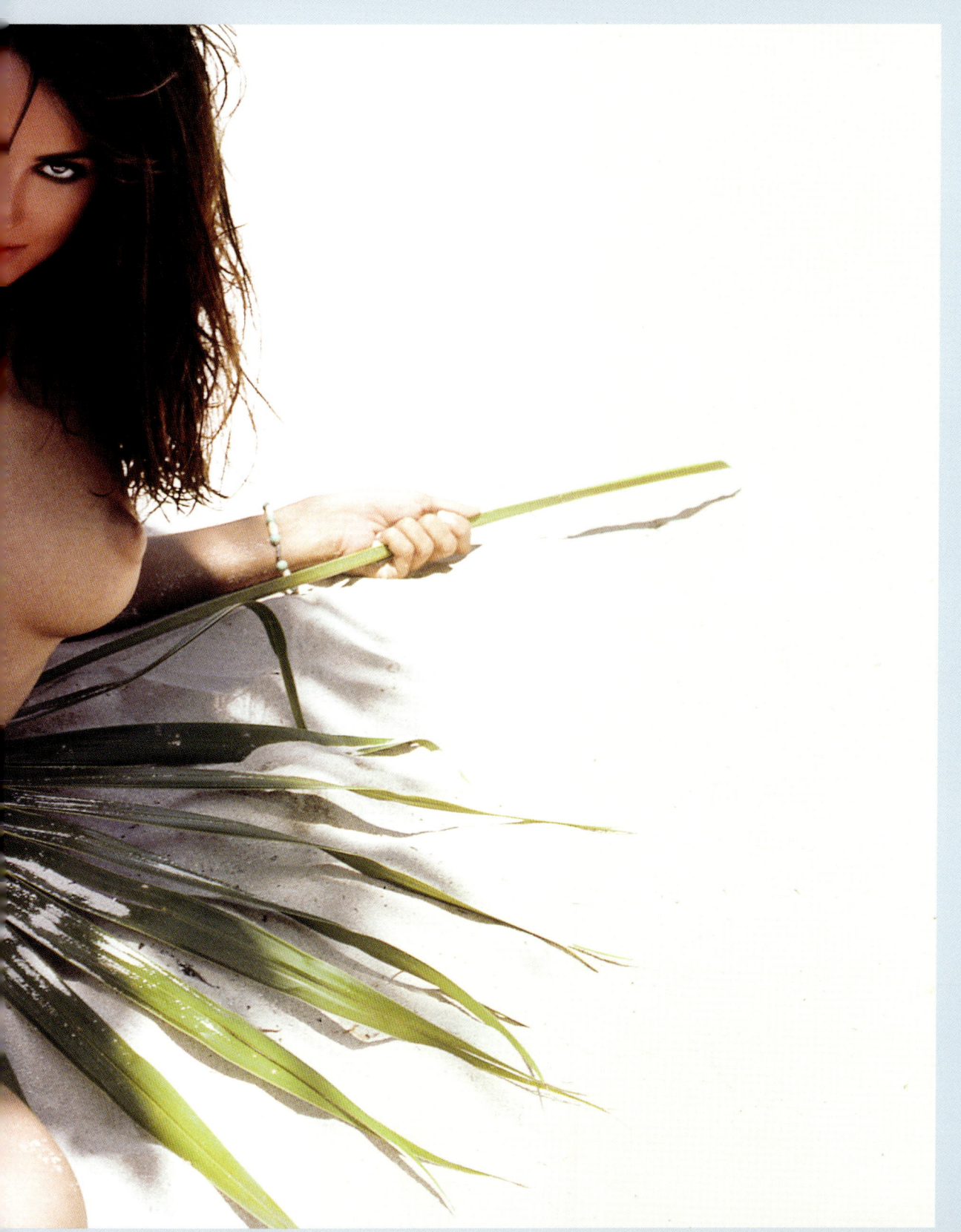

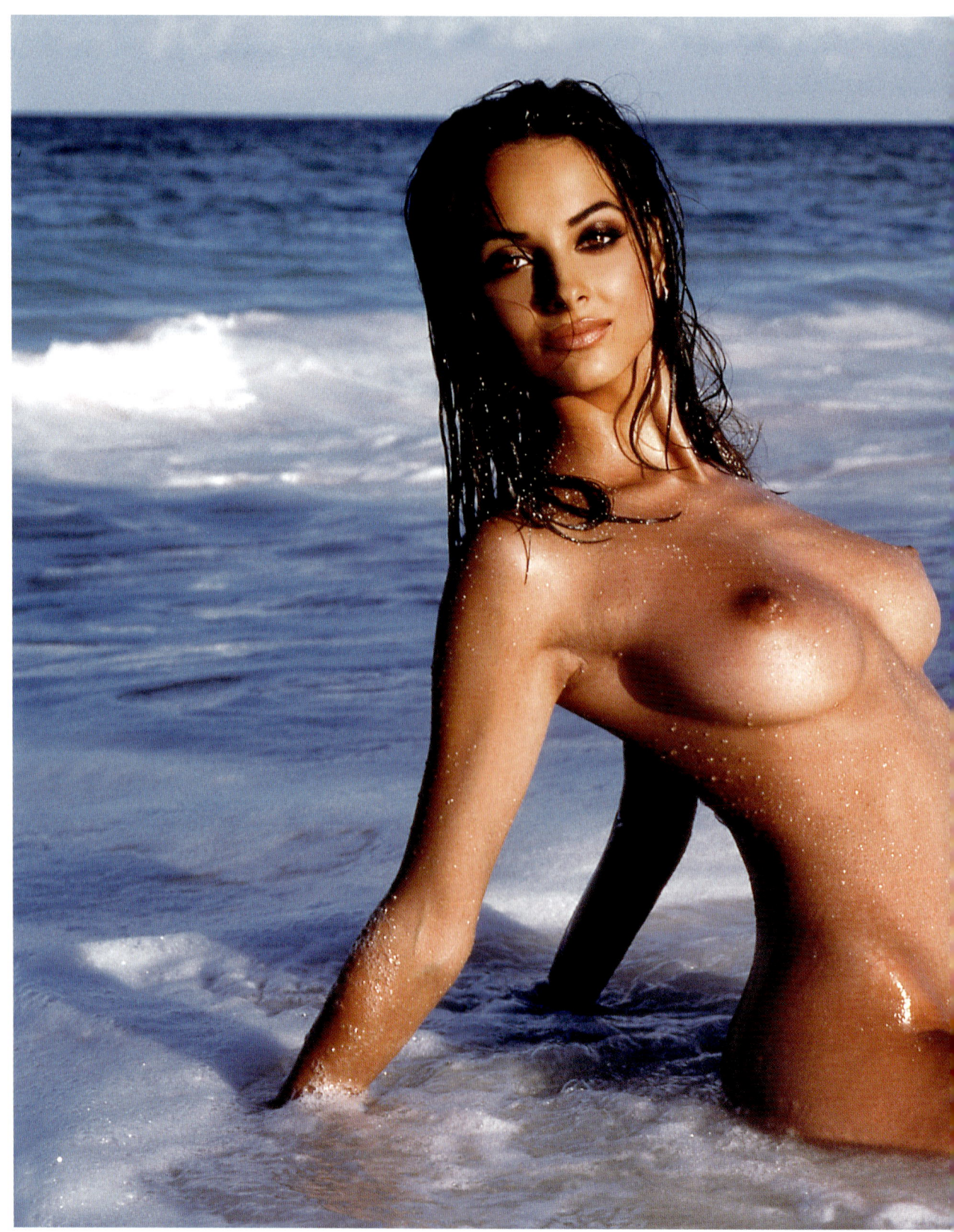

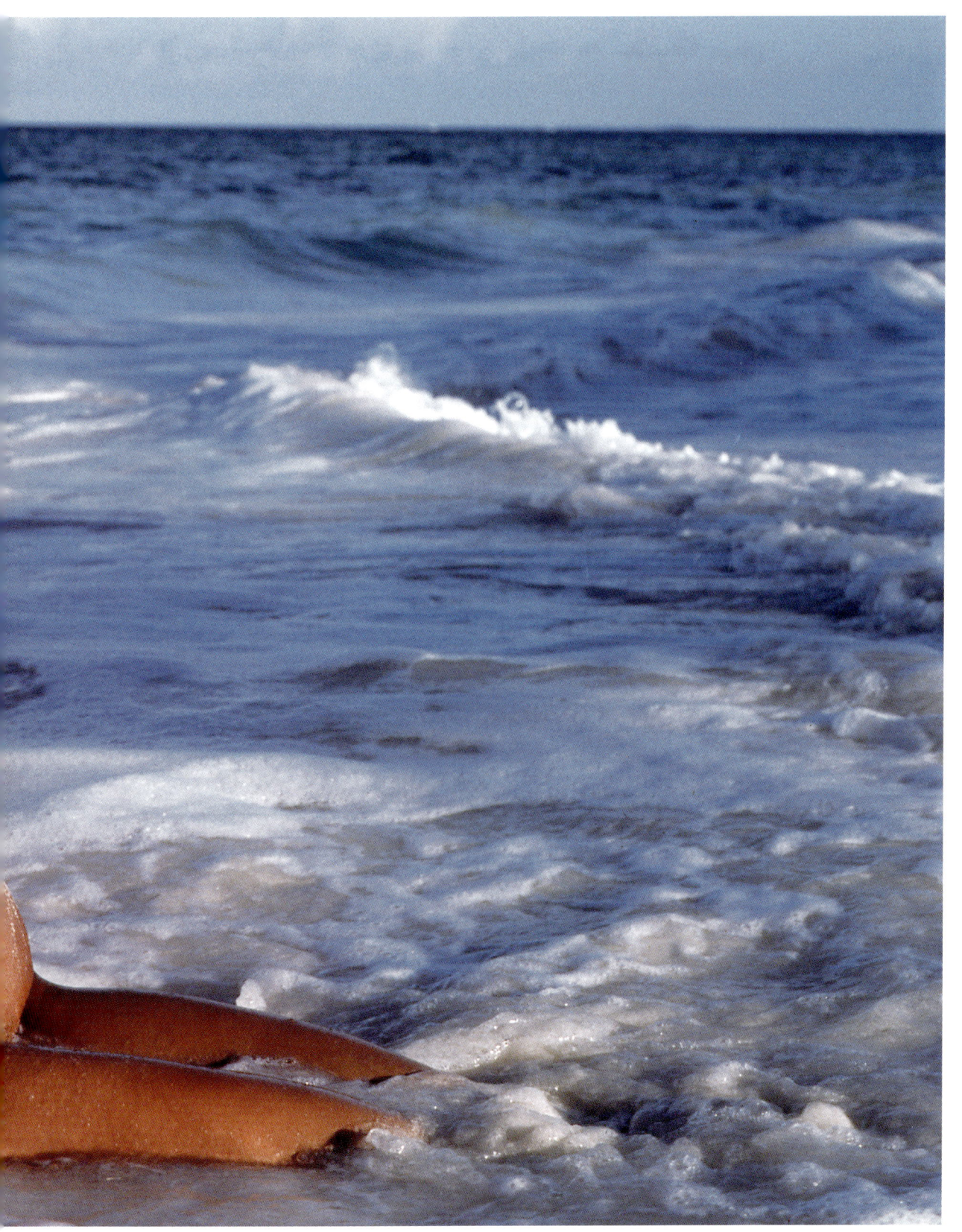

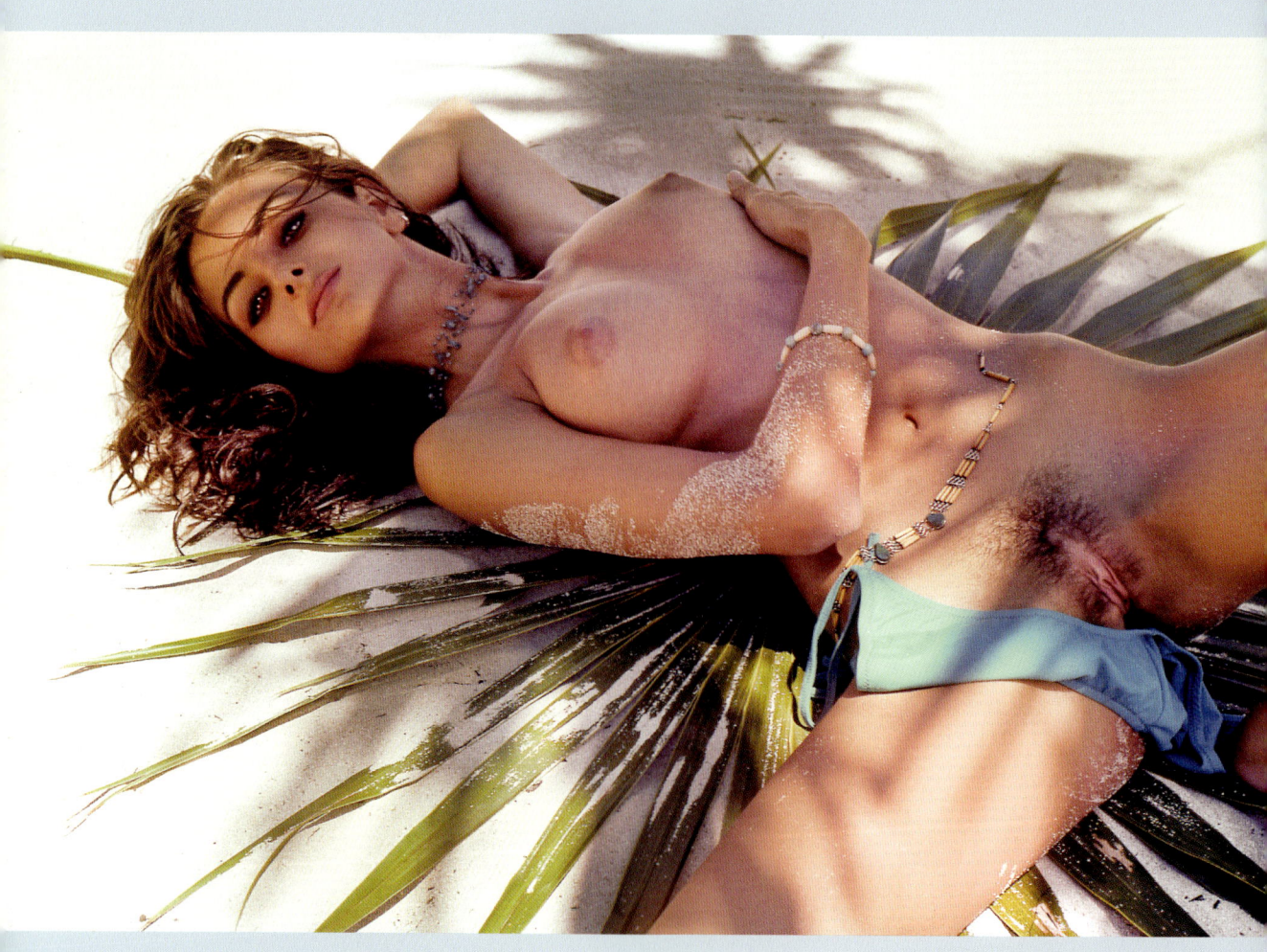

SANJA

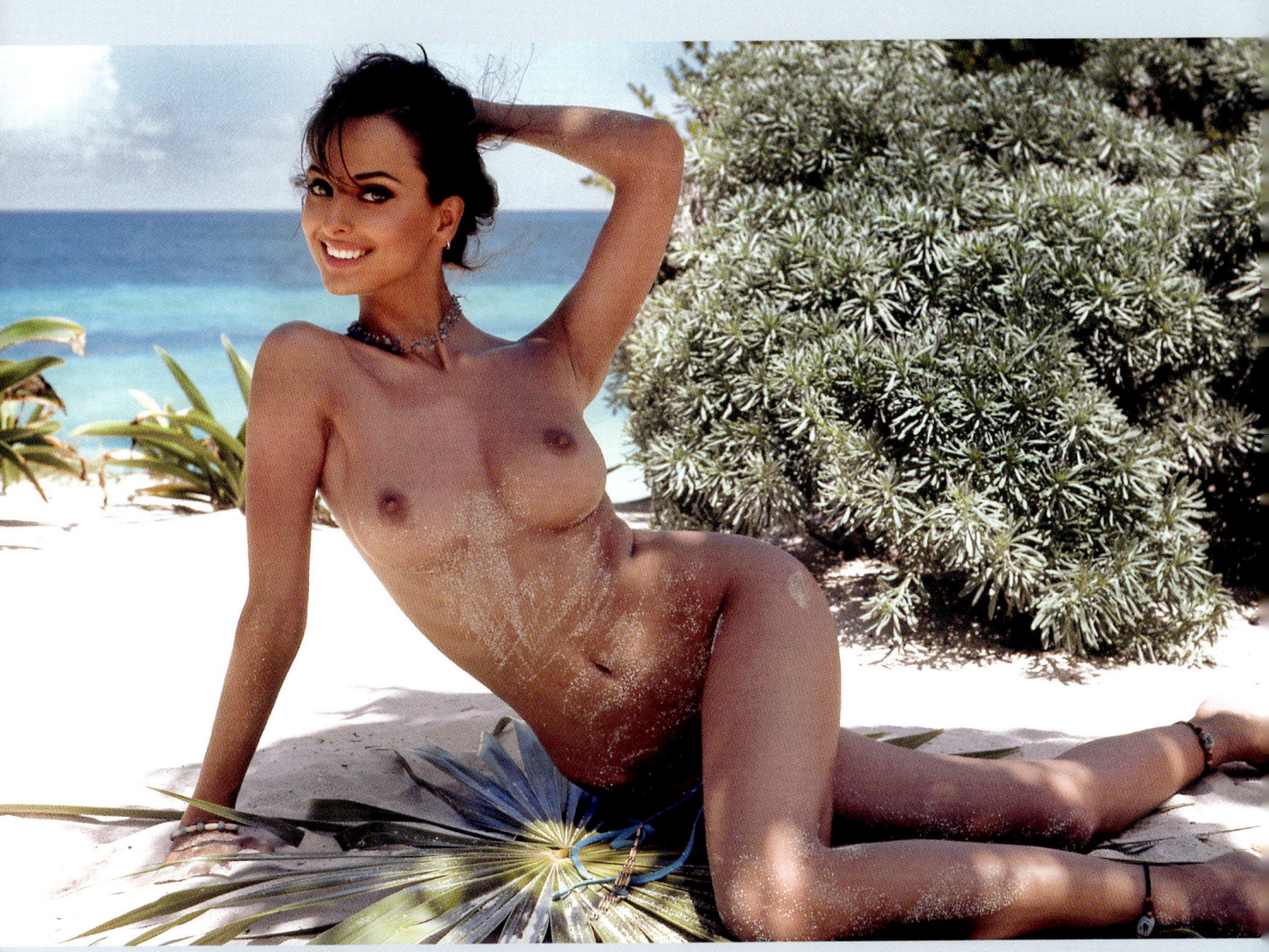

SANJA

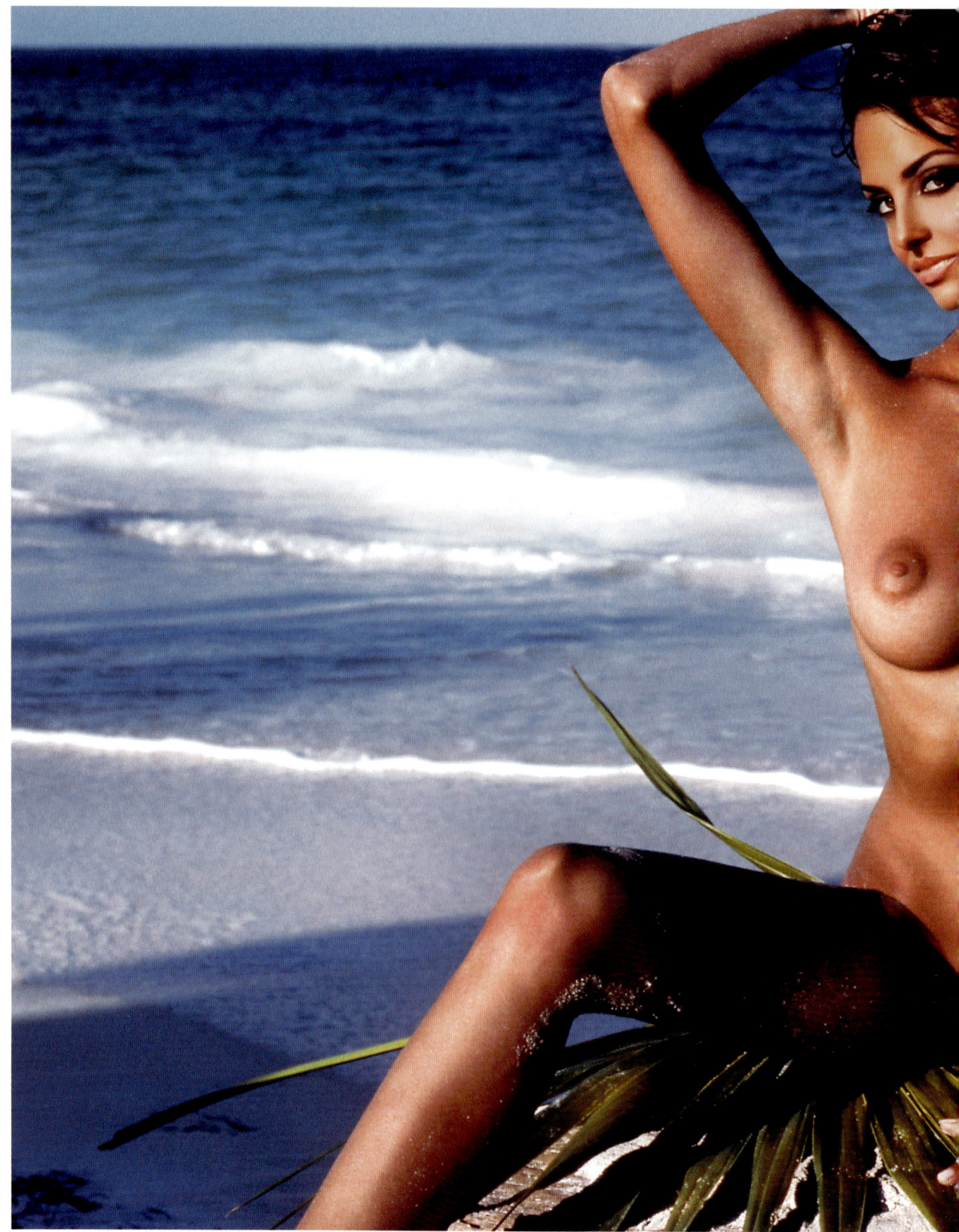

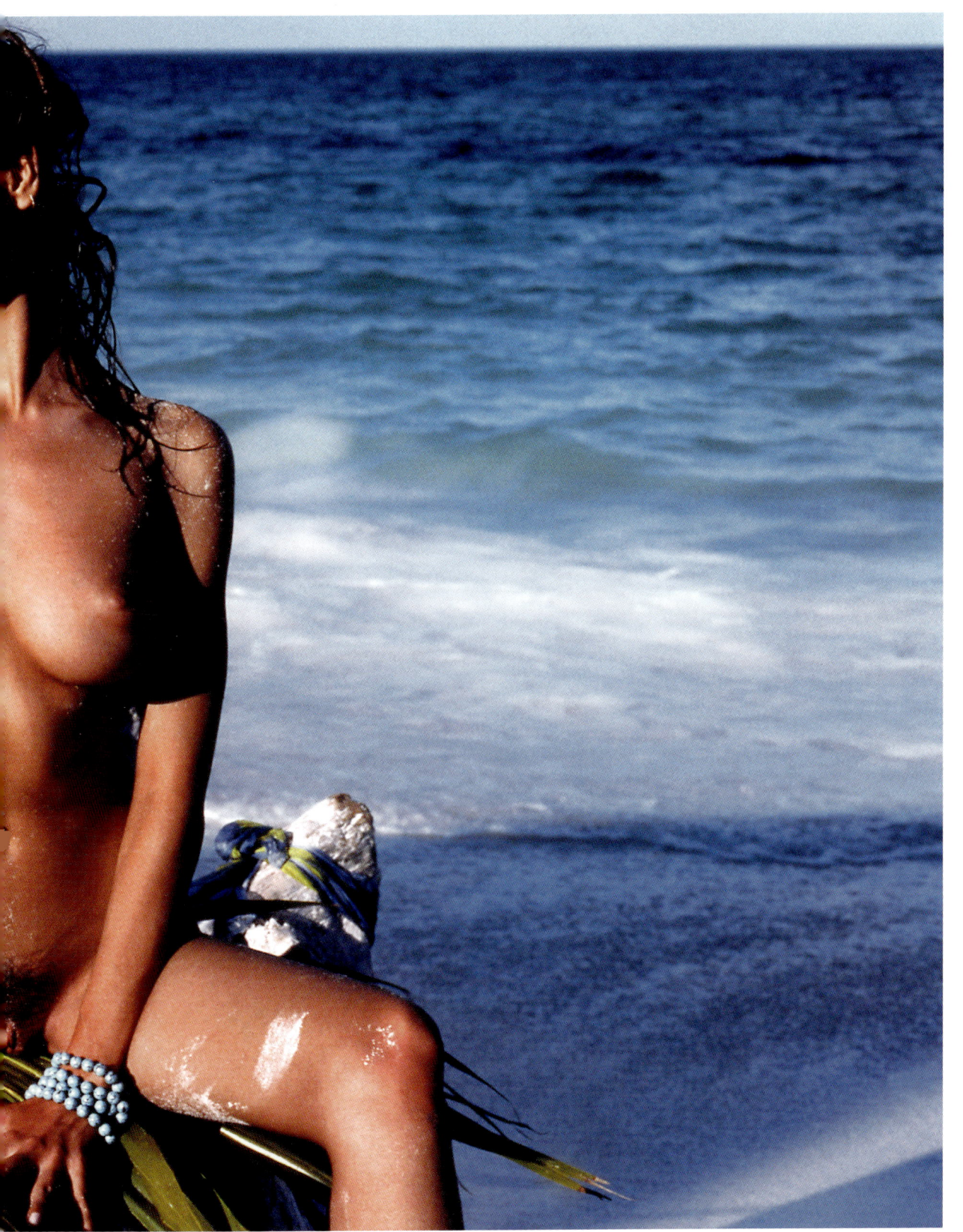

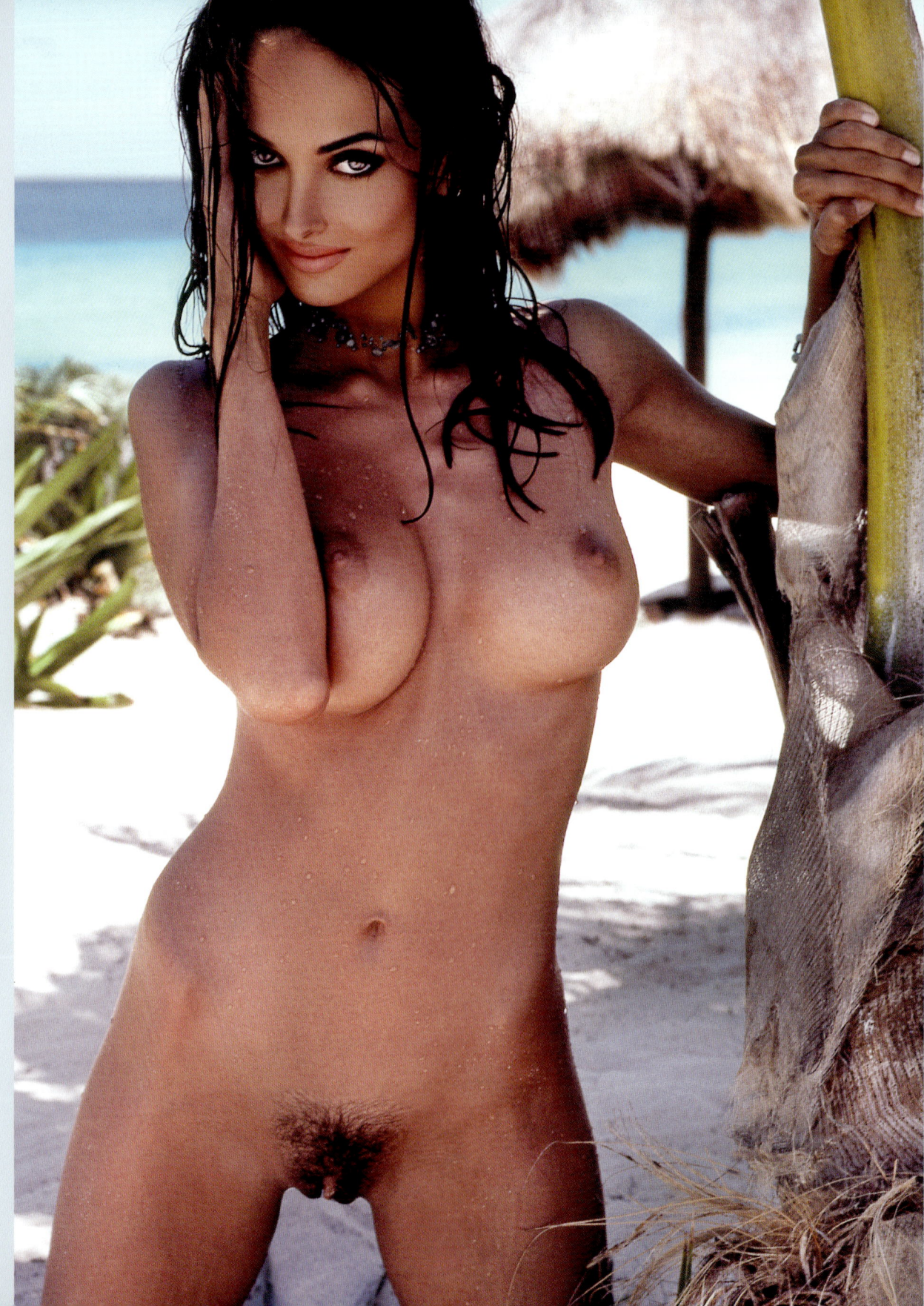

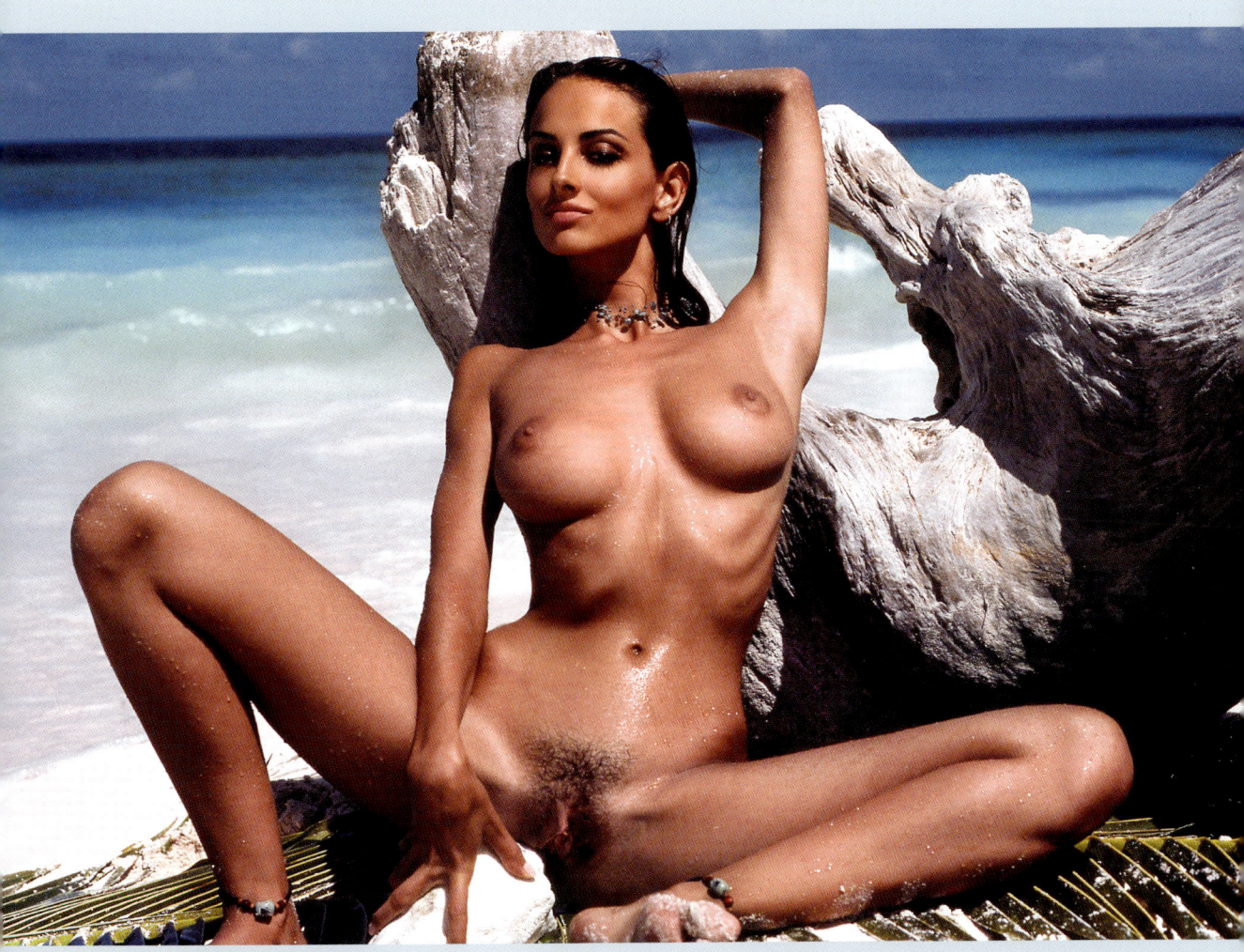

SANJA

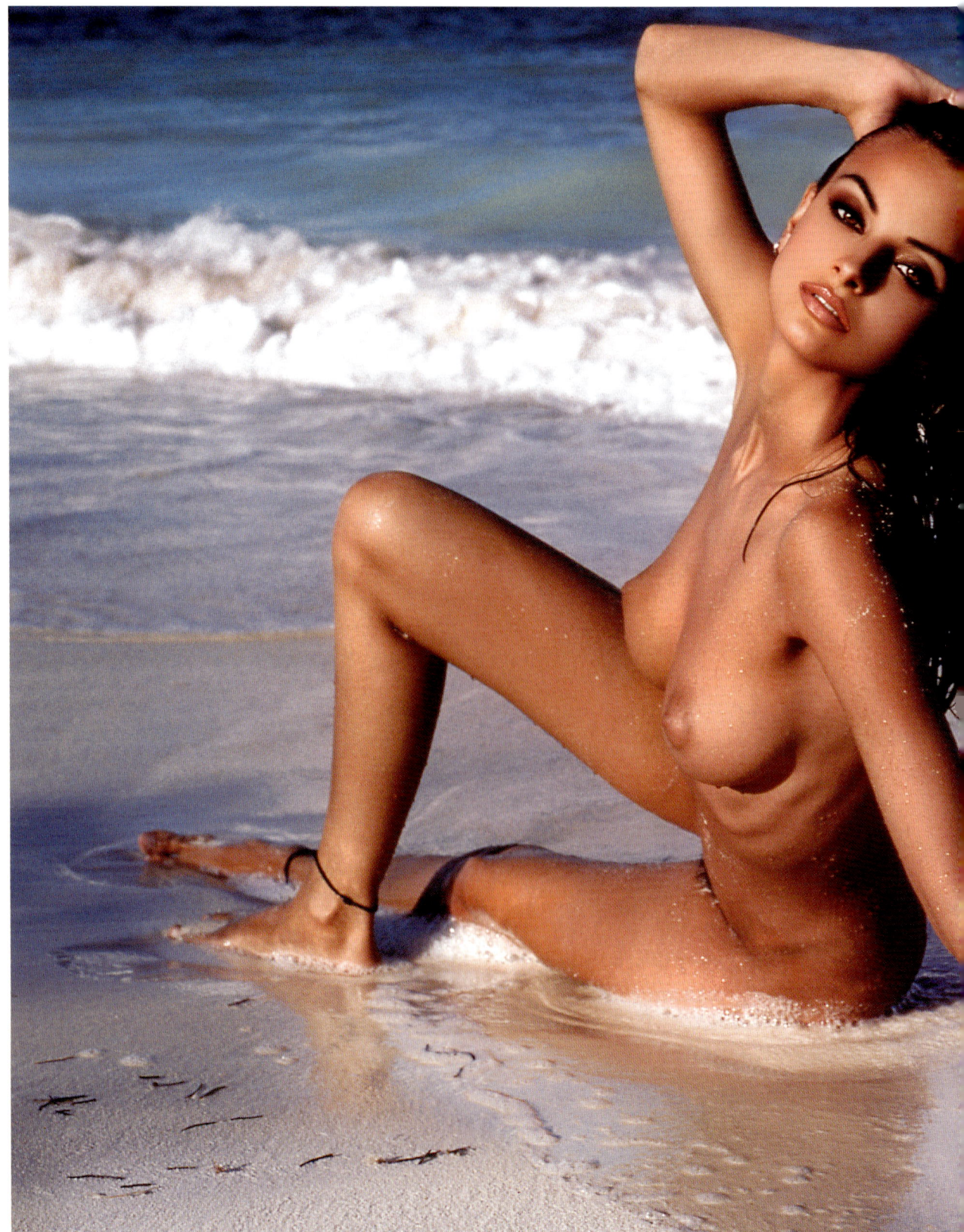

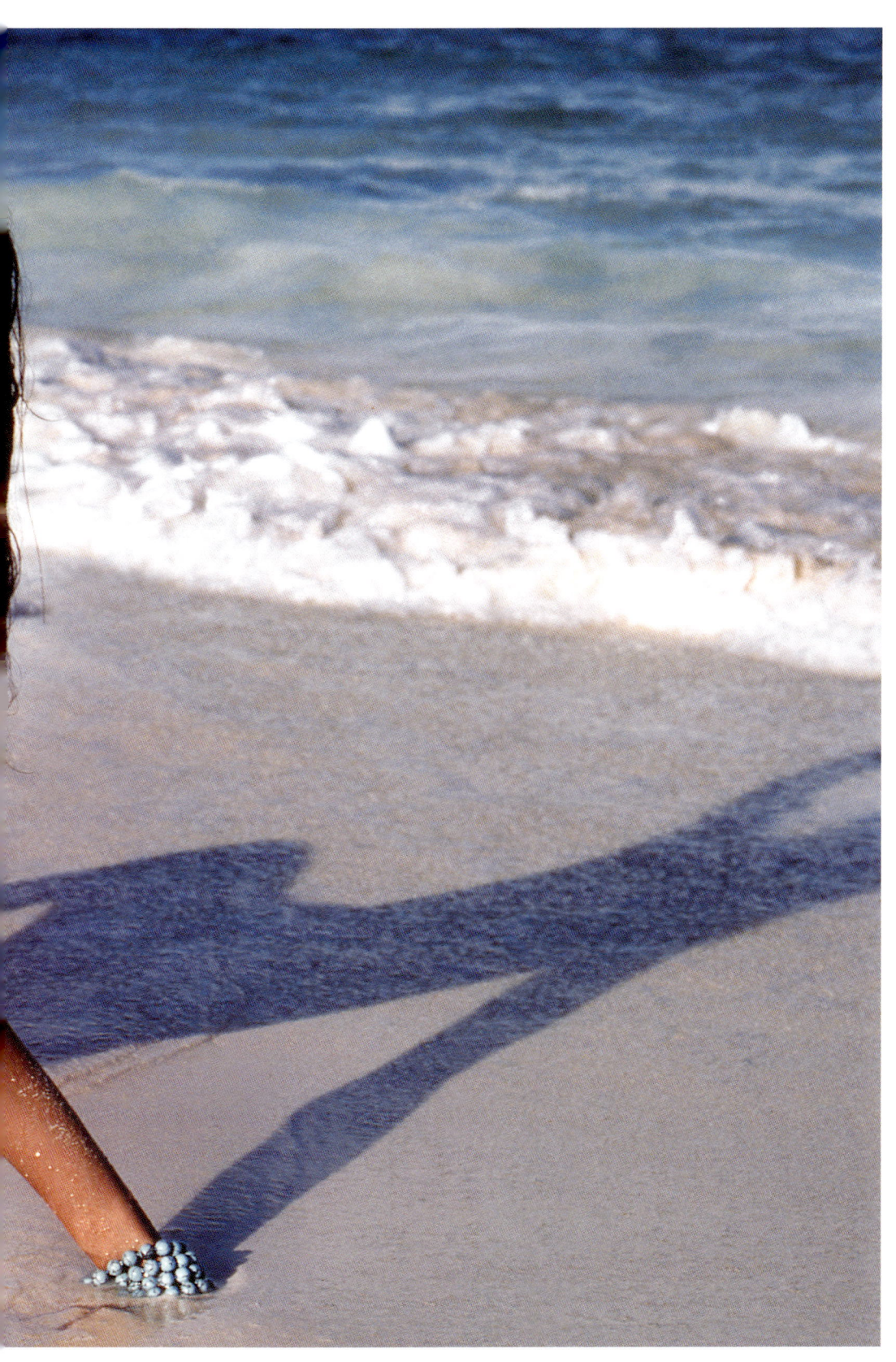

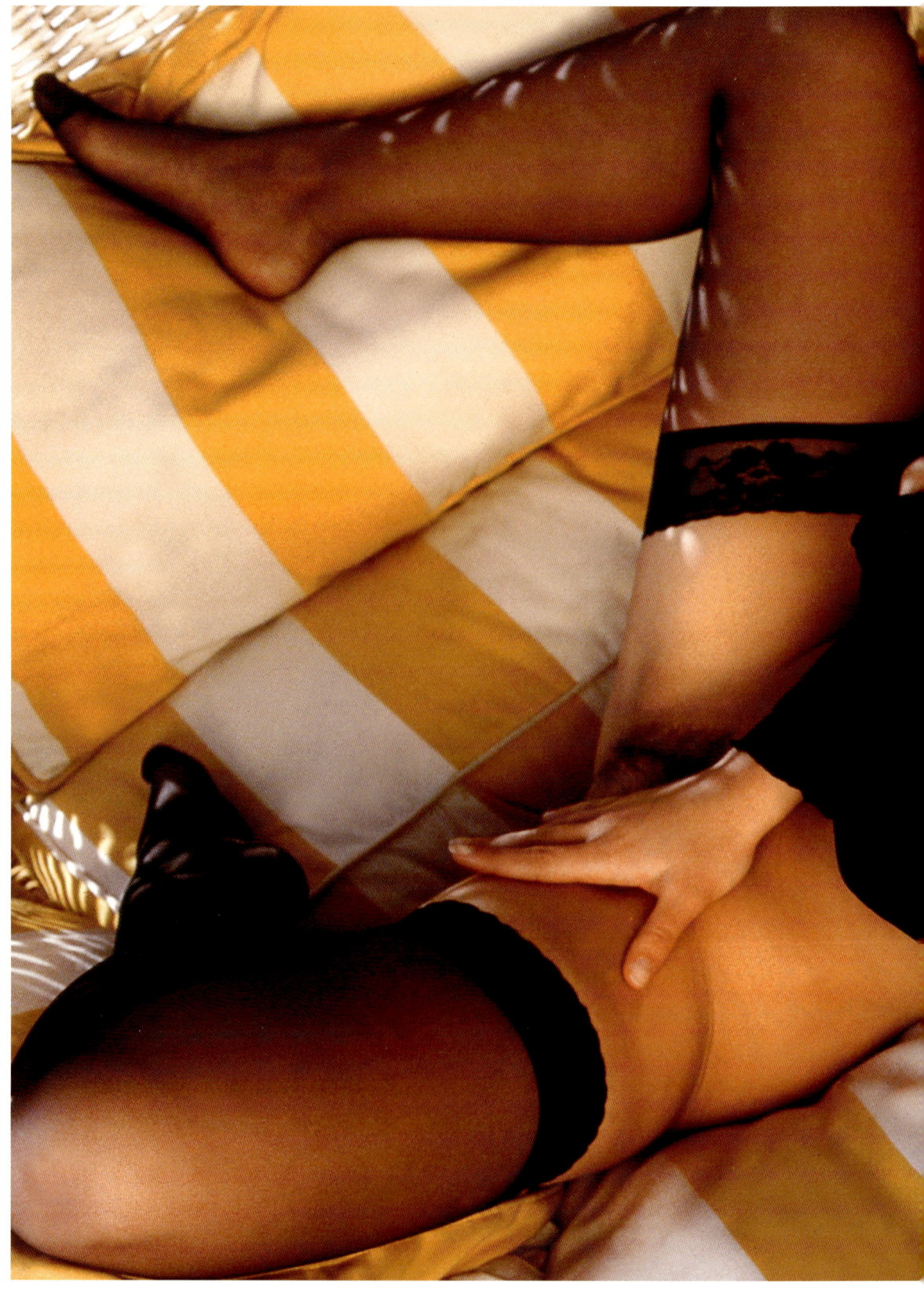

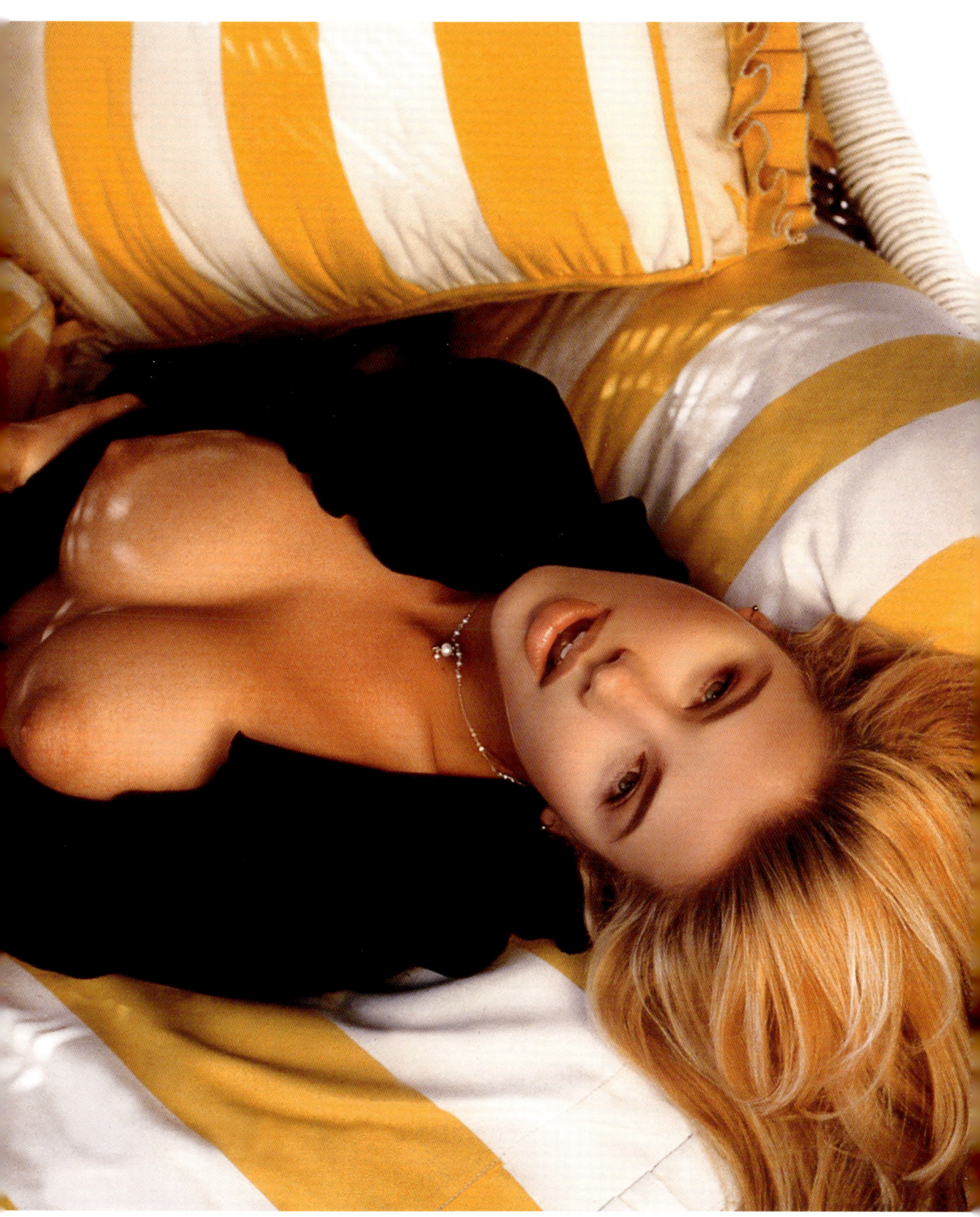

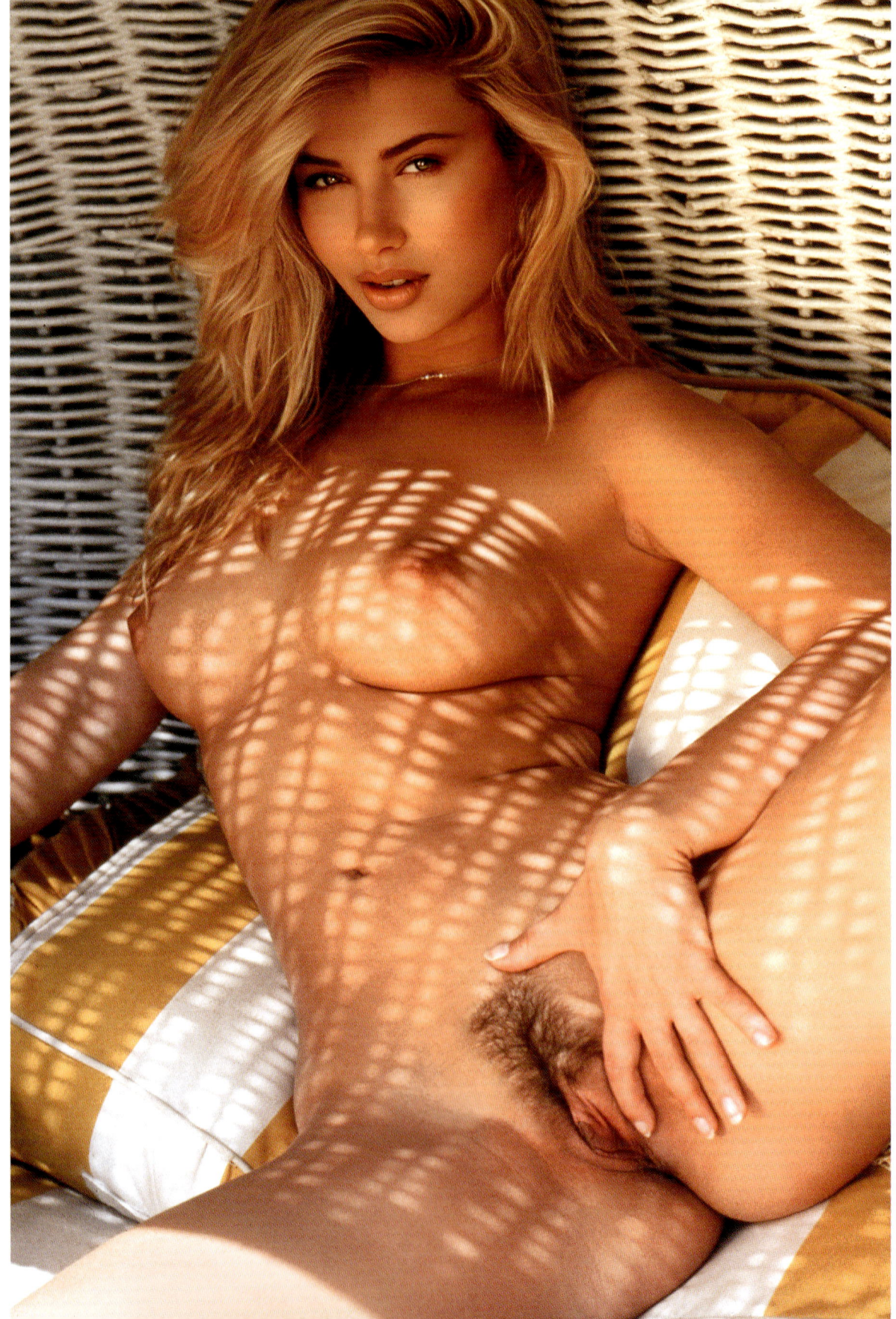

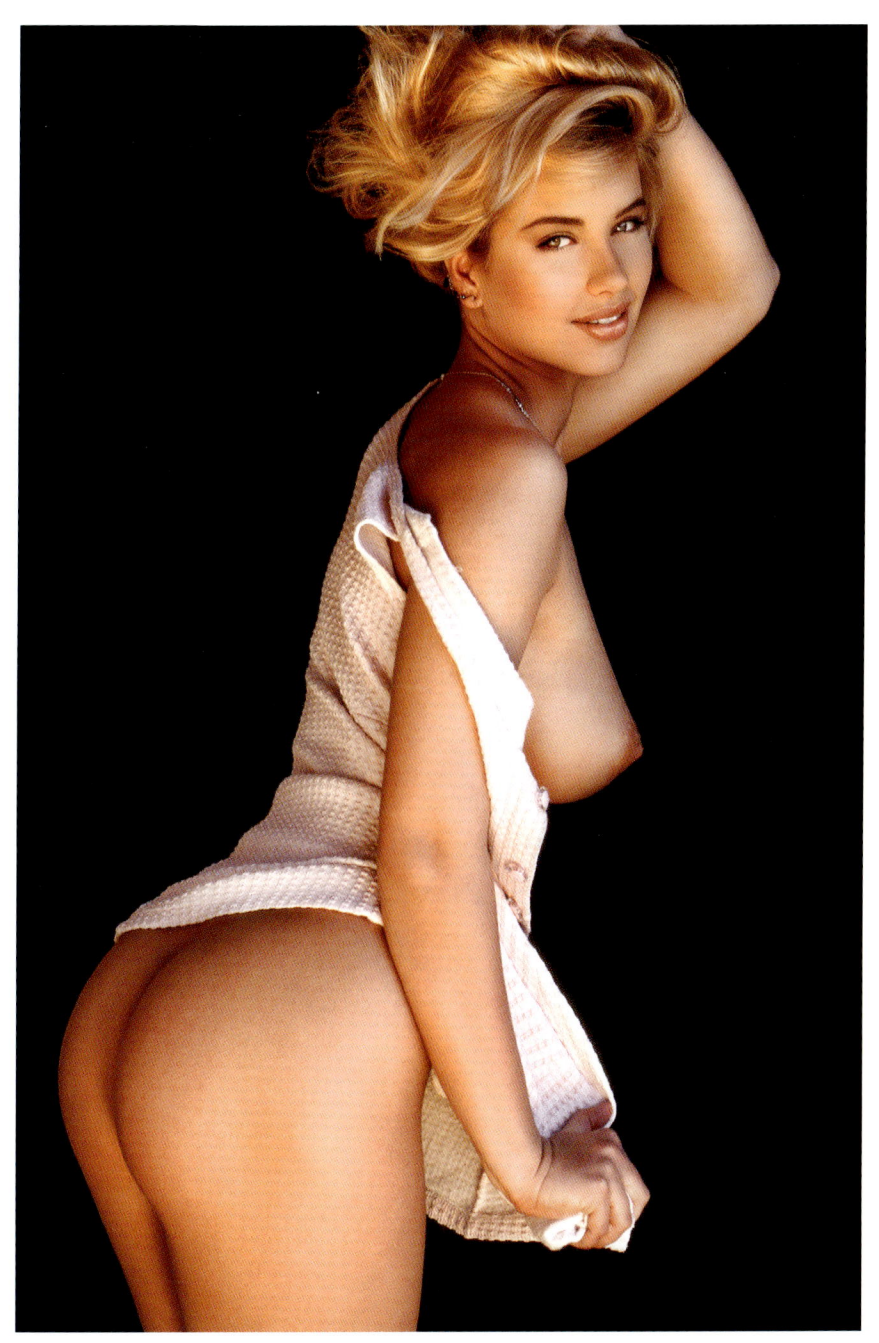

TEREZA

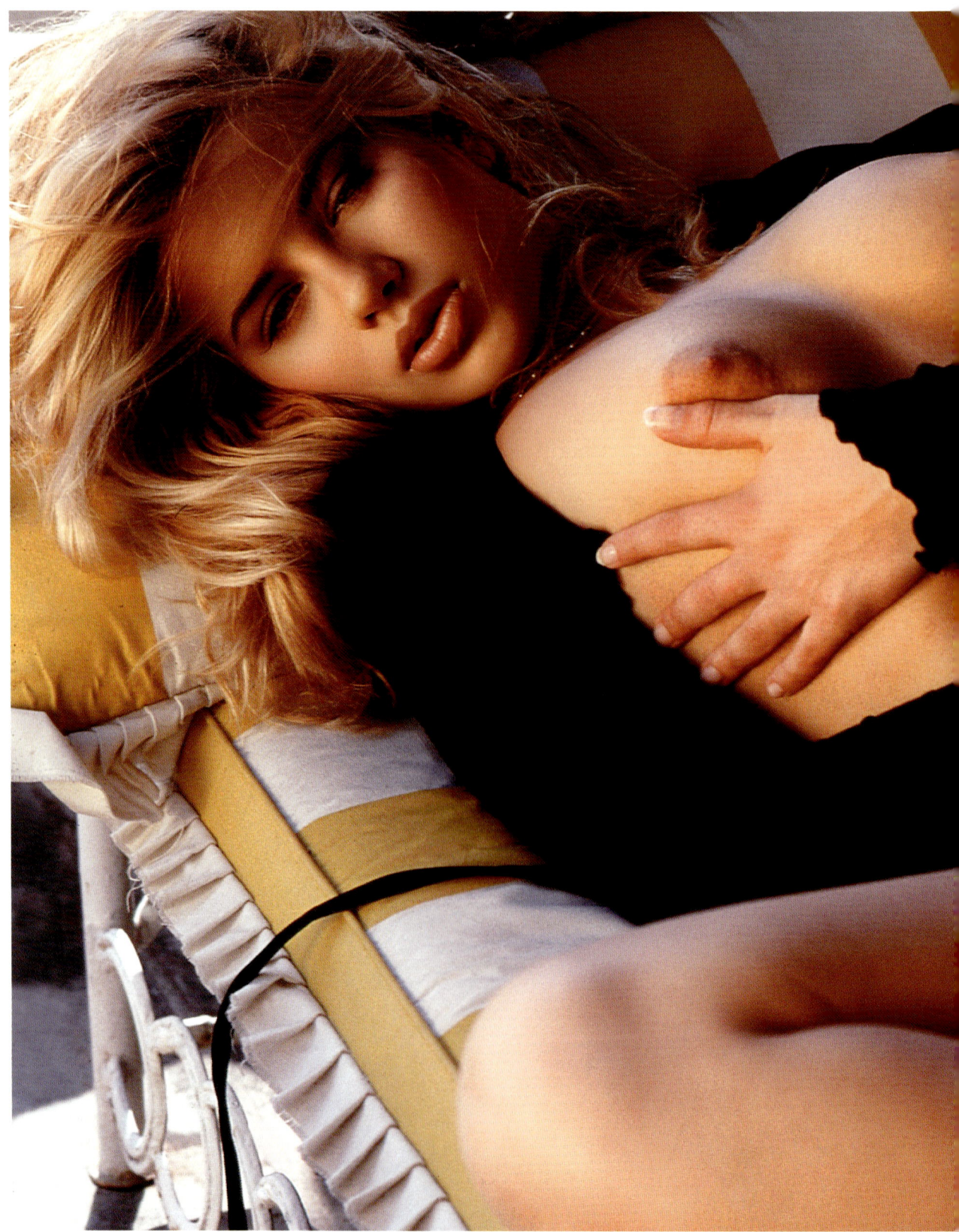

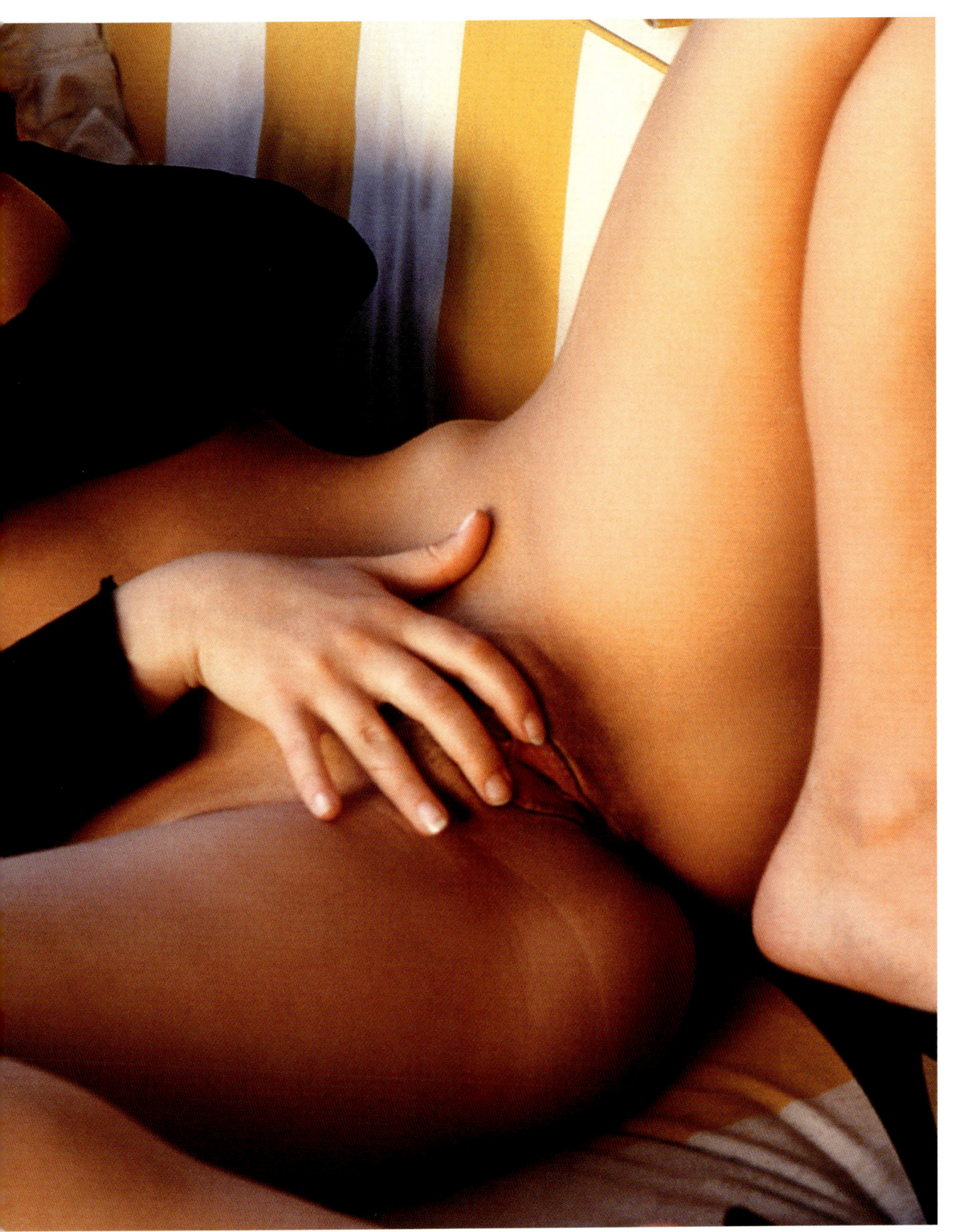

TEREZA

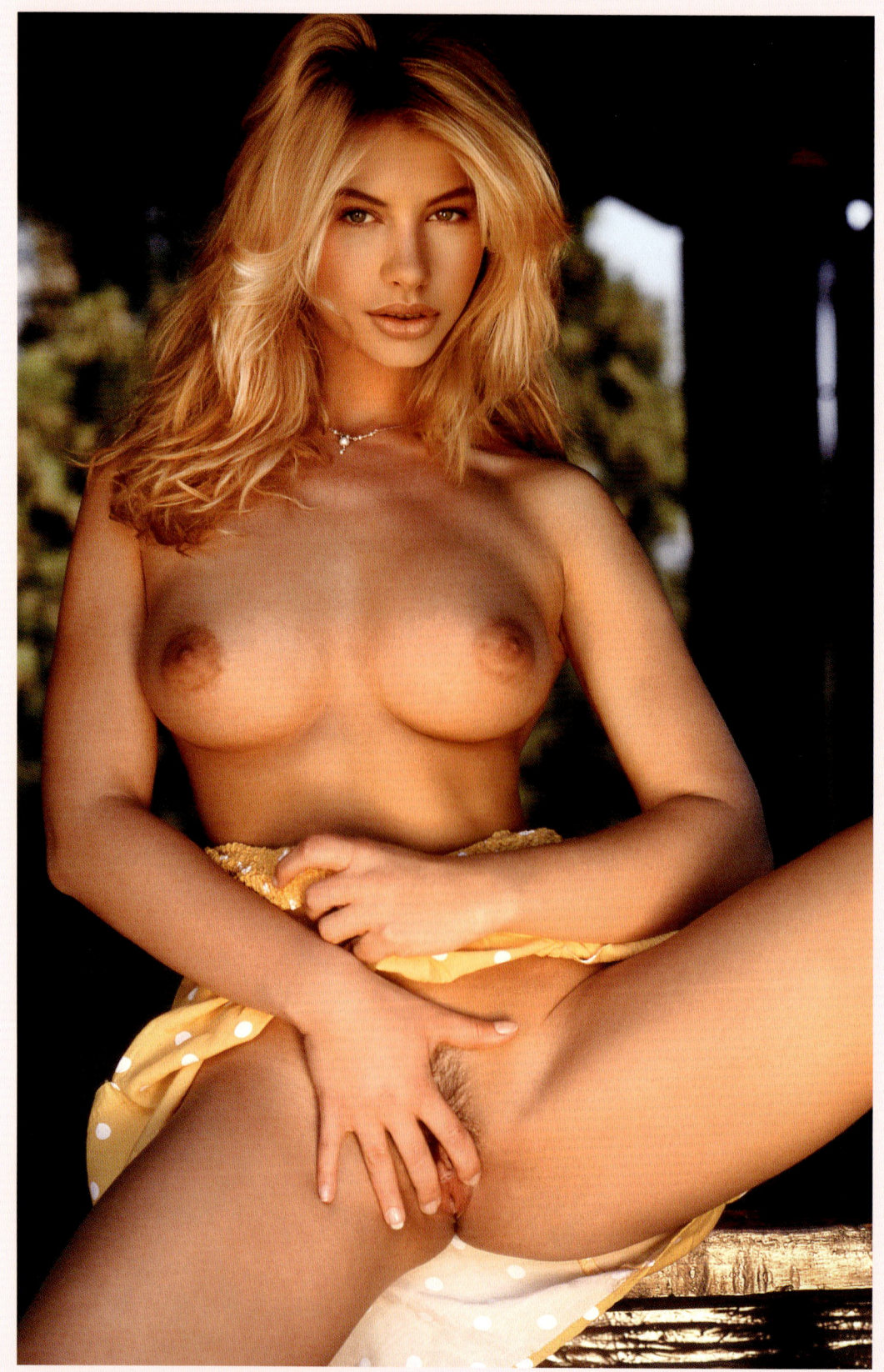

TEREZA

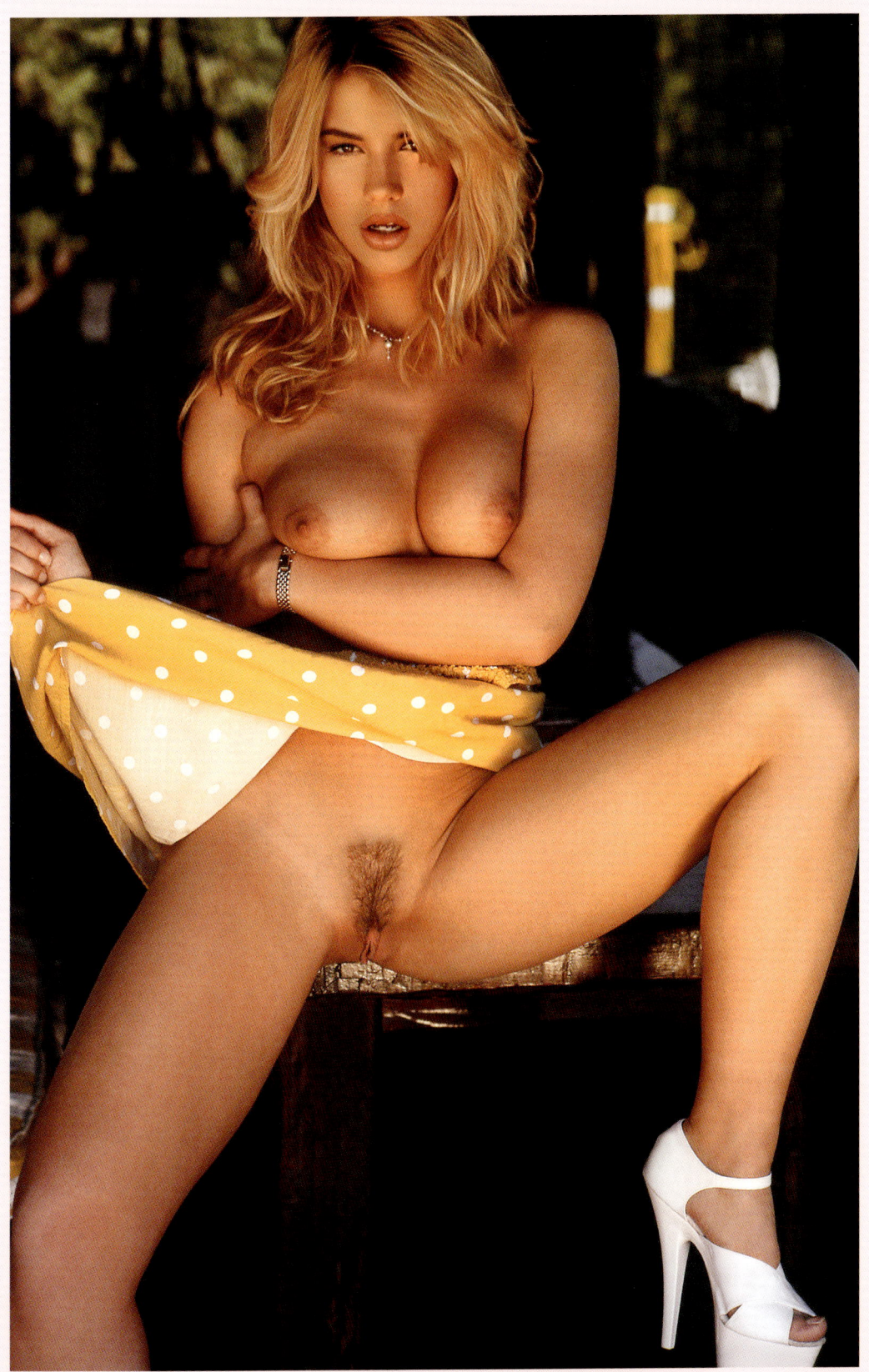

TEREZA

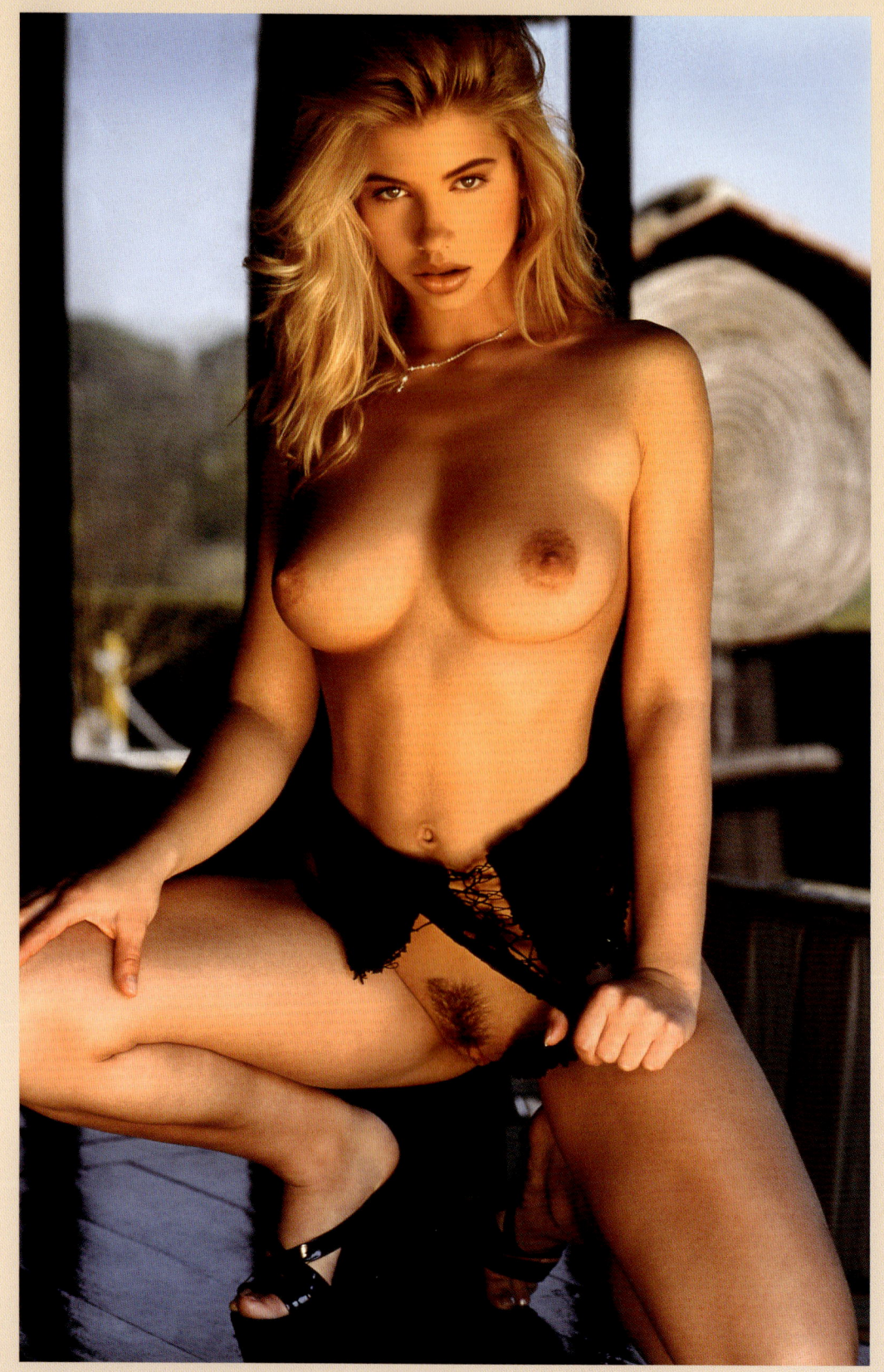

TEREZA

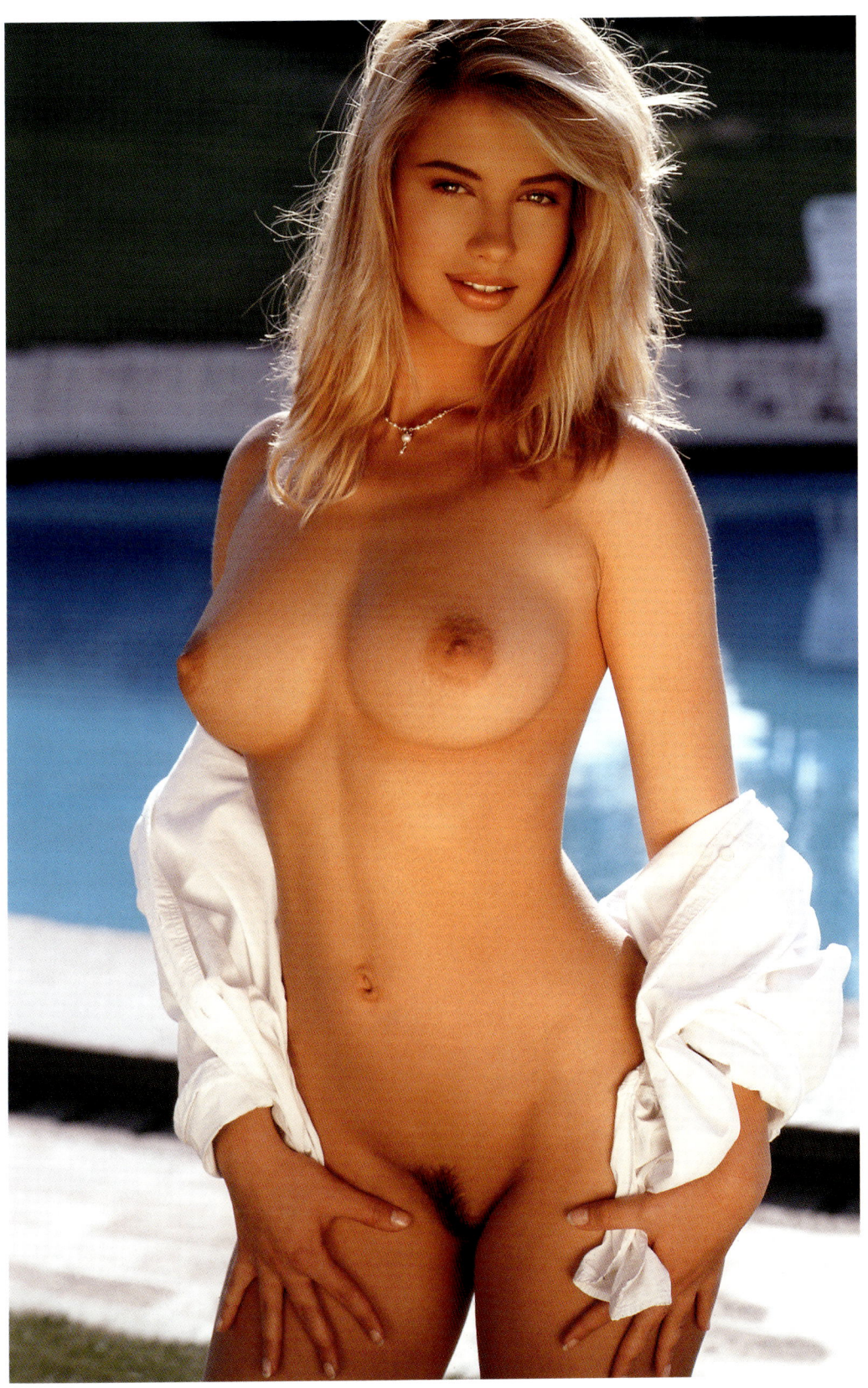

TEREZA

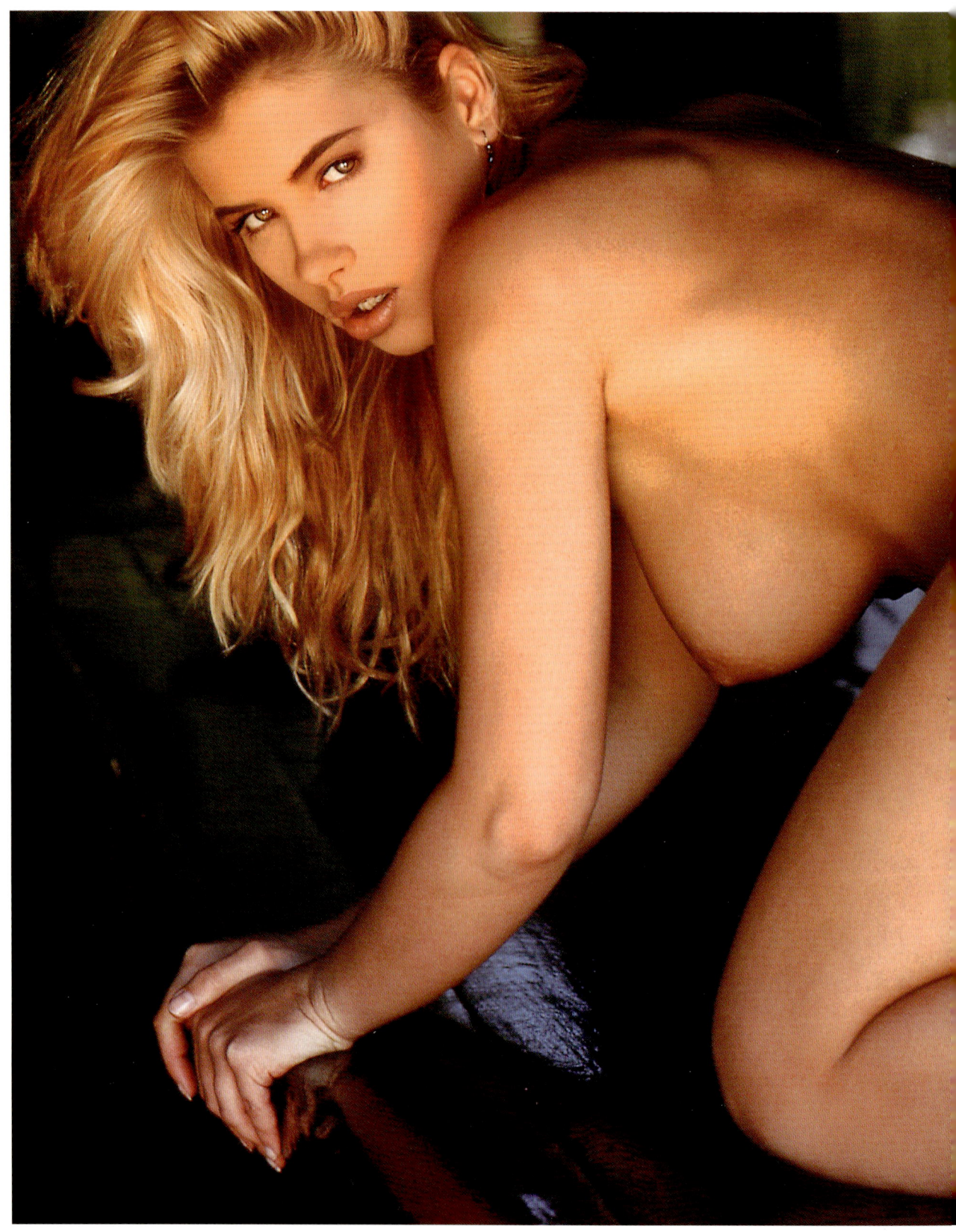

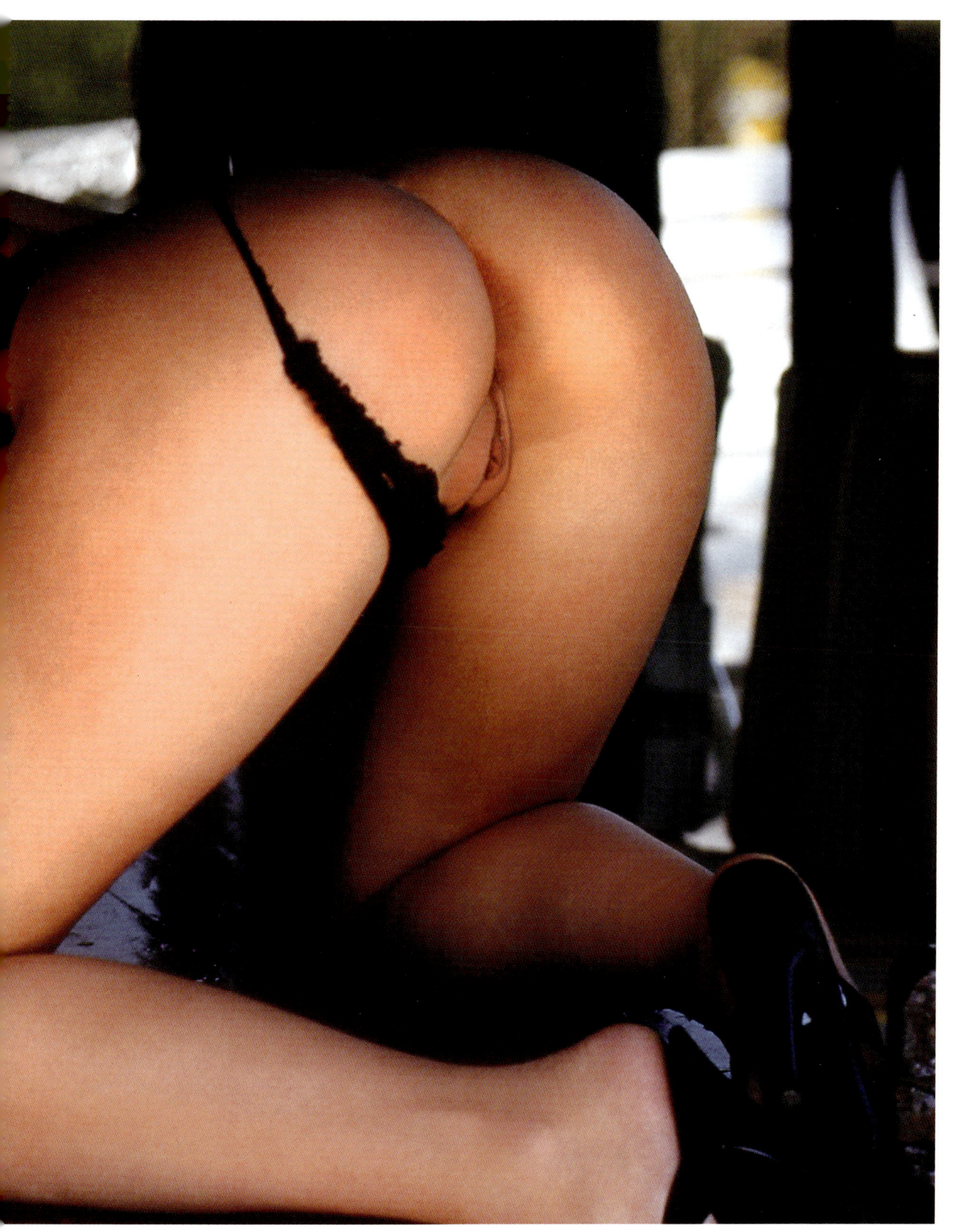

TEREZA

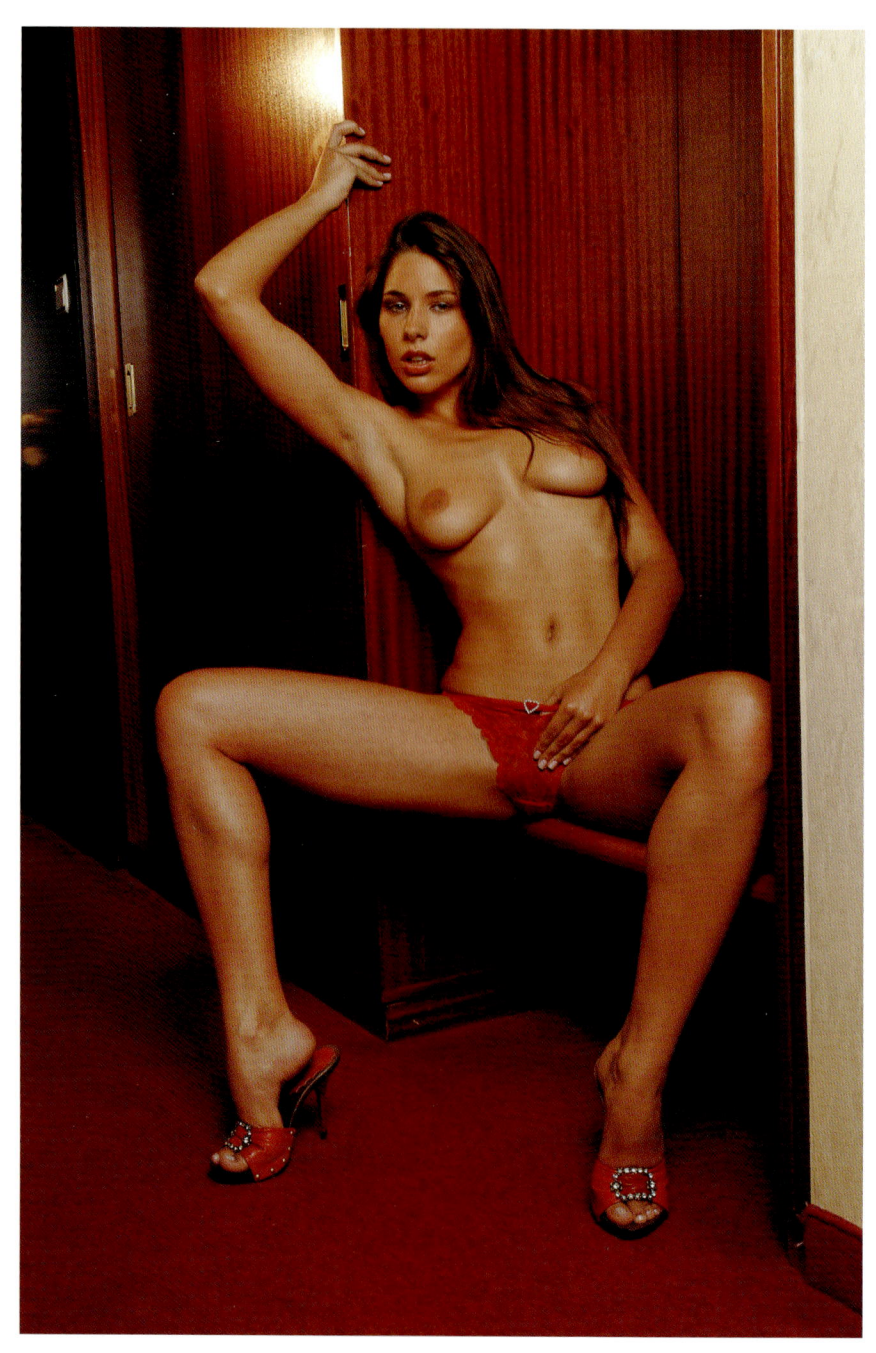

ZAFIRA

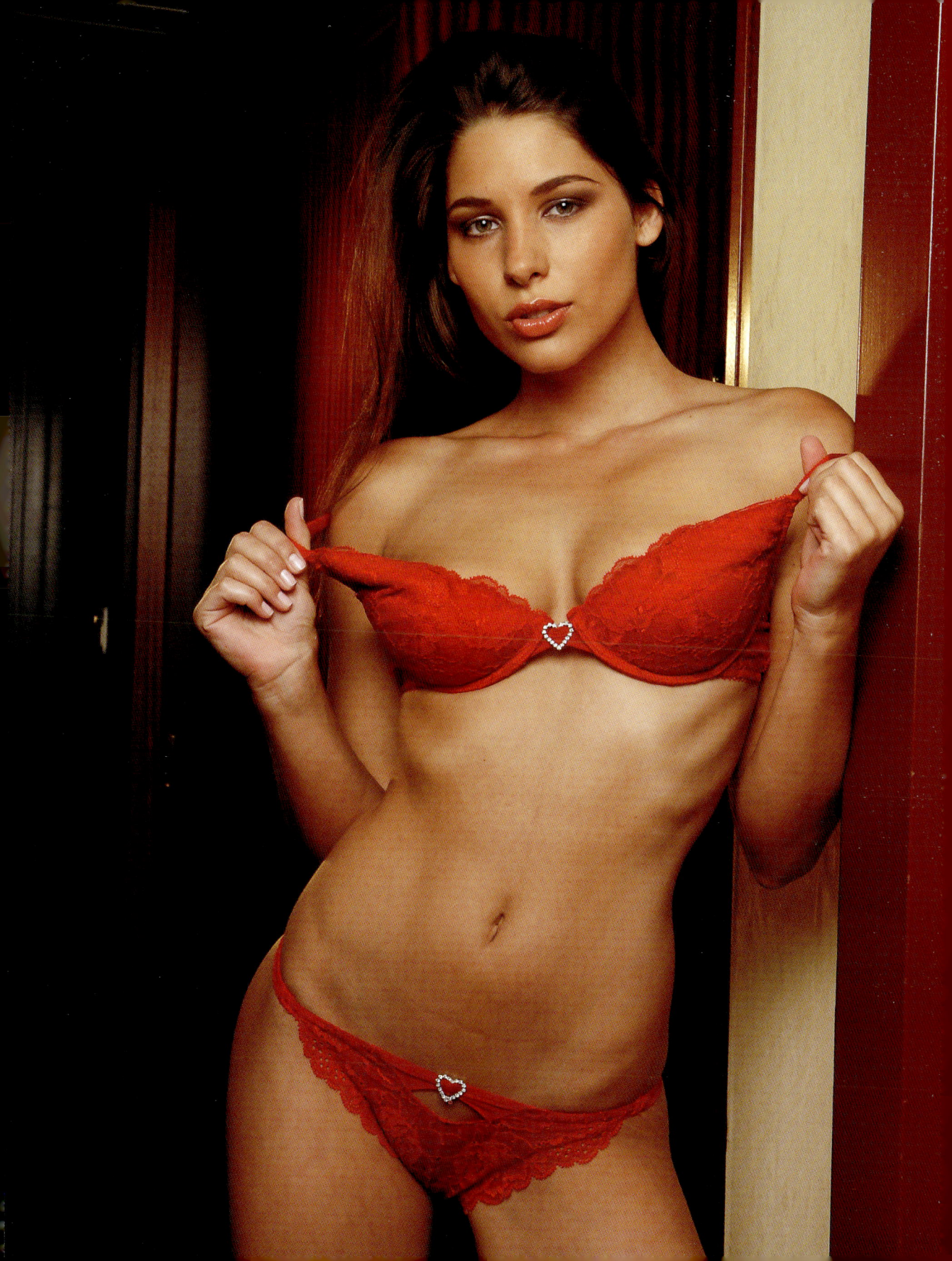

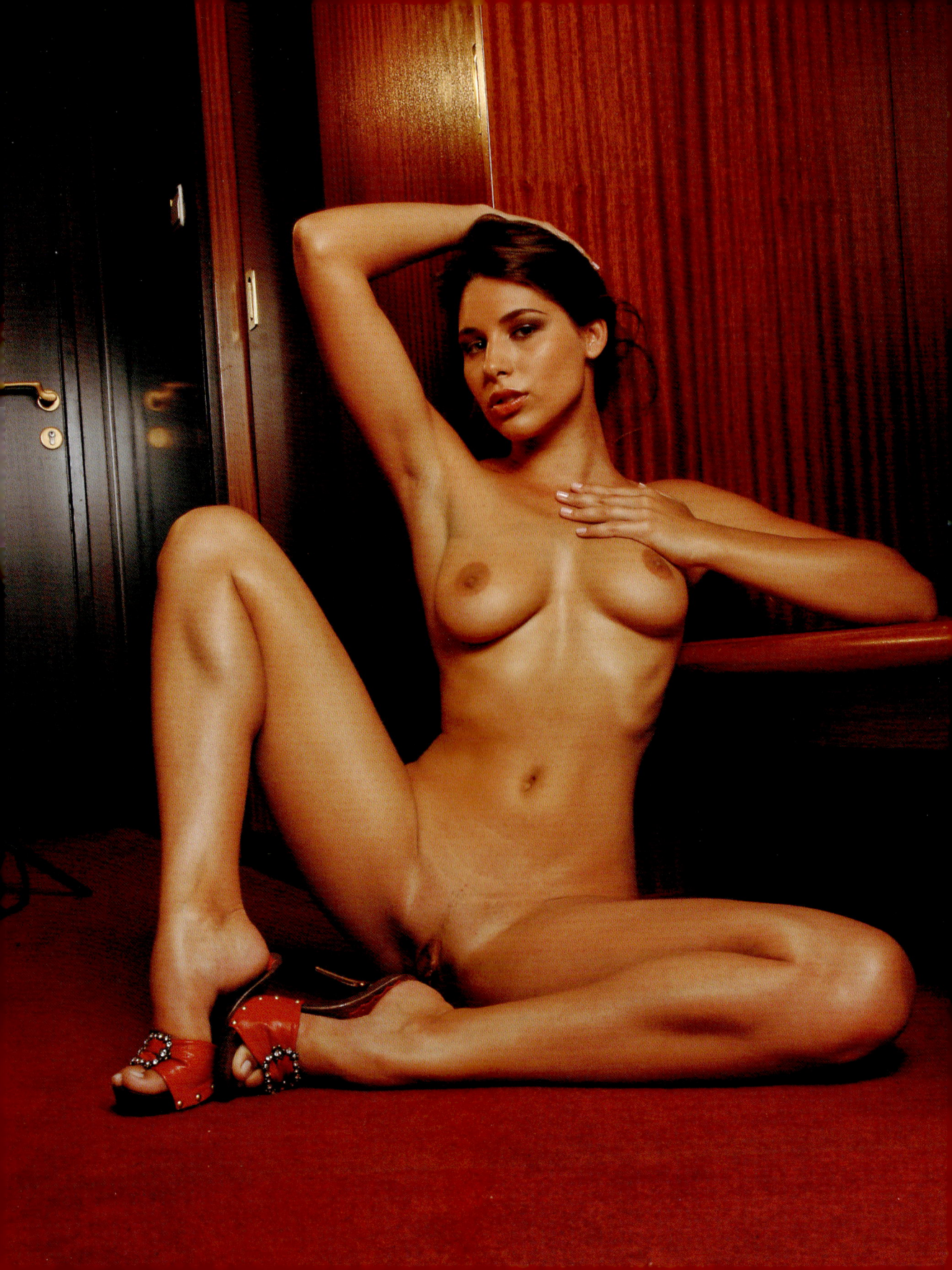

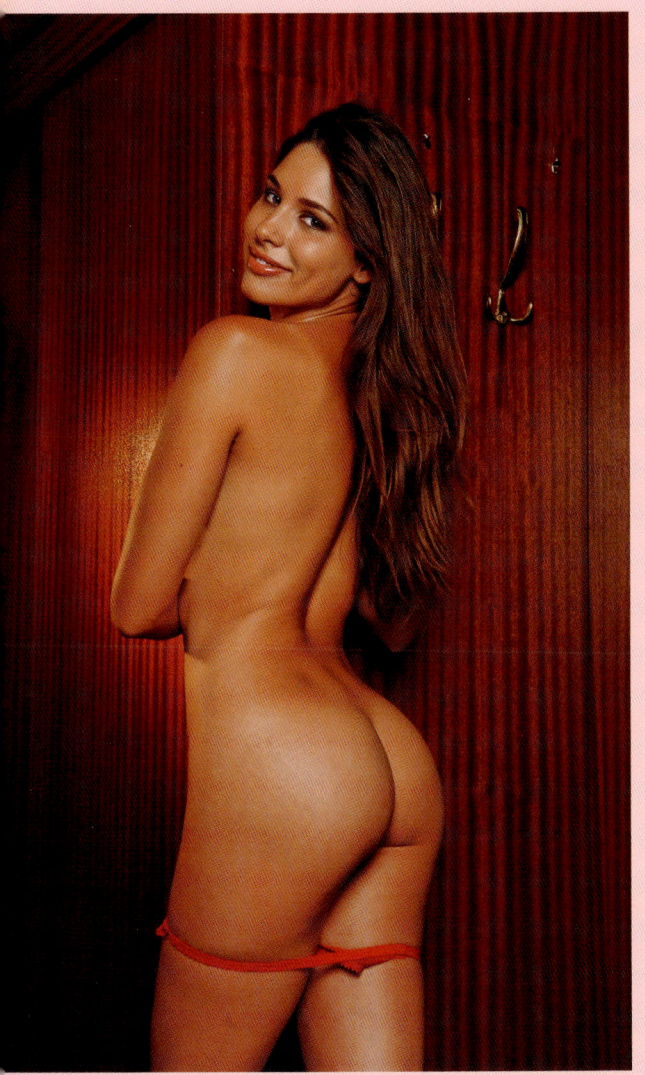
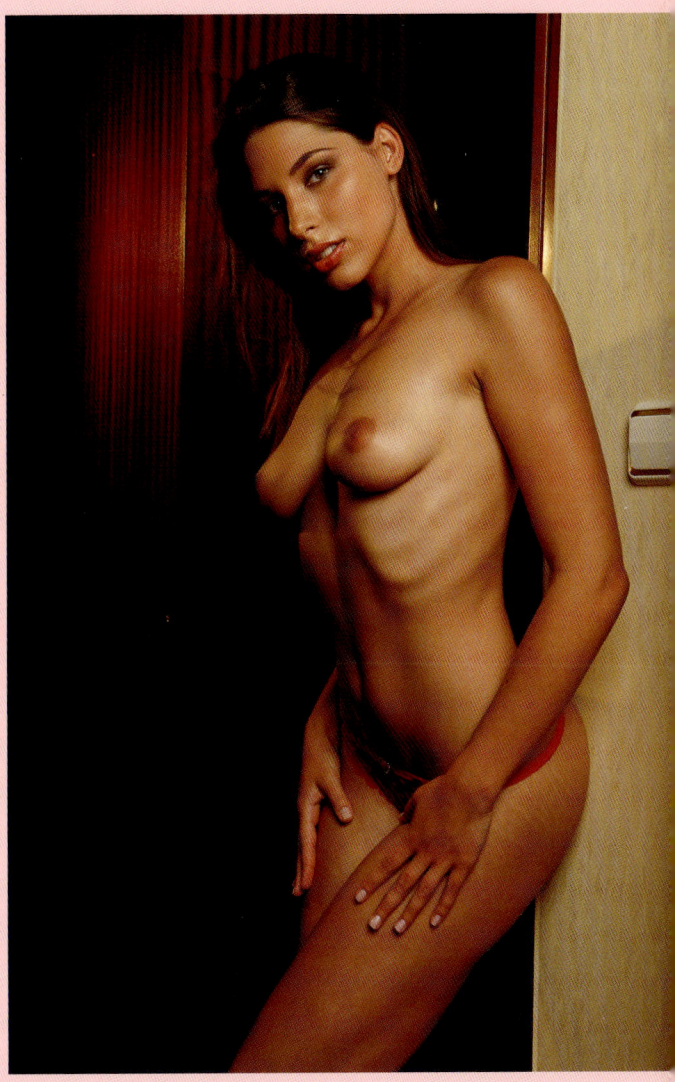

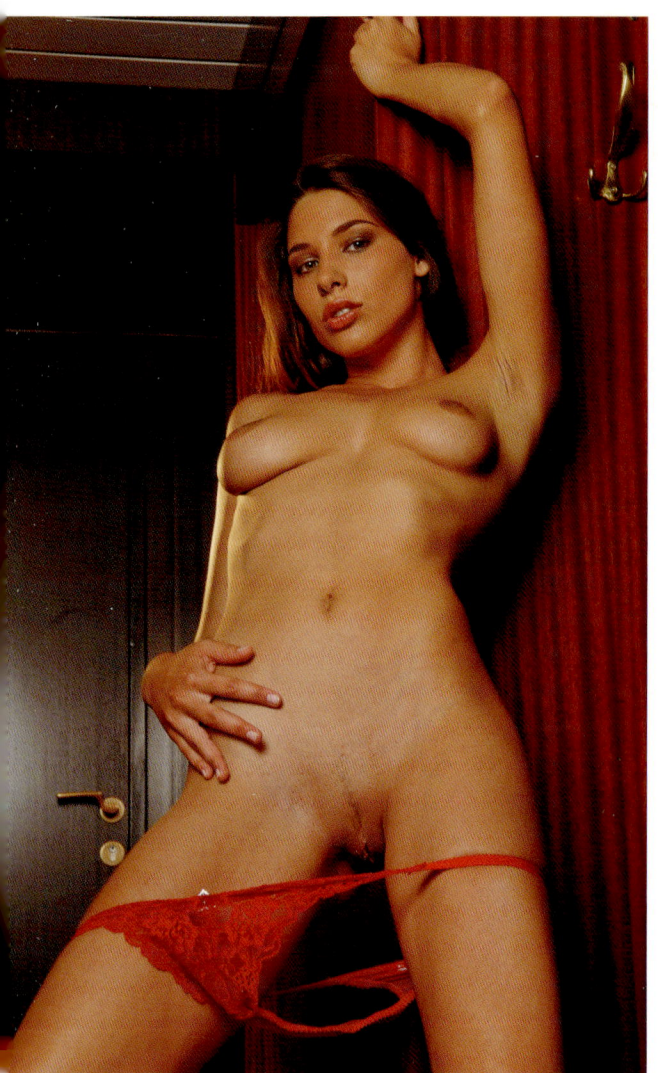
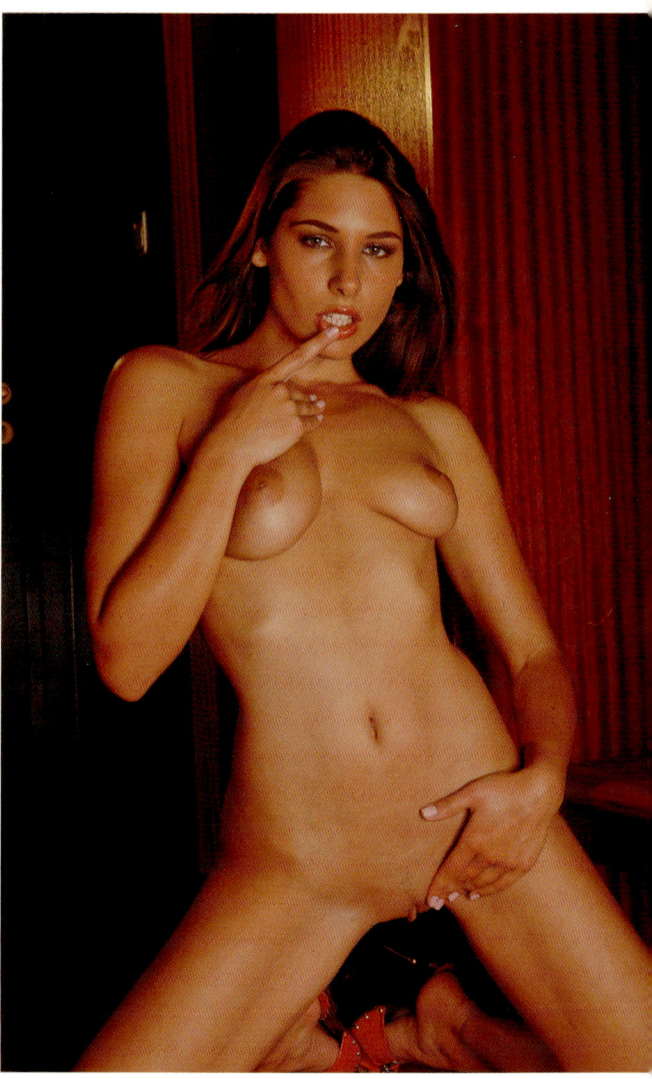

ZAFIRA